Champions of the Poor
The Economic Consequences of
Judeo-Christian Values

Champions of the Poor
The Economic Consequences of Judeo-Christian Values

BAREND A. DE VRIES

Foreword by
ARCHBISHOP REMBERT G. WEAKLAND, O.S.B.

GEORGETOWN UNIVERSITY PRESS / WASHINGTON, D.C.

Georgetown University Press, Washington, D.C.   20007
© 1998 by Georgetown University Press. All rights reserved.
Printed in the United States of America.
10 9 8 7 6 5 4 3 2 1 1998
THIS VOLUME IS PRINTED ON ACID-FREE OFFSET BOOKPAPER.

Library of Congress Cataloging-in-Publication Data

De Vries, Barend A.
    Champions of the poor : the economic consequences of Judeo
-Christian values / Barend A. de Vries.
            p.   cm.
    Includes bibliographical references and index.
    1. Economics—Religious aspects—Christianity.   2. Economics—
Religious aspects—Judaism.   3. Church work with the poor.
4. Poverty—Religious aspects—Judaism.   5. Judaism—Doctrines.
I. Title.
BR115.E3D36   1998
261.8′5—dc21
ISBN 0-87840-664-6.   —   ISBN 0-87840-665-4 (pbk.)
                                                                97-37200

To
PHILIP S. LAND, S.J.
IRVING S. FRIEDMAN

Contents

Foreword

Professor Barend A. de Vries asks the right questions about the influence of an economic system on our society and all societies around the globe. He is genuinely concerned about the poor and those who are not making it. It is consoling to find today an economist who is willing to take such an impassioned stance for the poor, a position usually reserved to religious advocates. The trend today among politicians and economic researchers is often to be less compassionate, even with hints that someone who is not making it economically is guilty of laziness or plain ineptitude.

Two special qualities recommend de Vries' approach and make it different from the many other books being produced on the same topic. The first of these is his approach to the international aspects of the economy. He does not limit himself to domestic issues but engages the question of poverty on a larger basis. His background permits him to do this with confidence and knowledge of the concrete situation. Given the world we live in today and the ways in which all nations have become economically interdependent, de Vries asks the right questions about how the whole of life on this planet is affected by our economic system. The book is a timely one, since it touches so many issues that we must as a world culture debate today. He is concerned not only about the poor in the United States but, rightly, about the poor around the world. The two are intimately connected. This work recommends itself for that approach, a vital one if we want to understand what is happening to us domestically and if we want to assume any kind of leadership beyond our own borders.

The second unique aspect of the work is the fact that it takes seriously the moral arguments that have been proposed by the various religious denominations. It is rare to find an author with the economic background and expertise necessary to confront the world situation who takes seriously the ethical positions that have been brought forth by the various churches and religious bodies. De Vries engages that theological discourse and does so in a way that is unique and most stimulating. He also does not limit himself to one group but gives a fair and unbiased presentation of positions taken by various different religious bodies. The book is unique in this respect not only because it takes the ethical approach seriously, but also because it brings together thinking from various ethical and religious sources. He does so also with a broad understanding and sympathy. One cannot fault him, for example, in the way he presents the moral and ethical positions of the popes over the last hundred years and that of the American bishops in their pastoral letter, *Economic Justice for All*, of 1986. At times, as one will see immediately, he puts his weight behind a different solution than that proposed by the churches, including the Catholic Church. However, his positions are not taken because he rejects the need for moral arguments in the economic field but because he does not accept other moral positions that impact on the economic ones. His positions are buttressed with strong reasoning and worth the reflection given them.

For those of us deeply concerned about the whole of this planet and the future of everyone on it, Professor de Vries offers hope. The lines of approach that are the centerpiece of this book—namely, an international approach to poverty and one with an ethical dimension—can only bring us closer to the right solutions. The worst of evils would be for us to abandon hope or to reach out for partial and ineffective solutions that would benefit our own country for a time but ultimately prove disastrous for the whole globe. Professor de Vries' book will help us to avoid such chimerical solutions.

REMBERT G. WEAKLAND, O.S.B.
Archbishop of Milwaukee

Preface

This book applies Judeo–Christian ethics to the critical economic policy issues that confront our society: poverty persisting in the wealthy U.S. economy, widespread poverty in the developing countries, and the problems posed by discrimination against women, environmental degradation, high military expenditures, and the excessive debt burdens borne by many of the poorest countries. The book grew out of a lifelong interest in applying biblical ethics to economic problems, a desire to see countries make the best use of their resources and give all people an equal chance.

I got the idea of writing this book during a series of meetings of economists who dealt with the interrelation of Christian ethics and economics. Among the various topics discussed were the U.S. Catholic bishops' comprehensive 1986 pastoral "Economic Justice for All" and the study paper "Christian Faith and Economic Life" of the United Church of Christ. Earlier I had become acquainted with the Vatican's "*Populorum Progressio*" ("The Development of Peoples"), the encyclical dealing with basic issues of economic and social development which drew wide attention among experts in the field in 1967.

Since the start of modern economics, poverty reduction has been of central concern to many eminent economists. Although a number of recent studies have focused on poverty, the problems of the poorest among us have largely been ignored in the national political debates of the 1990s. In the 1980s, the churches and the Jewish community took a stand on poverty reduction in the United States and applied their ethical views to American economic policies. In assessing the economic feasibility and the realism of the churches' positions, I necessarily deal with the conflict between the selfishness that prevails in many quarters of our society and the Judeo–Christian message of love and care for one's neighbor.

This book could not have been written without the enthusiastic help of my family, church, and numerous friends, economists, and ethicists who taught me the depth and history of social testimony in a broken world.

My wife, Dr. Margaret Garritsen de Vries, advised me on many questions of the economics of prosperity and poverty, and helped to keep the book's economic reasoning on a sound path. She suggested the title *Champions of the Poor*. My daughter Chris, whose master's thesis examined the impact on remuneration of the entrance of women into a profession, was an inspiration for Chapter 3 ("Women: The Poor of the World"). She gave me a better understanding of women's contributions to, as well as their problems in, the marketplace.

Dr. Jo Marie Griesgraber, James E. Hug, S.J., and Philip S. Land, S.J., of the Center of Concern all were very helpful in various stages of the study. Phil Land and Jo Marie Griesgraber commented on an early draft of the manuscript and introduced me to the wealth of Catholic social teaching. Martin McLaughlin, who worked for several years with the Catholic bishops and now with the Center of Concern, made detailed comments on the entire manuscript and introduced me to additional documents. Professor Henry W. Briefs of Georgetown University and Jack Maddux, formerly with the World Bank, also gave useful guidance. The office of the Apostolic Pro-Nuncio in Washington was always ready to send me important Vatican publications. More generally, the Catholic community opened new doors of understanding and knowledge.

Professors J. Philip Wogaman and Alan F. Geyer of Wesley Theological Seminary gave me the benefit of their views on Christian ethics and the social gospel of earlier Protestant theologians. The excellent library at the seminary was a key source of information for me.

At the Bethesda United Church of Christ, the Rev. Jean Alexander advised me on the chapter on women, introduced me to feminist theology, and referred me to a number of sources. Jay Lintner of the UCC Washington office, Audry Smock, and Charles McCollough explained the thinking behind the UCC's paper "Christian Faith and Economic Life." The Rev. Lon Dring, founder and executive director of the Community Ministry of Montgomery County, gave essential information and encouragement at the very start of the project.

The national offices of most mainline Protestant denominations and the National Council of Churches all gave complete and quick replies to my queries and made available a broad range of social justice statements. Episcopal Bishop John H. Burt familiarized me with the work of the Urban Bishops Coalition. Professors Elton J. Bruins and Robin Klay of Hope College in Holland, Michigan, introduced me to the actions on social justice undertaken by the Reformed Church in America. Lee Anne Skoogland Huffard made available documents of Interfaith Action for Economic Justice. James W. Skillen of the Association of Public Justice commented on an early version of Chapter 12 ("The Evangelicals"). Harriet Baldwin introduced me to the studies on liberation theology written by her brother, Robert McAfee Brown.

Professor Sumner M. Rosen of Columbia University encouraged me in all phases of the study. He gave advice on the impact of the military on the civilian economy and the current thinking on full employment and job creation in the U.S. economy. He also introduced me to the important contributions to social justice action by the Jewish community.

Julie Youdovin, Mickey Meyers, and Jennifer C. Friedman of the Religious Action Center of Reform Judaism sent me essential documents. Rabbi Ian Wolk read the draft of Chapter 8 ("The Jewish Roots of Social Justice") and introduced me to important works on Jewish ethics. At the Temple Har Shalom in Potomac, MD, I received guidance from Rabbi Leonard Cahan and help from Jack and Shirley Dominitz and Oskar Weitzberg. At Temple Sinai in Washington, DC, librarian Deborah Taga helped me with important sources. Carol Davidson of the Jewish Theological Seminary in New York made detailed comments on the chapter and suggested essential further reading, which I was able to undertake at the library of Temple Har Shalom in Potomac, MD.

At a number of seminars and conferences I received valuable reactions to my presentation of the main themes of the book. The deliberations of the Study Group on Debt and the Environment, chaired by Dr. Jo Marie Griesgraber and Professor Danny Bradlow at The American University, broadened my understanding of the consequences of excessive indebtedness and environmental degradation for the poor. Others in the Washington nongovernmental organization (NGO) community, especially Nancy Alexander of Bread for the World, were also helpful to me.

The book draws freely on the publications of the World Bank on many aspects of development. Jim Feather, then publications director of the World Bank, gave useful advice and encouragement on publication of the manuscript. John Kay, formerly with the International Monetary Fund, brought the work of the Fourth World Movement to my attention.

John Samples, director of the Georgetown University Press, was not only an understanding publisher from the very beginning, but showed me many ways of improving the manuscript. I thank the anonymous reviewer of the manuscript for suggesting that the book include a chapter on Jewish thinking on social justice. Joan Leibman gave unstinting help in editing the first three chapters.

*   *   *

This book is dedicated to the memory of two eminent workers in the Lord's vineyard: Father Philip S. Land, S.J., and Dr. Irving S. Friedman. Both of them were an inspiration to me in writing *Champions of the Poor*.

Phil Land (1913–1993), both a theologian and a professional economist, led the way in applying economics to Catholic social teaching. After being active in helping the underprivileged in the American Northwest, he taught economics at the Gregorian University and worked in the Commission of Justice and Peace of the Vatican. At SODEPAX (Society for Development and Peace) he played a leading role in the collaboration between the Vatican and the World Council of Churches on international development issues. He was a leader in the 1968 Beirut Conference on Church and Development and in the 1969 Montreal Conference, which was a focus for the subsequent formulation of liberation theology. After his service in the Vatican, he was a pillar of strength at the Center of Concern in Washington as an expositor of Catholic social teaching. He was an inspiration to numerous younger people in their work on social issues. His life was a long and bright "day that the Lord has made."

Irving S. Friedman (1915–1989), an accomplished international economist and aspiring theologian, was dedicated to an equitable international financial system that benefits all, regardless of economic standing or racial origin. He served in senior capacities in the International Monetary Fund, the World Bank, and Citibank. He helped to establish the Center of Concern, an international action group on social justice issues, and served as its chairman. In the IMF he led the fight for removing controls on international payments and established a policy of regular consultations with member countries. He helped the World Bank focus on social–economic issues as the economic adviser to then Bank president George D. Woods and strengthened the professional base for economic analysis and research. In Citibank he broadened the horizons of commercial banking, helping the bank to get a better understanding of the needs and problems of developing countries. In his later years he was an advisor to the president of the African Development Bank and was active on population issues as chairman of the Population Resource Center. In all his activities he proved to be a helping friend to the many people who worked with him.

I gratefully acknowledge permission from publishers for quotations in various chapters:

Barbara R. Bergmann: "The Economic Emergence of Women." New York: Basic Books (1986).

William R. Cline: "International Debt: Systemic Risk and Policy Response." Cambridge, Mass.: M.I.T. Press (1984).

Hans Kung: "On Being a Christian." New York: Doubleday & Co. (1976).

United States Catholic Conference: "Economic Justice for All: Pastoral Letter on Catholic Social Teaching and the U.S. Economy" (1986).

J. Philip Wogaman: "Economics and Ethics: A Christian Inquiry." Minneapolis: Augsburg Press (1986).

Introduction and Overview

This book focuses on the economics and ethics of fighting poverty, and aims to assess the economic consequences of the ethical views expressed by the Judeo–Christian community. Part One starts out with a review of poverty issues in the United States and the developing countries, followed by a discussion of the special problems experienced in various segments of society. Part Two follows up with the ethical response to widespread poverty, the views on poverty issues expressed in the Bible and by Jewish and Christian ethicists, and the economic reasoning pursued in the ethical positions and the feasibility of their policy recommendations.

The fight against poverty deserves high priority in the spectrum of economic and ethical debate. Opinions on the extent of poverty and how to deal with it vary with one's position in society, political outlook, moral conviction, awareness of the facts, and many other factors. Some are inspired by America's agricultural past, when the less fortunate could find their fortune on the Western frontier. But while our people are still highly mobile, modern industrialization and urbanization have taken their toll in increased poverty. To gain perspective, it is necessary to look at the spread and causes of poverty, to explore the measures that might be taken to improve the conditions of the poor and the underlying moral questions.

In U.S. society one person in every seven is poor, and the proportion of children is even higher. The poor are on the margin, out of the mainstream, and miss the benefits of our wealthy society. Minorities, blacks in particular, suffer more than whites; women suffer more than men. Much of U.S. poverty is hidden. One can drive on superhighways from the Atlantic to the Pacific without encountering poverty. But one who takes a local road often sees many signs of poverty and decay; many of us fear to enter our blighted inner cities. We cannot ignore these realities. The poor can be brought into the mainstream, become fully productive, and contribute to their own well-being and that of the entire community.

1

In reality, people who have experienced poverty make up far more than the official estimate of one-seventh of the population, for millions move in and out of the world of the poor. More permanent is a smaller hard core, much of it concentrated in black urban ghettos or rural areas like the hollows of Appalachia and the barren planes of the Southwest. Most people who are poor at some point in their lives are poor for only a few years. But there remains the hard reality that millions live on the margin, out of the mainstream, deprived of the benefits of our wealthy society.

The story is often sad. Despite progress like lower inflation and lower unemployment in the 1980s, the nation suffered a double calamity as the poverty rate went up and the public debt quadrupled. Cuts in social services and erosion of the safety net aggravated the plight of the poor. In 1980–1983 alone, poverty in the United States rose by 6 million to 35 million. After 1983, although the economy improved, the condition of the poor worsened—the first time such opposite movement had occurred. Income disparity got worse as real wages tumbled in many sectors.[1]

As economic performance improved in the 1990s, the official poverty rate has come down somewhat, but by historic standards the overall growth rate of the American economy has remained low. Moreover, large numbers of middle-class and professional workers had to shift to lower paying jobs or feel deeply insecure about their economic future. While official statistics show that unemployment dipped well below 6 percent, in reality the total unemployment is much higher. Allowance must be made for the millions who have been able to find only part-time jobs or have become discouraged and dropped out of the workforce.

In the developing countries poverty is much more extensive than in the industrial North. It deeply divides the world with a seemingly permanent and intolerable separation, with a minority of rich and a majority of have-nots, a situation drastically different from the Judeo–Christian ideal that all people be equals. More than a billion people, one out of five, live in the kind of abject poverty which makes human life hardly worth living. They are often starving or suffer from severe malnutrition, illiteracy, and substandard clothing and housing.

What measures can be taken to tackle the worst poverty and lay the basis for greater productivity of all? In the developing countries, how can general growth be combined with action to improve primary education, health, and nutrition, and, most importantly, to reduce population growth? Actions in these areas often reinforce each other; for example, slower population growth will free resources for better education, and improvements in education will help to raise incomes and are associated with better health and smaller families.

Four areas, in both industrial and developing countries, further illustrate the complexities of poverty and the diverse nature of policies needed to overcome it. In each of these areas we will see how confrontations between ethical and economic considerations call for actions and policies of reconciliation.

- *Women* suffer worse economic conditions than men; they are often severely disadvantaged in the marketplace, even though they are essential to maintaining the health of their children.

- Greater attention to *the environment* is critical to improving basic conditions for the poor, for they suffer most from environmental degradation. The formulation of environmental policies involves a thorough rethinking of development priorities and of many strands of economic analysis.

- *Military programs* negatively affect the efficiency of manufacturing industries and hence the country's ability to sustain vigorous growth in the civilian economy and to maintain competitiveness in world markets. They reduce resources available for poverty alleviation. The conversion of military to civilian production raises special problems for employment, but also opens up new opportunities for helping the poor.

- *The international debt crisis of the 1980s* had dire consequences for poverty conditions and growth in the developing countries. It highlighted the dependency of poor countries on the global economy and the often-difficult relations between debtors and creditors. Substantial progress has been made through policy reform in many debtor countries, various kinds of debt relief, and a resumption of private lending and investment, but it is worthwhile to consider the lessons that must be learned to prevent the recurrence of such a crisis in the future. The Mexican crisis of 1994–1995 showed once again that the interrelationship between external finance and the policies of developing countries is critical for maintaining financial stability compatible with poverty eradication.

The global economy has experienced major changes in the last two decades, with a strong market-friendly drive toward reducing state intervention. In Europe, the unification of Germany and the end of state socialism in Central Europe and the former Soviet Union set a new economic agenda. Latin America saw the rise of representative government, accompanied by a lessening of state influence over the economy. East Asian and Pacific countries have demonstrated remarkable growth, often a persistent 8 percent even in major countries like China and Indonesia. The progress in many developing countries has been sufficiently impressive that the validity of the group term "developing countries" has been brought into doubt.

Despite global developments, poverty has persisted and even increased in some situations. The banks and corporations that are the primary movers in the global economy pay little attention to poverty conditions. Globalization itself has increased unemployment in some industrialized communities. Europe suffers from stubborn high unemployment. The transition toward market economies in Central Europe has turned out to be more difficult than originally anticipated. Even in the United States, poverty in the early 1990s continued at a high level despite good growth and a decline in official unemployment data. And at well over one billion persons affected, there is no abatement in poverty in the developing countries. All this means that the goal of poverty eradication continues to deserve special attention, especially in a rapidly integrating global economy.

In brief, when society faces difficulties, it is the poor who suffer most: they pay the highest price for environmental degradation; when developing countries have to adjust to unfavorable external circumstances, the measures are often hardest on the poor; military programs divert resources from programs to improve the productivity and the condition of the poor. The predicament of the poor calls for attention beyond the realm of economics; it is essential to establish the ethical base for action and the importance of personal responsibility.

ETHICAL VIEWS IN THE JUDEO–CHRISTIAN COMMUNITY

Faced with the consequences of persistent widespread poverty, the Judeo–Christian community has repeatedly issued testimony and urged government, business, and individuals to take action. It has been guided by the message of the Bible, which confronts poverty with simple but penetrating rules:

- It expresses concern for the poor and the conditions in which they live, and urges that the poor be an integral part of the community;

- It proclaims the rule of love above the rule of money, profits, and power;

- It recognizes the dignity of the individual, created in the image of God. In God's world all people are equal; there is no place for a downtrodden class or race;

- It proclaims that all of creation's resources belong to God, that they are good and we must care for them with love; and

- It calls for reform of financial and property structures when they become oppressive.

The call for social justice is an ancient one. It was expressed by Moses and his laws of moral behavior and care for one's neighbor, based on the veneration of God the Creator. Even the stranger in our midst is to be cared for. Throughout the Old Testament the prophets pointed to the injustices that the rich and powerful wrought on the poor and neglected. Isaiah projected a society of justice where behavior was based on care and faith, not on economic value and profits.

The New Testament teaches the value of the ultimate sacrifice, the central role of faith and love in our personal and social behavior, and the importance of a deep, life-changing personal commitment.

These intrinsic values of moral social behavior continue to be proclaimed by both Jews and Christians. In this century they have spoken out whenever society, government, or business have failed in their moral duty of bringing justice to the poor. They have been truly the *Champions of the Poor* by taking on the moral issues posed by pervasive poverty.

In its social witness, contemporary Judaism builds on thousands of years of teaching and applying the rules of *social justice for all*—not just the Jewish community. What the Jews have to say is accentuated by the realities of the centuries of oppression they have suffered. Based on the teachings of the Old Testament and the Talmud, the Jews have applied their convictions to concrete situations as they arose in the United States. Judaism is opposed to racial segregation and discrimination; it believes in the unity of humanity, in the dignity of each person as a child of God. It has placed special emphasis on the fight against discrimination, which it regards as a critical cause of poverty. It stresses the importance of education and productive and remunerative work. In its view, poverty constitutes a destruction of human dignity, and it proclaims that all must work for the eradication of poverty.

Christians have a strong tradition of speaking out for justice in the twentieth century. Protestants preached the Social Gospel in the progressive era at the turn of the century. William Jennings Bryan spoke for Evangelicals when he called for the protection of workers against the monied interests early in the century.

The Catholic Church has dealt with the ills of modern society, starting with Leo XIII's 1891 encyclical *"Rerum Novarum"* ("The Condition of Labor") and continuing through the many statements of John Paul II addressed to the social ills of contemporary society. It proclaims that the Bible takes the side of the oppressed, and that much of the biblical story is the story of the oppressed, their suffering and victory. This "liberation theology" was inspired in part by the work of priests among the poor in Latin America and has been a strong unifying force in the ethical vision of the Catholic Church and many Protestant churches. In the 1960s the Catholic Church first explicitly addressed the social issues posed by the developing countries, stressing that development of nations must contain more than the creation of material wealth. The U.S. bishops' pastoral "Economic Justice for All" urged in the mid-1980s that domestic fiscal and economic as well as foreign policies be tested by their impact on the poor. In their view, "neglecting the poor, the outcast and the oppressed is like rejecting Jesus himself." Still the most comprehensive and authoritative moral statement on poverty in the United States, the pastoral has had an influence far beyond Catholic circles and our own borders.

Like the Catholic Church, the mainline Protestants have articulated the Christian faith in the context of contemporary economic and social conditions. On U.S. issues Protestant positions and theology have often been similar to Catholic views, with the exception of the role of women and the nature of population policy. Most mainline Protestants are perhaps more outspoken on the equality of women and men in church and society, and agree with secular experts on the need for artificial birth control in moderating population growth, of crucial interest in fighting environmental degradation and poverty in general.

Evangelical and Fundamentalist Protestants are divided on poverty issues. Some give full recognition to the priority given by the Bible to caring for the poor. Others, however, have placed a good deal of trust in the workings of free-market capitalism in reducing poverty, without recognizing the conflict between Christian love and the self-ishness prevailing in our society.

In many instances, ethical arguments confront economic reality and call for changes in economic policy. Ethical concerns also govern the selection of economic topics for analysis in Part One—for example, unemployment, slow growth, income distribution, the case for development assistance, and the special-sector problems of women, environmental degradation, military programs, and international debts already mentioned. Moreover, the economic analysis in each of the chapters in Part One is concluded with a review of the ethical response to the economic issues identified. Examples of important issues in which economic and ethical arguments must be brought together to reach satisfactory solutions are topics well-known to many policy analysts concerned with poverty:

- population problems and policy, and the moral case for and against birth control;
- uneven income distribution and the case for progressive taxation;
- the equality of all people and the inferior position of women in many situations;
- the integrity of God's creation and environmental policy;
- the ethical call for peace and the question of the levels and nature of military spending;
- the moral case for debt forgiveness and the management of international development debt; and
- the urgency and justice of poverty reduction, personal responsibility, and welfare policy.

Integrating economic and ethical viewpoints into sensible approaches is the challenge of our society to which this book seeks to make a contribution.

Most social observers and ethicists recognize that the problems of poverty are deep-seated and pervasive. They can be tackled most effectively when there is a moral personal and community commitment and when the effort receives the priority it deserves, which requires close collaboration among all groups in society. The churches have made the case for economic justice, but have not articulated specific economic policies. Yet their views have far-going consequences for the role and functions of the private and public sectors.

THE ROLE OF THE PRIVATE AND PUBLIC SECTORS

Social objectives set by moral considerations require that the state reach beyond its traditional functions, beyond the maintenance of law and order, healthy market competition, and a sound banking system, and give priority to action against poverty. For this to be possible, sufficient jobs must be available so all can be productively engaged, thus laying the material base for integrating the poor and marginalized into society as a whole. And these jobs should pay wages that are adequate to meet the needs of families.

The private sector can take primary action on these social objectives, including provision of productive jobs, health facilities, education, and nutrition. But when the private sector falls short, government must take action in the interest of recognized social objectives so all can live as full citizens of the land.

Most of the religious community calls for full employment, but some economists do not believe that this objective is either feasible or acceptable. One Protestant denomination even called for a constitutional amendment that would assure all adults a job. Jews believe that the purpose of society and government is to provide for the sharing of the earth's resources to ensure the security and rights of the disadvantaged and the needy.

To see and grasp the opportunities around them, people who have been downtrodden need more than jobs. They must be empowered into a new self-worth and self-respect so essential for a new economic beginning. This is recognized in liberation theology, but its consequences for government action are not entirely clear. It would require that government favor the poor in the allocation of public resources. But in reality, once the representatives of the poor are themselves in government, they must face up to a wide variety of economic problems. In addition to reducing poverty, they have to deal with the many demands of economic policy such as exchange rates, interest rates, the price of food, and the structure and level of trade protection. They may have to pursue simultaneously free-market policies and special action in favor of the poor. They will also have to seek a redistribution of income and at the same time maintain robust growth lest their policies end up penalizing the poor.

Policies that favor the poor must at times intervene in markets to ward off severe adverse consequences. When financial structures or property patterns become oppressive, government will have to take action to bring necessary reform in financial markets or agriculture. Not all reforms will work, and governments tread on dangerous ground when they seek to bring drastic change. Agrarian reform has suffered many failures because food production will decline when the new owners are not productive users of resources. Likewise, changes in financial structures need to be managed and implemented with caution. For example, large-scale allocation of bank loans to socially desirable targets, as has been practiced in some developing countries, can easily distort credit patterns and be harmful to the entire economy. Subsidization of any kind must aim at well-specified targets if it is not to discourage production. The harm that can be done to the poor by the absence of judicious intervention was amply demonstrated by the debt crisis in the developing countries during the 1980s, when a more forthright public policy toward debt accumulation in the preceding years might have avoided much of the subsequent crisis. The poor in the developing countries suffered most from the debt crisis of the 1980s.

The question of how the market forces and intervention should be balanced, of course, remains. Here, too, the role of the state deserves central attention. One may ask whether the system should be capitalist or socialist. Christian ethicists accept neither capitalism nor socialism, even less communism, as the uniquely chosen system for bringing economic justice. While capitalism sets free the spirit of innovation and liberty so fully practiced by early Calvinism, it may do damage through excessive competition, instilling an ethos of selfishness, and leave some behind in the wake of progress. Private property, a pillar of capitalism, is according to Catholic social teaching encumbered by a social mortgage: owners are to use their property in the interest of the community. For its concern with the well-being of individuals in society and the distribution of income, some Protestants tended to favor socialism, more so than Catholics. In a prophetic spirit Pope Leo XIII warned against the abuses of socialism a hundred years before its breakdown in Eastern Europe. John Paul II spoke of the shortcomings of socialism, but also cautioned against the faults of capitalism. On balance, he favored the free market, but warned that markets should be compatible with human freedom and dignity and that labor must not be treated as a commodity. In the end, Christ stands above all economic systems in the sense that love and personal responsibility must rule all systems if they are to work and be fair to the individual.

Social justice requires measures that must be both financially and economically feasible. Achievement of the objectives of social justice depends in practice on both the dedication of individuals and the outcome of the necessary policies.

CRITICAL QUESTIONS TO BE CONSIDERED

The economic feasibility of reaching the social objectives envisaged by ethicists hinges in large part on the ability of our society to achieve vigorous growth while maintaining reasonable price stability. Although many of the questions that must be considered have no simple answers, it is useful to enumerate some of the more important ones.

People are bound to disagree on whether measures taken should be direct or indirect, or whether action should be at the federal (central) or the state and local level. But there should be agreement that any measure or policy must be financed responsibly, lest the very objective will be defeated by the adverse impact of additional inflation or of excessive taxation that penalizes productive endeavor.

In recent decades, growth in the U.S. economy has fallen below historic levels. What, if anything, can be done to raise the growth rate and maintain it at a satisfactory level? Who has the primary responsibility, the private or the public sector? Is there agreement on the objectives of policy, if not on the means to achieve these objectives? Special consideration must be given to further reduction in total unemployment, including the role of part-time workers who get no benefits and of discouraged workers who are no longer included in the official unemployment data. Can new jobs be provided at just wages—i.e., pay that meets families' material needs and their requirements for adequate social insurance?

In the promotion of economic growth, is there a trade-off between full employment and price stability? Is the dilemma between growth and price stability primarily of short-term concern? Lower economic growth of the U.S. economy in recent years has reduced the

government's ability to increase tax revenue. With diminished reve-
nue-raising ability and in the absence of higher growth, government
has sought to solicit greater contributions for fighting poverty from
charity and other private sources. Can such voluntary and private-sector activity effectively reduce poverty, and how can government best
supplement private activities?

In the public sector, the present trend is to move action from the
central or federal government to lower levels of government, the state
or municipality. In antipoverty action, which functions and responsibilities can be 'moved down' and which should remain at the center?

Industrial restructuring has involved shedding thousands of
workers. How can higher productivity achieved by restructuring be
combined with an increase in the numbers of well-paying jobs? What
can be done to reduce insecurity among the people affected by restructuring, while continuing the increase in industrial efficiency?

A number of additional questions are of special interest to the
United States. What can be done to raise savings and investment to
more adequate levels? When general growth policies fail to lift certain
groups from poverty, what more can be done to assist them? Welfare
measures serve at best as a stopgap. What policies can do most for
improving the productivity of the poor and get them to join the mainstream? Why has poverty in the United States been so persistent in
recent decades, despite comprehensive action and attention since the
1960s?

Many of the questions raised are also appropriate for the developing countries, which have weaker governmental institutions, often
suffer more inflation, and have had more state direction in industry. Of
special interest is the interrelation between the growth rates of the
United States and other industrialized countries and those of the
developing countries. In recent decades the developing countries
have in fact grown more rapidly than industrialized countries, except
for some of the poorest nations in Africa. Despite these favorable
growth records, many ethicists have maintained that the poor countries are poor because the rich ones are rich. To what extent does
growth in the rich countries actually penalize the poor countries? How
can the developing countries maintain vigorous growth in combination with attention to the poor?

In fighting poverty, education and health policies are important
supplements to overall economic policies. Thus we would like to

know what types of education investment have the highest payoff in terms of improving the conditions of the poor, how investments in health can be made more productive, and how the developing countries can overcome malnutrition. Finally, the methods of slowing rapid population growth deserve central attention, for it is a major obstacle to poverty reduction.

The analysis of poverty conditions throws light on the need for comprehensive action on both economic and moral grounds. Thought should be given as to what kind of contribution the now-subproductive poor, when brought into the mainstream, could make to total output and income of the United States and the global economy. Could they, in fact, be an overlooked source for increasing economic growth? This would constitute an economic reward for doing what is ethically right. But this does not mean that economics and ethics cannot be in conflict in a short-run perspective. The best way to sort out the conflicts and consequences of ethical and economic considerations is to take a closer look at poverty in the United States.

PART ONE:

The Economy of Poverty

We are best able to observe poverty in our own immediate environment. We begin therefore with a look at poverty in our own country, which, despite being rich and prosperous in many respects, harbors millions of poor. Yet the poor are entitled to the same opportunities as everyone else.

We have selected those economic topics that are of special interest to our analysis of the causes and extent of poverty. The poor deserve priority in the policies of the nation and the personal attitude of its people. We must recognize that many of our fellows are much worse off than we are and subsist on the fringes of society. We hope that public programs will aim at improving the lives of the poor and making them equal partners in our national community. But we often do not know how to adapt our lives and policies. For we know but few, if any, of the millions of poor among us, nor do most people really care to know them.

1

Fighting Poverty in America

Effective action against poverty must be based on a clear understanding of the conditions and extent of poverty in our country: its key characteristics, the capacity of the economy to serve as a base for antipoverty action, and the impact of specific measures that have been taken to combat poverty. We must also address some broader questions such as how our economic system may best be organized, the importance of overall economic performance, the role of economic policies in creating jobs, and the contributions of the free-market capitalist system. The economic discussion leads to a consideration of the moral and ethical issues raised by poverty prevailing in a rich society like ours: the overriding moral issue of the urban ghetto, the relation between economics and morality, and the ethical framework for action against poverty adopted in this book.

THE FACE OF POVERTY

Effective pursuit of antipoverty policies requires an understanding of the nature of poverty, who the poor are, where they live, what obstacles they face, and the economic and social conditions under which antipoverty policies must be pursued, as well as the moral underpinning of these policies.

Key Characteristics

Is this the best of times for the great majority of Americans? Don't they enjoy the highest standard of living in the world? Yes, and are they not mostly busy maintaining or raising their own earnings, their consumption, and their leisure time? And in their prosperity have they tended to forget those Americans who live in poverty? Yet poverty is pervasive.

American poverty has many faces. It is widespread and not confined to particular regions. Many people move in and out of poverty, and many of the poor have full-time jobs. Long-term poverty is concentrated among racial minorities and families headed by women. We find the poor in our backyard, in our inner cities, in the hollows of Appalachia, and in other rural areas of the South, North, West, and East. One-fifth of America's rural population lives in poverty. We can drive on interstate highways from coast to coast and see the beauty of our land without ever noticing poverty. But leave the main highways and try the secondary roads on the Olympic peninsula or in West Virginia, and suddenly we face the ugly scenes, substandard housing surrounded by shacks and littered yards, abandoned rusty cars and trucks, underemployed and undernourished people. In the Sunbelt, allegedly one of our most prosperous regions, thousands of African-Americans continue to live in rural poverty. In Pennsylvania's Monongahela Valley and elsewhere, steelworkers and manufacturing workers are left in despair, bypassed by multifaceted industrial change and unable to find suitable work. It is even worse in the city slums where few of us venture, for there misery is intensified by filth, fear, violence, and the bleakest of prospects for a way out.

The poor find themselves in many different circumstances. People become or stay poor for many reasons: location, discrimination, lack of education or family support, the ups and downs of employment, the disintegration of the family, personal attitude, and moral fiber. Because of these basic factors, the poor are more vulnerable to a deterioration of economic, environmental, and other conditions. They are hard put to work themselves into the mainstream.

The multifaceted problems posed by poverty have been receiving fresh attention. In the early 1990s a new administration focused on a range of social issues like health insurance, crime in the cities, job creation, and welfare reform. After the 1994 elections a new majority in congress raised critical issues about the country's financial ability to continue antipoverty measures. It gave top priority to balancing the budget, even at the risk of endangering the safety net for the poor. The deliberations seemed to ignore the plight of the poor, especially children, which merits full attention in a rich society.

The public debate takes place against the fact that one-seventh of our people are living in poverty, and many more on the margin are hungry or underemployed or work at wages far below what they had been used to.[1] They are joined by thousands of formerly high-paid workers and technicians who have been laid off by large corporations that are restructuring and striving to survive in a rapidly changing environment, or have not survived and have gone bankrupt. Even in the mid-1990s environment of falling unemployment, few in the prosperous majority can fail to notice that many in their own surroundings have been affected by adverse secular trends in our economy. Are those in the center of things willing to do much about their unfortunate fellows, especially the poorest? They seem to care little about what happens on the fringes of our society. The poor are really out of it. And unless you know one of the poor personally or become one of them, you can never feel their pain and become realistic about extending a helping hand.

Most distressing is the growing number of children in poverty. One in every four American children under six is poor, and for blacks it is even worse: one in every two black children live in poverty.

Poverty is worst among the weakest of our fellows—women, African-Americans, and other minorities. Women are at a disadvantage the world over, and the United States is no exception. The past three decades have witnessed a dramatic increase in the number of women in poverty. They include women raising children alone and older women without adequate income following divorce, widowhood, or retirement. One-third of all female-headed families are poor; among minority families headed by women, the rate is over 50 percent. Women get paid less than men for comparable work, even if the law rules otherwise. They tend to be passed over when really good opportunities for promotion open up. They seldom receive reliable compensation when men walk out of the marriage.

Poverty increases when minorities suffer from discrimination on the job or in the marketplace. Although two-thirds of poor people in America are white, poverty is most severe among racial minorities. Blacks are three times more likely to be poor than whites. One in nine white Americans, one in three blacks and Native Americans, and one in four Hispanics is poor. Three decades of civil rights action have brought mighty improvements everywhere, yet often we encounter racial prejudice with dire consequences for people's livelihood and chance of improving themselves. Black family income is only 55 percent of white family income. Discriminatory practices in labor markets, hiring practices, educational systems, and electoral politics create major obstacles for blacks and other minorities in their struggle to improve their economic status, and we are left with the difficult question of what can realistically be done about it.

The poverty problems of minorities are highlighted by the conditions in the inner city. In the Bronx and other such urban ghettos, people encounter a combination of severely adverse situations:

- The family has been utterly shattered.
- People die of AIDS and suffer from many other diseases in much higher proportions than the rest of the population.
- There is virtually no medical care. Conditions in hospitals are totally unacceptable.
- The murder rate is out of bounds. The ghetto is a place of death, not of life.
- Neighborhoods are infested with drugs and drug pushers.
- Prostitution is rampant.
- Schools are run down and operate on highly inadequate budgets. Teachers are unqualified, and a high percentage of students are expelled.
- The ghetto is entirely divorced from a normal working existence. There are no job opportunities (Kozol, 1995).

Action against these intolerable conditions is barely contemplated by the vast majority of politicians and their constituencies. Yet vigorous action by government and business could reverse the progressive deterioration one now observes. A number of interconnected steps, substantive public attention, and finance are needed to counteract the present state of affairs:

- Move employment opportunities into the urban ghettos. Induce manufacturers to move into these areas by giving them essential overhead and protection, and by providing funds for job training. (This can be undertaken in part through "enterprise zones," which have worked well in many developing countries.)
- In the absence of sufficient job creation in the inner city, find suitable opportunities elsewhere and provide adequate transportation, or resettle people into new locations closer to their work.
- Upgrade schools. Spend at least as much on schools as on prisons.
- Provide opportunities for ghetto prisoners to earn good wages.
- Plan and execute these and other measures with full participation of the people directly concerned, as well as the clergy and social workers who spend their lives in the ghetto.

A truly national effort is required to tackle such a momentous task. However, the United States can be confident that comprehensive action is feasible. The success of action toward reducing poverty among the elderly bears this out. They have greatly benefited from improvements in Social Security and Medicare and are major beneficiaries of Medicaid. The elderly in many localities absorb the bulk of antipoverty spending. Even so, despite considerable progress, poverty among the elderly (15.7 percent) remains substantial. To eliminate it altogether, Social Security benefits would have to be increased. Whether or not that is feasible hinges in part on the prospects of the Social Security system itself. It is important to note that the federal government has been using Social Security taxes to cover its budget deficits. If the Social Security system is to be kept strong, the tax proceeds ought to be set aside for the security of future generations and no longer be used to conceal the true magnitude of the federal deficit. Other measures may also be necessary, as for example confining the benefits to people with low incomes.

Social Security is, of course, only one of many measures that come into play in a comprehensive antipoverty policy, which is not easy to start or to sustain for political as well as economic reasons. It will be appropriate therefore to now consider the strengths and weaknesses of the economic foundation on which the poor can be brought into the mainstream.

Strengths and Weaknesses of the U.S. Economy

None of these observations about the current state of American poverty should detract from the many achievements of our society and economy. It is good to recognize from the start the enormous strengths and advantages we enjoy, socially, economically, and culturally. *The strength of the American economy affords strong economic action and the maintenance of a moral stance, often against many obstacles.*

First, American society has many *political* strengths. The following examples can put our analysis in some perspective:

- Freedom of expression and the advantages of a free press.
- Stability based on a constitution that all can respect after more than 200 years.
- The advantages of recognized processes through which to work out differences and achieve new understandings and

compromises. These processes extend to the rights of the minorities with which antipoverty action is centrally concerned.

The stability derived from our constitution has enormous consequences in the economic sphere. Compare the benefits from the U.S. constitution with what has been happening in the former Soviet Union, where people have lived without the protection of an enlightened constitution, and where existing differences among social and ethnic groups were suppressed rather than settled over time in a peaceful manner.

The American government has been instrumental in helping our economy and society to make significant material and cultural strides (Shields, 1991):

Despite many complaints about our environment and related policies, for over a hundred years our country has built a solid record in conservation. To mention just two examples of progress: in 1970, only one-third of our rivers were clean enough to tolerate swimming and fishing; today the number of clean and healthy rivers has more than doubled. Through our government regulations we have freed the air we breathe from deadly lead.

Acting through our government, we have built a system of state universities and land-grant colleges. Higher education has been made available to students from every economic background, not just the privileged few. Today these schools award almost half a million degrees annually, including three-fifths of all our country's doctorates and more than one-third of bachelor's and master's degrees. We can thank these state institutions for discoveries and achievements such as the Salk and Sabine vaccines, streptomycin, the first digital computer, the first atom smasher, and more than 100 Nobel Prize winners.

Head Start, besides boosting the child's chances of graduating from high school, has been shown to reduce both teenage pregnancy and welfare dependency.

Second, the U.S. economy has repeatedly demonstrated amazing strength and resiliency. Who could forget that World War II brought an unbelievable expansion of output, through the effort of all the people, both women and men, making America the arsenal of democracy? Half a century later, despite the comeback of Germany and Japan, the U.S. economy has continued to grow to such an extent that the World Bank's *World Development Report 1994* shows that the purchasing power of output per capita in the United States exceeds that of all other industrialized countries. Small business has made a dynamic contribution to U.S. performance. In the early 1990s, after a slowdown of some years, U.S. growth and employment once again improved. Monetary authorities succeeded in restraining both inflation and economic growth so that the economy was able to expand at a pace compatible with capacity and relative price stability.

But our economy also has weaknesses. Regardless of its overall performance, it has suffered from persistent structural unemployment. While many large corporations have gone through a vigorous program of restructuring, manufacturing growth has been handicapped by a decline of entrepreneurship and innovation.

Of special importance is the fact that our economy continues to be marked by a very uneven distribution of wealth and income. In fact, over the past ten–fifteen years inequalities have become greater. Of all net wealth, 28 percent is held by the richest 2 percent of families; the top 10 percent holds 57 percent of net wealth. Distribution of income is also unequal: the upper 20 percent earn 42 percent of all income, as against only 5 percent for the lowest 20 percent. One million families have incomes over $350,000. The richer families reaped three-fourths of the nation's real income gain in the past decade, while the bottom 60 percent were actually losing ground.[2] The government in the United States has reason to counteract economic inequality and can do so through various measures, such as more progressive taxation and investment in education, health, and infrastructure for the poor.

Rising wage inequality is one of the most important changes in modern economic history. Technical change has favored skilled labor in production. While the supply of skills has increased, the increase has not, in fact, kept pace with demand. Moreover, the workers on the bottom of the scale have fallen behind: while the highest ten percent of wage earners received ten percent higher pay in the past twenty-five years, workers in the lowest ten percent saw their earnings go down by 26 percent. Overall, the average real weekly wage for male workers in 1994 was actually lower than in 1973 (Gottschalk, 1997 and Topel, 1997).

Our economic and social fabric also suffers from the fact that large corporations and big government often make crucial decisions that upset the economy of less powerful communities. Not all large corporations assume their social responsibility when they decide on the location of their plants. Why not keep a plant at home and modernize it, if a move to Mexico only saves a few pennies in earnings per share? Why not factor in the cost of destroying our local communities and the lives of our workers and their families? On the other hand, and on a more positive note, in actual practice firms may stay in the United States despite the lure of lower wages abroad if it offers better infrastructure, technological support, labor skills and wider home markets. Moreover strong growth in competing countries will induce higher levels of trade in both directions as long as these countries also maintain open markets.

To fight poverty, many different initiatives by government, community, and individuals are needed. Measures must remain in effect over a period of years and address the many causes and circumstances of poverty. The nature and impact of these measures are critical to an understanding of antipoverty action.

THE IMPACT OF ANTIPOVERTY MEASURES

Since President Johnson's War on Poverty, the United States has introduced a battery of antipoverty measures or increased outlays on existing ones, often strongly motivated by moral considerations. Most of these expanded and survived recurrent budget constraints until the mid-1990s, when congress turned fresh attention to the justification of ongoing programs and the urgency of balancing the budget (Sawhill, 1988).

The government's helping hand has provided means-tested assistance (21 percent of total outlays) and social insurance of various kinds (79 percent). Under the first category have come cash assistance like the former Aid to Families with Dependent Children (AFDC) and Supplemental Security Income (SSI), as well as in-kind help like Medicaid, food stamps, school lunches, public housing, and social service, which make up 70 percent of means-tested assistance. Most social insurance (especially Social Security) is provided in cash, with some 18 percent, including Medicare, in kind.

Welfare expenditures grew especially rapidly in the late 1960s and early 1970s. But a steady upward trend in real terms, both per capita and as a proportion of the gross national product (GNP), has continued. New programs required new outlays: food stamps in 1964, Medicare and Medicaid in 1965, and SSI in 1974. Expenditures also increased with extended coverage, higher participation rates, and

TABLE 1.1 Federal Appropriations in 1994 for Welfare

Items	Number of Programs	Appropriation ($Billion)
Food and nutrition (incl. food stamps, $23.7 bill.)	10	38.0
Employment and training	154	24.8
Housing	27	17.5
Cash welfare (incl. Aid to Families with Dep. Ch., AFDC, $12 bill.)	7	17.2
Child care (incl. Head Start, Title 1)	45	11.8
Social services (incl. VISTA vol., help for runaways.)	33	6.6
Child welfare and child abuse	38	4.3
Health	22	5.1
Total	*336*	*125.3*

Source: *Washington Post*, Jan. 7 and 13, 1995.

more generous benefits in existing programs. By 1994 the total federal appropriations for welfare, other than social insurance, were $125 billion (see Table 1.1).

Isabel V. Sawhill, the Urban Institute economist, observes that in-kind benefits, especially for medical care, have grown more rapidly than cash assistance. The expansion of food stamps, Medicaid, and public housing has caused means-tested programs to increase more rapidly than social insurance programs. On the other hand, means-tested cash assistance (like the former AFDC and SSI) have grown only relatively modestly; as a result, the average real benefit to families has tended to decline. Real AFDC for a typical three-person family declined by 47 percent in 1970–1994 (Sawhill, 1995, p. 6). The slowdown in cash welfare coincided with the deceleration in long-term economic growth since 1973, which made the pressure of welfare expense more keenly felt.

The steady pressures on government budgets caused by the growth in welfare expenditures raises pertinent questions about the causes of the increase, the effectiveness of the programs, and the best

way of funding welfare. Detailed studies show that the various measures have reduced poverty, but not all are equally effective and some
indirect effects have reduced their full impact.[3]

In the 1980s there were significant changes in government policies toward poverty issues. The federal government cut social services
and permitted an erosion of the safety net, widening the gap between
rich and poor. The 1980s saw unfavorable shifts in the work environment that depressed the earnings of many workers, families that could
only survive economically by working longer hours in more jobs, an
increase in farm foreclosures, escalation of housing costs, an increase
in homelessness, and persistent hunger among many poor groups. The
experience of the decade is of particular importance to the debate in
the 1990s about health insurance and antipoverty measures.

The persistence of poverty in face of the steady rise in antipoverty
expenditures raises critical questions about the effectiveness of particular programs. The causes of the persistence of poverty are therefore
important for both analytical and political reasons.

Demographic change, especially the increase in female-headed
families, and years of poor economic performance kept poverty up. It
remains high in the growing urban underclass, which often proves less
amenable than others to traditional solutions. Education and training
programs designed to improve the productivity of the poor are not
always sufficient or effective. The growth of income transfers is important, but transfers caused people to work less, so that the poverty-
reducing effects could be less than 80 percent of the transfers. Transfers
also tended to reduce the savings of the recipients. Larger cash transfers directly reduced the poverty rate by about 3 percent; the side
effects cut this to less than 2 percent.

Another important policy aimed at poverty reduction is investment in human capital. Many new programs were introduced in the
1960s: the Job Corps and the Neighborhood Youth Corps (1964), Head
Start (1966), improvements in elementary and secondary education,
grants, and the Manpower Training Act. Even though these programs
were aimed at improving the productivity of the poor, inequality in
actual earnings continued to rise.

According to Sawhill, careful economic analysis suggests that
many of the education programs were ineffective in reducing poverty.
The evidence is mixed on Head Start, a widely praised and popular
program. Employment and training programs proved neither a great
success nor a complete failure: their most positive result was helping

adult women return to the work force. The Job Corps had good results, but was an expensive program.

In short, a large proportion of expenditures were not well-targeted and some education programs were not well-designed. Most of what economists call human capital investment goes on within the family, and institutions like schools have little hope of offsetting the powerful influence of the home environment.

This brief overview would not be complete without mentioning the critical importance of better health care for the poor. Medicare and Medicaid increased access to health care for the underprivileged and the uninsured, resulting in a sharp drop in infant mortality since the late 1960s.

Overall, the many measures taken reduced poverty, but it is difficult to say by how much. The design and effectiveness of education programs for the poor should be kept under review and, where necessary, improved. Reduction in poverty among the elderly, brought about by social insurance programs, is the greatest success story.

It seems clear that the special programs for assistance to the poor alleviate the problem but do not solve it. *In the end we must rely on changes in social structures as well as general economic policies* that benefit the entire society and work without reliance on government largesse. These include macroeconomic policies, improvement in saving and productivity, and the maintenance of well-functioning markets. Macroeconomic factors, especially high unemployment rates, contributed to keeping up poverty rates until at least 1990. Hence we will look in more detail at the performance of the U.S. economy and what can be done about it.

POVERTY AND MACROECONOMIC PERFORMANCE

Healthy overall economic performance and the maintenance of free markets that encourage growth are of fundamental importance to poverty reduction. We will examine the record of the U.S. economy and the essential features of our economic system that make for dynamic development.

Economic Policies and Job Creation

Programs dealing with poverty or helping workers move to new employment are more successful when jobs are plentiful. World War II

TABLE 1.2   U.S. Economy in the 1960s and 1980s

U.S. Economy	1962–1973	1973–1986
Average unemployment rate (percent of civilian labor force)	4.7	7.4
Inflation	4.1	6.7
Real GNP growth rate	3.9	2.3
Real after-tax income per cap. (growth)	3.4	1.4
Average growth of productivity	2.6	0.9
Real wage rate (growth)	2.6	0.3

Source: Alan S. Blinder, 1987, p. 40. The growth rate may have been underestimated somewhat as a result of the overestimation in the deflator of current income estimates, i.e., the Consumer Price Index.

taught us that when there is a strong demand for workers, even "unemployables" can get jobs. So how has the American economy performed in recent decades?

Since the early 1970s the U.S. economy has put in a much poorer performance than in the decades of the 1950s and 1960s. In much of the 1970s and 1980s growth in output and productivity declined and inflation was higher, while real wages stagnated or declined and unemployment increased (see Table 1.2).

The strong inflationary overhang from the 1960s and two rounds of oil price increases caused the U.S. economy to sputter in a stop-and-go pattern in the 1970s. America's manufacturing industries needed time to adjust to the many changes in the world economy. Toward the end of the decade of the 1970s, the economy suffered pressures shared with other industrial countries, including a run-up in commodity prices. In the United States these pressures manifested themselves in inflation accelerating into double digits.

Inflation worries notwithstanding, new job opportunities must increase substantially to combat poverty more effectively. For the purpose of analysis, the concept of unemployment should be expanded beyond the official definition to include the large number of part-time workers, as well as the discouraged workers who are in effect involuntarily outside the labor force. For example, in 1992 there were 9.4 million officially unemployed persons (7.4 percent of the labor force), and in addition 6.4 million persons wanted full-time jobs but involuntarily settled for part-time work (on average twenty hours per week); 6.2 million persons wanted jobs but had become so discouraged they were no longer actively looking for work. Including these latter categories, there were some 22 million fully or partially jobless persons. Moreover, one also has to keep in mind that in 1992 there were 21.4 million persons who were jobless some time during the year. Unemployment was worse for minorities.[4]

In all, the number of new jobs required is much higher than the number of officially unemployed persons. If the economy were to return to full employment conditions of the type prevailing in World War II, the number of new jobs to be created would be less than 22 million, since many part-time workers would convert to full-time work, and some would drop out of the labor force as family income rose.

The problems of the unemployed were made worse by the consequences of the acceleration of inflation experienced in the late 1970s. In the fall of 1979 the Federal Reserve, under newly appointed Paul Volcker, started giving top priority to price stabilization.[5] Unfortunately, the immediate effects of the Federal Reserve antiinflation policy under Volcker were undesirable: interest rates over 20 percent, a severe recession, and a sharp increase in unemployment. Americans, especially the poor, paid a high price for the Fed's success in squeezing inflation out of our system. Meanwhile, the "supply-side" economists of the early 1980s promised that lower taxes would so enhance economic activity that in reality government revenue would rise. But when tax rates were actually lowered at a rapid clip, revenues did not rise sufficiently, and the simultaneous rise in military and other expenditures (e.g., for transportation) bloated the budget deficit.

Except for a markedly more favorable trend after the mid-1990s, unemployment in the United States has averaged between 6 and 7 percent, well above levels compatible with effective antipoverty action. The cost of unemployment in terms of output lost is astounding. The Princeton economist Alan Blinder, who considered unemployment over 5.8 percent excessive, calculated that the output loss of unemployment over 5.8 percent totaled $1,892 billion in 1975–1986. Had this lost output been actually produced, saved, and invested in government bonds, everyone in the United States would be $11,500 richer (Blinder, 1987, p. 34). Losses of this kind can never be made up.

Among various measures to improve employment conditions, some have suggested that available employment may be spread by shortening the workweek to twenty-four hours. This would run against the current business practice of encouraging longer hours for full-time workers with benefits. Any move toward shorter hours would require full cooperation of business. In our contemporary environment, propositions like these must also be considered in an international context, for whatever we do at home must remain competitive abroad.

Other proposals contemplate wider use of labor-intensive technology. Talented and skillful workers with initiative can find a place in more labor-intensive production, as for example in high-quality furniture building. But one can reasonably doubt that less capital-intensive technology can be applied to mass production of consumer goods like cars and electrical appliances. Whatever is tried must be compatible with the forward surge of technology, even when jobs are at risk. The public sector may have to come up with proposals to create employment and training for displaced workers. In a technologically advanced society, education—at all levels—must be a growth industry, essential for maintaining an innovative environment. Much of education is labor-intensive. Moreover, it is entirely possible that the systemic absorption of new technologies, including computers, will make intensive use of labor. But such labor will have to be highly trained and educated.

Authorities have been reluctant to pursue policies of new job creation for fear that they would engender inflation, a fear widely shared by economists. The emphasis on containing inflation is motivated in part by the experience of the 1970s, when high inflation rates were thought to curb growth and job creation, as well as by the fear that a little inflation creates expectations of more inflation and becomes harder to control. In fact, a little inflation is like being a little pregnant.

Even so, the damage of high unemployment to efficiency is enormous and inadequately appreciated. By contrast, the harm that inflation inflicts on the American economy may well be exaggerated. Under inflationary conditions, prices paid by the poor rise neither faster nor slower than the prices paid by the rest of the population. Generally, inflation does not raise incomes of rich people faster than the incomes of the poor. Conversely, when jobs are lost as a result of restrictive monetary policies, minorities suffer most. For example, when unemployment for prime-age white men rises by 1 percent, unemployment for nonwhite males and teenagers rises by 2.2 percent and 2.6 percent (Blinder, p. 37). The poor and the underprivileged are devastated when unemployment is used to fight inflation, and they are the big winners of a more resolute full-employment policy.

Unemployment not only represents a net economic loss to society, it demoralizes and marginalizes the afflicted, and it may severely impair their health, their life expectancy, and even the health of their families; their poor health weakens their chances of finding new employment.[6] Unemployment insurance assists the jobless and helps to stabilize the economy, but it is costly in terms of budget outlays and was cut back sharply in the 1980s. The government can combat the adverse effects of unemployment in a more cost-effective way through a program which provides productive jobs. It puts the idle back to work and enables them to realize projects needed by our communities. Upon completion of the job program, the idle have had a wholesome experience and society has gained some badly needed infrastructure. The cost may be somewhat higher than unemployment insurance, but the extra expense is well worthwhile since the jobs program produces badly needed infrastructure that is justified on purely economic grounds.[7]

Over the *long term*, the strength of our economy will depend on better performance of both savings and productivity. National savings fell sharply from 7 percent of GNP in the 1960s to 2 percent in the 1980s, when the rising federal government deficit preempted the savings of the private sector. In addition, household savings suffered from increased consumption financed by debt (Krugman, 1990, p. 67). The most direct way of improving national savings is for the government to get its deficit under control. The deficit was cut in 1985–1988 (from 5.3 percent to 3.2 percent of GNP), and has been reduced further in the first half of the 1990s. From the vantage point of the poor, it is unwise and impractical to achieve better balance by cutting expenditures across the board. Some restructuring of expenditures, especially the replacement of military outlays by expenditures for infrastructure, technological development, and continued industrial renewal, is necessary and feasible. Unless the government reduces nonsocial expenditures, the deficit will remain a debilitating depressant on the country's ability to deal with critical poverty issues.

Improvement in productivity is the second pillar of stronger growth. Output per worker grew at a healthy 2.5–3 percent in the 1950s and 1960s, but in the 1970s and 1980s productivity growth slumped to less than 1 percent. The encouraging feature of the 1990s is some upturn in productivity. However, by historical standards, productivity and growth have remained low. When some economists' recommendations to make adjustments in the consumer price index are implemented, the statistical measurement of U.S. growth and productivity will show an increase, but of course such a change will do little to relieve the real incidence of poverty.

The causes of the slowdown in long-term economic growth may well be related to technological and attitudinal factors beyond the direct reach of economic policy.[8] The 1950s and 1960s benefitted greatly from the absorption of new technologies such as improvements in road and air transport, refrigeration, and food marketing. But these had worked themselves out by the early 1970s. Some years may be required before a new wave of technological innovation is felt in the economy. Computer technology remains to be fully absorbed in business methods and organization. Moreover, the generation of the 1960s now entrenched in the workplace may have laxer standards than its predecessors (Krugman, 1994, p. 60). Environmental policy may also depress growth, although there is much contrary evidence. Others will point to the cost of excessive regulation and of liability suits as possible causes of slow growth.

We may be able to take some essential productivity-boosting steps as part of a viable program for restoring and maintaining our economic health. It is important that labor be provided with more capital equipment and that our children and workers receive better training and education. In addition, as industry is restructured, the economy can be bolstered by continued strengthening of industries that have economic potential, as well as by relocating and retraining workers. This means finding the best ways of keeping management and workers on their toes and essential reform of job-training programs.

When the economy achieves healthy growth, the poor can fully share in its benefits through stronger employment conditions and, where necessary, steady progressive action involving both public expenditures and fiscal policies. On the other hand, if we fail and experience very slow growth or simply bump along from one recession to another, then the poor are bound to suffer more than the rest of the population and will require specific antipoverty actions.

The overall economic policies discussed so far can be most effective in well-functioning markets and in an environment of private property and initiative. We next turn our attention to these systemic factors.

Poverty and the Market

Against those who favor government intervention to assist the poor stands a powerful group of advocates of the blessings of the free market. They believe that market forces can bring about social justice compatible with efficient use of resources. Actions that run against the force of the market will necessarily bring distortions and in the end may harm those we want to help. We draw here on publications of economists, whereas in Chapter 12 we return to similar views expressed by conservative Christians on moral grounds.

Several professors of the Economics Department of the University of Chicago have been among the leading advocates of the supremacy of the market. Most "Chicago economists" bring a useful and powerful message. The market is indeed the most effective instrument for resource allocation, and we cannot ignore it with impunity.

Professors Frank Knight and Milton Friedman deserve special attention. Frank H. Knight (1885–1972), perhaps the most revered and authoritative of the free-market philosophers, drives home the point that when wages are set at what ethicists call a "just level," they may in fact be set above market levels. This would encourage an employer to replace the less productive workers with more productive workers. The latter may then be better off and less discriminated against on racial grounds than those who are laid off. The intervention could have the opposite effect of what was intended. So his key advice is: don't tinker with market wages and prices. On this ground, he also objected to the reasoning in two church declarations issued in the 1930s, the papal encyclical *Quadragesimo Anno* of Pius XI of 1931 (which stressed the importance of justice in setting wages) and the Report on Christianity and the Economic Order of the Oxford Conference of World Protestantism of 1936. According to Knight, "The least familiarity with the laws of economics—a much abused term which properly means only the general facts—will show that any general pressure on the employers to pay wages appreciably above the market value of the service rendered is in the first place certain to be injurious to the interests of wage workers—but more especially to those wage workers who are already in the weakest position" (Knight, 1982, p. 148).

Milton Friedman, a powerful debater and a teacher at Chicago from the 1940s through the 1960s, basically follows the same tack as Knight in advocating the autonomy of free markets. Friedman titles his commentary on an earlier draft of the U.S. Catholic bishops' 1986 pastoral dealing with the U.S. economy "Good Ends, Bad Means" (Gannon, 1987). He notes that the bishops do not deal with relative prices; in his view, this is in economics tantamount to not mentioning God or Christ in a theological treatise. He does not believe that full-employment policies work, and draws attention to the poor results achieved in Europe. Nor does he believe that rigid central planning works, a view shared by most economists and social justice advocates. And he joins other conservatives in denying there is much of a poverty problem, pointing out that U.S. poor are better off than those elsewhere.

Friedman considers government policies as the cause of residual poverty in the United States. In this context he points to the low quality of public schooling, the setting of the minimum wage at too high a level, and the fact that public housing exacerbates an already bad environment because it puts together people on relief. Thus Friedman's critique goes well beyond the finding that many welfare programs have some negative indirect effects.

Believers in the self-sufficiency of the market see little role for government in the economy. They are apt to overlook the fact that to function well markets need, in Thurow's phrasing, "supportive physical, social, mental, educational and organizational infrastructure" (Thurow, 1996, p. 276). And, as both Adam Smith and today's Evangelicals emphasize, the market system needs operators with moral strength and fiber.

Friedman does not persuade us that free-market forces would eliminate poverty from our country. Left alone, the free market has many undesirable effects that somehow must be dealt with through countervailing action. It leaves pockets of severe poverty, a phenomenon first articulated by Gunnar Myrdal in his "An American Dilemma" (1944) and again, more generally, in his "Asian Drama" (1968). At the same time, however, free markets and private initiative inspire essential innovation, a topic to which we turn next.

The Essential Contribution of the Capitalist System

Free markets, essential for efficient resource allocation, work best in a capitalist system of private ownership such as we know in the United

States and other industrialized countries. Capitalism encourages innovation and the development of entirely new products and production processes. And, as one of the greatest economists of the twentieth century, Joseph Schumpeter (1883–1950), so eloquently taught, innovation is the mainspring of long-term growth and hence a weapon against poverty. It is worthwhile to focus on the advantages of capitalism.[9]

"Capitalism," of course, has different meanings in different hemispheres. In the United States it implies free enterprise, free initiative, and the right to work out one's own destiny, valued principles associated with the entrepreneurship that grew in American soil. In Europe, on the other hand, the development of industry was often under the control of an elite group of bankers who had state support, and capitalism thus was equated with the exploitation of the common people. In Latin America, capitalism is often plainly synonymous with social injustice, in particular as seen by intellectuals and the masses. Markets dominated by a few do not benefit the many. When only a small segment of the population can gain market access, a social revolution is needed to make markets function for all.

Kenneth E. Boulding made a penetrating contribution to the understanding of capitalism in a series of studies commissioned by the Federal Council of Churches in the 1950s. His vision of the central role of economic progress in our society puts the American economy and its ability to combat poverty in proper perspective. He points out that "one of the main justifications for the free market as an institution is that it permits rapid displacement of one process by another."[10] "Another institutional factor on which economic progress depends is the ability of innovators to acquire control over the resources necessary to make the innovation." This is one of the main tasks of the financial system in a capitalist system. The virtue of capitalism has been its decentralization (op. cit., pp. 76–77). By 1989 it had become clear that bureaucratic socialist institutions were not up to the task of promoting economic progress and stimulating innovation.[11]

How can capitalism benefit the most people? Boulding was among the first to recognize the essential role of human capital: "Education, training and health services may easily be by far the most profitable kinds of investment." Turning to poverty, he recognizes that "there is no avenue to the abolition of poverty save through the increase of productivity." Writing in the 1950s, he attributed the income disparity between the North and the South of the United States to the low productivity of the South, which in turn was due to its low rate of economic progress. Inequality in income distribution must be overcome through greater production. "Methods of achieving equality which involve leveling up rather than leveling down, which involve raising the levels of the poorer without lowering the levels of the richer, are much more likely to find social acceptance than methods of forcible redistribution" (op. cit., pp. 76–77). But he adds that "certain methods of forcible redistribution, for example progressive taxation, are entirely feasible and desirable within limits. Even these methods, however, will meet much less resistance in a society which is rapidly increasing its wealth than in a stationary society."

Anyone interested in social objectives is bound to note that capitalism is short-sighted when action must be taken on the needs of the community at large. Business typically has a planning horizon of only three to five years and expects a 10 percent or higher return on capital. The justification of social investments may require longer payoff and lower returns. Because of the differences between business and social investments, government has had to rescue or supplement capitalism in numerous ways (e.g., free public education, free lands under the Homestead Act, land-grant universities, antitrust legislation, the GI Bill of the 1950s, and in the 1960s the National Defense Education Act, the War on Poverty, and affirmative action). Besides these important government initiatives, public investments have historically assisted the functioning of the economy in many areas (viz. musket research, building of the National Road [1815], cross-continental railroads West of the Mississippi, the interstate highway system, use of the mails to subsidize airlines, public airports, atomic energy, and the exploration of space).

The capitalist economy today faces strong headwinds. One may point to the difficulties of making allowance for the ongoing large-scale immigration, the decline in investment, the reluctance of the population to pay taxes for socially essential purposes, and the decline in real wages and the stagnation of productivity of the large majority of U.S. workers, which eventually are bound to threaten the prosperity of the few at the top and of the economic system itself. All this takes place while political forces are moving authority and functions from the center downstream to states and municipalities, where local politicians may act on their own narrow interest. We also witness the rise of self-righteous religious fundamentalism and the lack of a common resolve that must inspire national action in favor of the poor in a world now free of the external threats that previously bound society together. Internationally, we see the end of the American and the Soviet alliances and the rise of feudal lords in several smaller nations like Afghanistan, Chechnya, Somalia, and the former Yugoslavia. All these forces are bound to weaken the way capitalism is working (Thurow, 1996, pp. 245 and 286).

Yet despite these problems, few now deny that our capitalist system, with its freedom of association and political decision and its urge to innovate, is by far the best system to raise output and productivity. The challenge we face is to keep our system strong and assure that the benefits accrue to all and that the poor will fully share in the general progress, something the capitalist system does not guarantee on its own. Economists are generally agreed on the benefits of free markets and free choice in the system in which both rich and poor must live and work. They also provide advice on fighting poverty.

Reflections on the Advice of Economists

The seekers of social justice must face the hard facts of economics. Economists have set warning posts along the road to a more humane society, warnings that cannot be ignored without paying a price in genuine progress for all. Frank Knight and Milton Friedman are entirely correct in saying that no government can with impunity interfere with prices and wages set by the market. Nonetheless, we can act against the injustice engendered by the free play of market forces.

In a recession the government must take many anticyclical measures. But to be able to take appropriate action, the government must have its budget in reasonable shape before the recession sets in, lest the recession aggravate an already-serious budget deficit problem. It is in everyone's interest that our government gets and keeps control over the budget deficit without imposing new burdens on working America and the poor or aggravating the condition of our children. Yet gaining such control is hard in an environment of low growth in which people object to higher taxes; it means cutting expenditures which by any reasonable standard are less essential.

Creation of sufficient job opportunities remains a realistic and justifiable objective, achievable without opening of the floodgates of government expenditures. Long-term structural policies that enable workers to get new and better skills and to find new jobs can be put in place through close collaboration among federal, state, and local governments, and private business. In the absence of such positive action, both government and business will seem to be uncaring.

Though economists have long argued that forceful action to reduce unemployment may bring forth inflationary pressures that should not be tolerated, the experience of the 1990s so far suggests that a judicious combination of monetary (Federal Reserve) policy combined with government attention to the working poor, moderate growth, and reasonable budget balance is feasible and can bring down unemployment.

Even if we succeed in macroeconomic policies that move the economy toward plentiful jobs, a broad range of specific supplementary measures will continue to be necessary. Single mothers need child care centers if they are to convert a life of welfare into one of well-paying work. Sweatshop wages must be fought by enforcing existing laws. We should also encourage developing countries to improve their own domestic employment opportunities and thereby reduce pressure from cheap labor immigration in the United States. Special assistance (cash, food stamps, Medicaid, etc.) must be available in adequate amounts to the needy, including the working poor. Welfare should encourage work and reduce dependency, and might best be administered by authorities most familiar with the conditions of the recipients. Some of these measures are already in place and have been working well in certain regions.[12] Even after reform, welfare is at best a palliative that should not distract from the importance of productive work in a healthy economic environment.

The government must take the lead in maintaining and enhancing job opportunities for all—and this requires active policies regarding growth, job creation, and price stability. If there are no jobs, people get discouraged and stop looking for work. Even with low interest rates, creation of sufficient job opportunities is not an easy goal, especially when the economy is in a state of turmoil from the forces of global integration, modernization, and computerization.

Global integration is a ruthless process which can easily depress entire regions and industries. The key players, multinational banks and enterprises, have little interest in pursuing social objectives. Globalization cannot be stopped, but its adverse employment and social effects call for countervailing measures initiated by government and business. International institutions can be encouraged to study the need, feasibility, and design of corrective measures. One would hope that business will start making greater allowance for the social impact of its decisions, especially as to plant location.

In the end, there is no simple set of rules or policies that will bring prosperity to the poor and lift all out of poverty. Government policies can only be the beginning; local and personal initiatives are the basis for genuine poverty alleviation. Government cannot be effective without the best efforts of individual citizens and communities. It is a matter of the mind and the heart, of government and business, of communities and people, of morals and economics. Moreover, unless politicians and their supporters are convinced of the need for forthright policies to help the poor, no job-creation schemes can get off the ground (Freedman, 1993). True integration of rich and poor must begin in the hearts of people and be nourished by families and communities. Personal commitment at all levels is indispensable, as will be clear from consideration of the moral and ethical base of our struggle.

MORAL AND ETHICAL ISSUES

Poverty in the United States is widespread, often hidden, and especially acute among African-Americans and other minorities in the inner city. Antipoverty action must necessarily be comprehensive and long-term. It calls for resolve and both general and specific measures. Our economy has the strength to mount effective action, but effective action requires a deep moral commitment on the part of citizens and decision makers at all levels of the community.

Economic measures alone do not suffice in the struggle against poverty. Antipoverty action must also rest on sound attitudes toward work, savings, personal hygiene, and aversion to liquor and other drugs. All these are basic to the ability to utilize new opportunities. When it comes to moving the poor off dead center, we may point to the efforts of a man on horseback: John Wesley tirelessly rode Britain's rural roads and city streets, evangelized the underclass, exhorted pride, and combated family disintegration by reforming behavior. Structural and economic measures must be combined with restoration of the moral and spiritual environment in which the poor live, which requires personal involvement through churches, unions, professional associations, and the like (Will, 1991). Many of these have done yeoman's work, often with sparse resources. Government can greatly enhance the impact of its programs by supporting the personal involvement of its citizens (Novak, 1993, p. 78).

Democratic capitalism has proven to be the most efficient system for improving the standard of living. But competition among institutions, businesses, and individuals has instilled a pervasive selfishness which must be counteracted by a spirit of caring.

The religious community has an obvious role in strengthening the spirit of charity and society's moral fiber, a role it can play on its own turf without getting into technical economics. But the churches must do more than preach morality. And indeed, as Wogaman points out, John Wesley had a much deeper and wider message. He wanted the rich to do more for the poor: "Gain all you can, in order to save all you can, in order to give all you can." "Every shilling which you needlessly spend on your apparel," Wesley wrote, "is, in effect, stolen from God and the poor." What gave his revival such transforming power was its refocusing of values beyond the self to God and the moral community of which we are all a part.[13] Moreover, the spirit of unselfishness affects our relations with all people, both rich and poor.

The churches have dealt extensively with the *moral* aspects of the causes and remedies of poverty. But it is to their credit that they did not confine themselves to the personal morality of the poor. They took a much broader approach in their call for social justice and action, and did not use personal morality as an excuse for public inaction. Economists must recommend specific steps to overcome poverty, conceived and executed in a comprehensive framework of ethical principles.

The Ethical Framework

The prevalence of poverty in a rich society raises profound ethical questions. How can contented and affluent Americans accept poverty when practical remedies exist? Economic recommendations should be complemented by ethical considerations that affect our attitude toward all people and govern the nature and persistence of just policies against poverty. The centrality of ethics makes economics a new and different science, not concerned merely with efficient resource allocation, but also with the impact of its policy recommendations on human beings. In this spirit one can accept classical economics as a means of understanding how to allocate resources efficiently, but with the added feature of special attention to ugly pockets of poverty and neglect.[14]

In reality, the principle of "perfect competition" of classical economics is put to work by individuals who may inflict harm on their neighbors in the exercise of their competitive rights, and hence is unacceptable without an ethical qualification. Each person must regard the common good in the management of his or her economic affairs: wealth must not be accumulated for its own sake; personal property must be managed in a way compatible with the interest of society at large, and carries in effect a social mortgage.

In the ethical framework adhered to in this book and developed in greater detail in Part Two, a basic first principle is that concern for the poor deserves a central place in all our social deliberations. This principle is compatible with lessons from the Bible, which frequently and in many different contexts considers poverty a critical issue deserving our urgent attention, and expresses God's love and concern for the poor. The recognition that the poor deserve priority attention is a central feature of twentieth-century theological thinking, for example, as expressed in liberation theology. Historically, it is comparable with the return to biblical teaching in the sixteenth century.

Second, the dignity of the human being, based on the idea of creation of people in the image of God, requires that those living in misery and inhuman conditions on the margin of society be entitled to the means to lift themselves from poverty and gain a place in the mainstream.

Third, social and economic policies must aim at poverty eradication and social integration. All policies must be tested by the impact they have on human beings, especially the poor. Domestic policies must use macroeconomic measures to improve conditions and, in addition, to improve wages, job opportunities, housing, health, and urban safety. Where needed, direct assistance should be provided to lift people beyond poverty into a productive life.

Up to this point we have dealt with poverty in the United States. But poverty—absolute poverty—is an enormous problem elsewhere in the world. We now turn to the plight of the poor in the developing countries.

2

The Poor in the Developing Countries

Our world is divided by a deep cleavage between very rich industrialized and poor developing countries, a division that presents a challenge to international policy for both economic and moral reasons. More than a billion people in the developing countries live in a state of misery unknown to most in the industrialized countries. The injustice inherent in such widespread poverty is of obvious deep concern to ethicists. It also poses fundamental economic questions, for in a real sense poverty of such expanse imposes a drag on the entire global economy and indirectly on the individual countries concerned. Poverty sets the developing countries apart from the industrialized countries, which nevertheless are interdependent with them.

The focus of this chapter is on the actions that can realistically be taken by individuals and their communities, by the private sector and a supportive government that shares the commitment of the community. We will look at a number of different aspects of poverty in the developing countries: the dimensions of poverty, including key characteristics and the importance of growth and income distribution; the impact of economic policies on poverty; social policy issues; the outlook for poverty reduction: and the case for international assistance. The economic analysis of poverty in the developing countries points to difficult ethical issues which are taken up at the conclusion of this chapter and in greater detail in Part Two.

THE DIMENSIONS OF POVERTY

Many developing countries have substantially reduced poverty within their borders over the past three decades. This is evident from trends in personal income and consumption, the proportion of the total population that lives in poverty, and the pace of social progress in education and health. But despite many improvements, the total number of poor continues to exceed one billion. Moreover many countries suffered severe setbacks in the 1980s, especially sub-Saharan Africa and the countries that had debt-servicing problems. Other countries (e.g., China, India, and many East Asian nations) made significant progress. Many of the debtor countries of the 1980s made significant policy improvements, and later in the decade and into the 1990s experienced higher growth rates which are bound to strengthen the base for attacking poverty.

By almost any standard of comparison with people in the less developed countries (LDCs), those of us living in the United States are very rich. We find it difficult to imagine what poverty in Calcutta or the slums of Rio de Janeiro really means, and to understand the deprivations suffered by millions of the poorest of the poor in developing countries. Our own standard of living is hundreds of times higher than theirs. Though over 30 million Americans live in poverty and the income distribution in the United States has become more unequal since 1980, we live in a world which has taken great strides in overcoming the worst of poverty. People in the industrialized countries are the beneficiaries of numerous measures taken to combat poverty and inequality: unemployment insurance, social security, various other kinds of social insurance and direct assistance, progressive taxation, and, since World War II, stabilizing monetary and fiscal policies. These measures, combined with political stability, have helped workers in the capitalist countries of the West to enjoy many of the material benefits of our society.

But what about the workers and peasants in the poor countries? They have the benefit of neither a long and general rise in living standards nor the countervailing measures taken to combat the inequities in property and income distribution. Indeed, much of the analysis we will draw on was first undertaken by Indian economists who around 1960 found evidence that inequality was actually increasing and that the fruits of development were not reaching the poorest groups in India. Since then, economists and others working with them have been asking what went wrong and what can be done to spread the benefits of development. They had much to learn about the characteristics of poverty and the policies and strategies to combat it.[1]

KEY CHARACTERISTICS

To mount effective and comprehensive action, it is essential to understand the characteristics of poverty, its nature and dimensions, and the way it is distributed within and among countries.

Generally, the poor live below a minimum standard which varies from country to country. The poor are deprived of what is enjoyed by others in the society in which they live, that is, by their "reference group." As development proceeds, the horizon of the poor is extended. Their reference group changes from the village to the better-off people in the cities, and perhaps beyond that to the richer industrialized countries. Modern communications greatly contribute to this expansion of horizons.

Absolute and Relative Poverty

Poverty is both a relative and an absolute concept. We can draw a poverty line for a particular country that indicates the per capita family income below which poverty starts. And we can draw a global poverty line below which people anywhere suffer absolute poverty, a state of starvation, severe malnutrition, illiteracy, and substandard clothing and housing. Based on the Indian experience, absolute poverty in the early 1980s was defined to start at a per capita income of around $75 per annum, less than a quarter per person per day.

Total world population is now close to 5 billion, of which 4 billion live in developing countries. The most severe poverty is concentrated in the poorest of these countries, those with annual incomes below $400 per capita. These countries account for about half of the total world population. The "absolute poor" now total around 1 billion, or one out of five in the world. This is a rough estimate, and in reality could be higher.[2]

The absolute poor suffer from such low levels of nutrition, education, housing, and access to resources (such as land or credit) that normal productive life as we know it is impossible. A cutoff point of $75 of annual income per capita is obviously a rough approximation, and in practice the income of the poorest inhabitants will vary with the income and wealth of the country and with the way it is distributed among the various groups and regions within the country (Chenery, 1974). Most of the poorest people live in countries with very low per capita incomes (like China, India, Bangladesh, and sub-Saharan Africa) and are found primarily in rural areas. Hence, improvement in agriculture is a primary step toward eradicating the worst poverty.[3] The poverty rate, the number of poor as a percentage of the population, averages 33 percent for all LDCs.[4] These data merely add up the numbers of poor; they do not describe the conditions and characteristics of the poor.

Special Features

Who are the poor and under what conditions do they live? We must be able to answer these questions, if we are to act effectively. They are best answered in concrete country situations rather than globally. Populations are heterogeneous, and the poor tend to live in a state of flux. Deprivation before the harvest may vanish temporarily when there is a good crop. A good crop or employment on a road project can pay for the purchase of new tools or clothing. But two years of drought and the lack of employment opportunity on some government-sponsored project pushes these people back below the poverty line. Rural poverty is often the critical issue. In many countries it may account for three-fourths of the total, with the rest of the poor living in urban slums.[5] This is so even in Latin America, which has achieved a high rate of urbanization.

The poor survive mainly by working long hours—men, women, and children—as farmers, vendors, artisans, or hired workers. Four-fifths of their income is consumed as food, often monotonous diets of cereals, yams, or cassava. They are malnourished to the point where they cannot work hard, and the physical and mental health of their children is impaired.

The poorest households also have the highest number of children or dependents because child mortality is high, and it is essential to ensure that some children survive to free adults from domestic tasks or eventually to support their parents. But many poor peasants don't have access to essential family-planning services and have unwanted children.[6]

Finally, most poor people are illiterate; they cannot read road signs or newspapers. Yet they learn about a better life from direct observation and hope their children will be able to climb out of poverty.

Regardless of type and pattern, poverty is most prevalent in countries with slow growth and unequal income distribution. It is worthwhile to look next at growth factors that influence the extent of poverty in different circumstances.

Economic Growth and Poverty

Vigorous and persistent economic growth helps to reduce poverty. Many believe that general growth benefits all groups and regions, in accordance with the so-called trickle-down effect. But this does not always work in practice. First, governments may spend excessive resources on monuments and military hardware. Second, much new public investment has been for heavy industry, often poorly conceived spending that does little to raise the income of the poor. Third, the rich may get most of the new output. Furthermore, even if greater output produces greater well-being for most, some regions and groups are left behind. Some argue that very rapid growth might make things even worse for the poorest group by producing greater inequality.

The Importance of Income Distribution

Though many hold that on moral and ethical grounds all people are equal and should have equal opportunities, in reality the distribution of income earned is highly unequal between and within countries. Ethicists join many economists in calling for policies that will bring about greater economic equality.

Per capita incomes of nations stretch over an astounding range. The U.S. per capita income of over $23,000 is more than a *hundred* times that of the poorest ($110) in Ethiopia and Tanzania. The growth experience of countries varies greatly with their economic characteristics. We can, for example, distinguish among those countries that depend predominantly on oil exports, those that have become important exporters of manufactured goods, those that had excessive external debts, and those south of the Sahara.

During 1950–1980 there was steady progress in poverty reduction (see Table 2.1). This long-term trend has generally continued, reflected in rising consumption per capita, life expectancy, and net school enrollments. The number of absolute poor has also come down in many countries. But in the 1980s many countries, notably in Latin America and sub-Saharan Africa, suffered severe setbacks. As a result, the poverty rate increased in a wide range of countries, although some continued to move people above the poverty line (e.g., Indonesia, India, and Malaysia) (World Development Report, 1990, p. 43). For almost thirty years there has been a decline in per capita income in several African countries. The poorest countries, with the exception of China and India, performed less well than those that were better off to begin with.

Income distribution in the LDCs is generally less equal than in the industrialized countries. Income distribution may be measured by the percentage of total national family income which accrues to the

TABLE 2.1   Economic Data for Low-Income Countries

	1950	1960	1980
Per capita income (1980 $)	160	174	245
Output growth (av. ann. percent)		0.6 1.7	
Life expectancy at birth	35	42	50
Adult literacy (percent)	22	29	38

Source: World Development Report, 1980, page 34.

lowest and the highest 20 percent of families. The 1996 Human Development Report, published by the United Nations Development Programme, shows a slightly different measurement, namely the average income of the poorest fifth as a percentage of the average per capita income of the population as a whole. This percentage ranges from 10.5 percent for Brazil and Guatemala and 12.1 percent for Tanzania to 24 percent for the United States, 41 percent for the Netherlands, and 44 percent for India.

What can be said about the relation between growth and income distribution? Income distribution data confirm the work of Nobel Laureate Simon Kuznets, the pioneer of national income data, who found that as countries developed and their income level rose, their income distribution actually became less equal. Only later, as countries develop more educational and health services and workers move from low-income rural jobs to higher paying jobs in the cities, does income distribution become more equal. But many doubt that Kuznet's findings represent a theory with general validity. For example, Sri Lanka and Uruguay had income distributions more equal than could have been expected from their per capita income, and Brazil, Mexico, Cote d'Ivoire, Kenya, and Peru had far more unequal distributions than could be predicted from their per capita income levels.

Some other factors besides income level that influence income distribution and the position of the poor in society are enrollment in primary and secondary education and rapid output growth. Some economists have found that, regardless of the pace of economic growth, a predominant small farmer sector may induce greater income equality.

Health, nutrition, and education are all important in influencing the well-being of the poorest segment of the population. As per capita income rises, the incidence of poverty and prospects for poverty alleviation improve: life expectancy and the number of physicians rise, daily supply of calories per capita improves, and maternal mortality at birth declines. A higher proportion of the relevant age group is enrolled in primary schools and relatively more women get schooling.

Enrollment into primary education has improved significantly. It is now relatively high everywhere, except in sub-Saharan Africa and other low-income countries besides China and India.

Different regions show wide differences. Sub-Saharan Africa lags behind in almost every respect: with a relatively high population growth rate, it has a severe shortage of physicians, high maternal mortality at birth, and lowest primary school enrollment. China does much better than other low-income countries, e.g., in life expectancy at birth, number of physicians per population, low percentage of underweight babies, and the lowest maternal mortality at birth. Mortality among children in Africa, South Asia, and the Middle East is much worse than in other undeveloped regions.[7]

It is clear then that economic growth may not always be associated with a lessening of poverty. However, steady growth of the economy is a positive factor in poverty alleviation. The question as to how growth can be vigorous and at the same time foster significant poverty alleviation deserves further discussion.

What Makes for Vigorous Growth?

Over the longer term, rapid growth has been good for the eradication of poverty. In the interest of alleviating poverty, the question of how to achieve and maintain growth is of central importance.

Among the main sources of growth, economists single out natural resources, physical capital, and human resources. Natural resources—soil, climate, and minerals—are given, but societies can adapt and do much to exploit scarcity. Indeed, some countries with few natural resources have put in a miraculous performance, while others favored by nature have squandered their resources and performed poorly. Policy, in short, can make a difference. Development of the human potential through education, training, and health measures is also of critical importance and will be taken up later in this chapter.

What about investment as a source of growth? The more the better? Here again, much depends on the quality of investment. Monument building and excessive concentration on heavy industry produce little improvement for the poorest groups. Despite high investment Brazil suffered severe inequality, while China established a much more egalitarian society. Thus, careful attention to selecting investment programs and projects is crucial. Return on investment is critical, but the calculation of return may have to be supplemented by special analysis of effects on the incomes and output of the poorest groups and regions.

A further factor governing growth is the *availability of land.* In many countries the pressure on agricultural land has become counterproductive and depresses income of the rural population, including the poor. The ratio of agricultural population to land in Egypt and Bangladesh is fifteen to twenty times *higher* than in the Netherlands, itself one of the most densely populated countries in Europe. Clearly, this situation calls for special efforts to create alternative employment opportunities for the rural poor.

Land reform can help to reduce the inequality of the distribution of land assets, but to be a success, it must be combined with credit and extension services. Studies in Brazil and India show that small farms are more productive than large holdings. But an illiterate peasant will have a hard time adopting new techniques or even managing his plot. In the alleviation of poverty we need a combination of interlocking policies, for single measures will not succeed in isolation.

It is clear that growth can be brought about by different factors and conditions; large capital expenditures and natural resources may not suffice. And growth alone is not enough to produce a significant reduction in poverty. A crucial ingredient is the nature of the policy that accompanies growth.

THE POLICY FACTOR

Differences in growth patterns are brought about by both structural and policy factors. The structure of the economy and the current level of well-being can influence the nature of growth. But the experience of many countries shows that the direction and effectiveness of economic policy is a major influence in translating economic growth into poverty reduction, and the strategy pursued by the country makes a real difference. We look first at differences in general development strategies and then focus on the specific measures countries can take to alleviate poverty.

Strategies of Combating Poverty

The difficult question is whether countries should first seek equity—that is, lift the income of the poorer groups in society and make overall growth secondary—or should first go for rapid growth in the hope that both poorer and richer will be better off in the process. Some countries that tried to redistribute before focusing on growth met with failure (e.g., Burma, Ghana, and Jamaica).

Three strategies of achieving growth with equity may be considered: first, the radical model represented, among others, by China and Ghana; second, the complex of policies called "redistribution with growth"; and third, the "basic needs" approach. These strategies can lead to considerable differences in economic performance, and the choice among them also raises moral issues because some strategies contemplate much more drastic measures (e.g., expropriation, forced migration, and limitation of family size) than others.

The *radical* solution strives first to achieve greater equality through drastic steps. In the 1950s Nkrumah of Ghana sought to speed up development by emphasizing large-scale state industry. He spent his country's reserves of sterling on this goal, and yet few Ghanains became better off. Nkrumah wasted large sums on overly ambitious manufacturing plants that turned out to be inefficient and poorly run.[8]

The People's Republic of China (PRC) was more drastic and in many ways more successful, although Mao's policies exacted a great cost in human lives. China began with large-scale expropriation of capitalists and landlords. Subsequently, following the example of Stalinist Russia, a close friend at the time, the Chinese built huge capital-intensive plants that were inefficient in the use of capital, materials, and energy, as well as labor. But the PRC turned out to be more balanced than the USSR; it "walked on two legs," meaning that in addition to heavy industry, it gave ample space to small and medium enterprises which require less capital and are easier to manage, more labor-intensive, and more in tune with the local community. At the same time the Chinese paid close attention to the human element through health, nutrition, child care, etc. These earlier policies put China in a stronger position to benefit from the subsequent greater reliance on free-market forces and more freedom in the agricultural sector.

The *"redistribution with growth"* strategy presents a broad and more gradualist attack on poverty that was first advocated by the World Bank in the 1970s and is still valid today. It envisaged an integrated set of government policies, operating through both the market and the government budget, to influence development in favor of the poor. These poverty-oriented economic policies include the following:

- Encouraging the use of labor-intensive rather than capital-intensive technologies. Price incentives induce businesses to use more local labor and less imported machinery.

- Channeling investment to areas where poverty persists or can best be attacked (such as land improvement, irrigation, and labor-intensive small industry). Many small entrepreneurs operate in the "informal" sector, away from government regulation and support; these type of activities have been highly efficient in improving economic conditions for the poor.

- Devoting more resources to education and training of the poor.

- Taxing the rich progressively (for example, through a sales tax on luxury products).

- Providing food for the poorest through targeted government grants or subsidies.

- Developing new technologies to make workers more productive and to assist small shops, and thereby attacking the problems of the poor with innovative methods adapted to their own circumstances. The importance of technology suitable to the economic environment of developing countries cannot be overstated.

More recent studies have confirmed the value of growth with redistribution policies (Squire, 1993). While development can create greater inequality, University of California at Berkeley professor Albert Fishlow (1995) found that a market-oriented approach and greater reliance on local self-governing institutions, community involvement, and autonomy of the poor can counteract this tendency. The process has been reinforced by the work of locally operating NGOs that have a capacity to reach people in poverty; they are currently working with as many as 250 million poor.

The *"basic human needs strategy"* supplements the redistribution with growth strategy by focusing on providing basic goods (staple foods, water, sanitation, health care, education, and housing) to the poorest groups and regions at affordable prices. Calling for special networks to make sure these services reach the poor, this strategy stresses that services must be suitable to the needs of the poor: elementary education rather than universities for the urban middle class and village clinics instead of intensive-care units in urban hospitals. This advice cautions against the widespread practice of overdesigning education and health facilities, a practice that benefits primarily the rich rather than the poor.

What Policies and People Can Do

Poverty is by no means an unavoidable fact of life. Governments and people can combat and defeat poverty by creating jobs; by encouraging personal responsibility and stimulating community action; by well-directed social policies, especially in education and health, in which the public and private sectors work together; and by lowering barriers to trade in the developed countries, creating export markets for the poor.

The principles of antipoverty lending by the World Bank are important here. The Bank recommends broad-based economic growth that uses the poor's most abundant asset, labor; access to basic social services that improve the well-being of the poor and enable them to participate fully in the growth of the economy; and safety nets to protect the most vulnerable. Policy action recommended on efficiency grounds may not make the most severely affected better off. The road to adjustment is paved with tough decisions and sacrifices.

Beyond the general policies aimed at economic growth, greater income equality, and poverty alleviation, specific measures in the area of human resource development, health, and education are needed to bolster the ability of the poor to become economically productive.

SOCIAL POLICY ISSUES

Economic growth can produce greater long-term benefits for the poor if countries also devote attention and resources to improvements in education, health care, and nutrition and slow down the rate of population growth. That is to say, countries must pay systematic attention to the well-being and development of all their citizens, without discrimination against the poorest groups or regions. By pursuing such people-oriented policies, they also come into closer harmony with the social objectives set by ethical considerations. These social actions do not come automatically with growth, although they may have greater impact in an expanding economy. The different measures reinforce each other; for example, slower population growth facilitates improvements in education, while better health and nutrition enhance efforts to reduce the number of children per family.

Education

Better education can help raise incomes and has in practice been associated with improving health and nutrition and shrinking the size of families. But education must effectively reach the poor and meet their needs.

In the 1960s and 1970s LDCs greatly increased their education efforts. In 1960–1976, for example, education expenditures of the LDCs increased from 2.4 percent to 4 percent of GDP. The dramatic increase in education drew attention to the costs involved. It turned out that costs of higher education were especially excessive in sub-Saharan Africa and the Middle East, where the outlay per student exceeded that of industrialized countries. Higher education in sub-Saharan Africa was 100 times more expensive than elementary education, compared with only double the cost in the industrialized countries. Ways had to be found to economize and rationalize higher education and to find better sources of finance. In many countries, tuition for middle- and upper-class students covered only a portion of the costs. Yet the educational opportunities offered to the more privileged enhanced their earning power, accentuating the already sharp differences between rich and poor.

To bring education more in tune with the needs of development, the results of different levels of education had to be studied in detail. Seen as an investment in human capital, the results of education can be expressed as the return on education investment. These results vary considerably, depending on the type of country and level of education (see Table 2.2). The highest returns on education investments are achieved at the lower levels, and in countries with lower incomes and rates of literacy.[9] Education at the lower levels also had a favorable effect on agricultural output. Studies in seven countries showed that

TABLE 2.2   Rates of Return to Education

Country Group	Primary	Secondary	Higher	Number of Countries
All LDCs	24.2	15.4	12.3	30
Low-income adult lit. rate under 50 percent	27.3	17.2	12.1	11
Middle-income adult lit. rate over 50 percent	22.2	14.3	12.4	19
Industrialized countries		10.0	9.1	14

Note: All figures are "social" returns: i.e., the costs include foregone earnings (what students could have earned had they not been in school) and both private and public outlays; the benefits reflect income before tax.
Source: World Development Report, 1980.

farmers who received four years of primary education were able to achieve much higher growth in farm output than farmers with only one year of primary education. Elementary education in the poorest countries deserves high priority.

Secondary and higher education produce the skills essential to help the poor make gains and to run the enterprises that raise incomes. It is, however, important that higher education be made more economical by streamlining curricula, reducing specialization, and having higher income parents pay more tuition. As experience in Brazil and Colombia has shown, on-the-job training and short-term courses can be more cost-effective than full-scale vocational schools.

Education can be made more effective by giving the poor greater access to schools, increasing the use of existing facilities, and improving the quality of education. It is sad to observe that students in lower income countries are in the bottom 5–10 percent of the performance range of industrialized countries. Teacher training and selection, curriculum improvement, and the quality and distribution of learning materials must also be improved.

Education and health are closely interrelated. Both are concerned with the well-being of individuals. Better health enables people to study more effectively, and better education helps in finding ways to improve one's health. It enables girls to find jobs, stay single longer, and have fewer children, leading the way to better health for many.

Health

Improved health contributes to economic growth in several ways. It reduces production losses caused by worker illness; it permits the use of natural resources in areas that had been totally or nearly inaccessible because of disease; it increases the enrollment of children in school and makes them better able to learn; and it frees resources that would otherwise have to be spent treating illnesses. The most obvious gains are fewer workdays lost to illness, increased productivity, better-paying jobs, and longer working lives. Healthier workers earn more because they are more productive and get better-paying jobs.

Several health parameters improve with rising incomes. While sub-Saharan Africa lagged behind badly, China performed well ahead of most other low-income countries.

Children suffer most severely from ill health. Some 20 percent of children die before they reach the age of five, in some countries it is as high as 30 percent, almost 50 percent in Brazil, compared with only 2 percent in industrialized countries and 1 percent in Sweden. Mortality among children in LDCs is twenty to thirty times above that in industrial countries. The high death rates among young children are mostly caused by diarrheal diseases and respiratory infections. Malaria kills one million children in Africa each year.

The health problems of adults in LDCs are more similar to those in industrialized countries. This is especially true for the cities, where physicians are typically concentrated. In Africa two-thirds of the doctors work in cities, even though only 20 percent of the population is urban.

However, substantial improvements, reflected in the rise in life expectancy in LDCs from forty years in 1950 to sixty-three years in 1990, have been achieved over the past forty years. Smallpox, which killed more than 5 million in the early 1950s, has been eradicated entirely, and vaccines have drastically reduced the occurrence of measles and polio. These successes have come about in part because of growing incomes and increasing education around the globe and in part because of governments' efforts, enriched by technological progress, to expand health services.

Many debilitating diseases transmitted by insects or snails are concentrated in particular regions, although malaria is still widespread and threatens 1 billion people. River blindness (onchocerciasis), which affects people in swift-water river valleys in West Africa and

TABLE 2.3   Health Facilities in Bangladesh and Germany

Number of Persons per:	Bangladesh	Germany
Physician	9,260	490
Hospital bed	5,600	80
Nurse	42,080	260

Source: World Development Report, 1980.

Central America, has depopulated entire fertile valleys. Control of these diseases requires a well-developed health service to monitor outbreaks of the disease and take remedial measures.

New technologies, the use of pesticides and vaccines, have improved health conditions and life expectancies in the LDCs. But further advances that hinge on improved sanitary conditions, nutrition, and personal health habits may be more difficult to achieve. Some communicable diseases have been spreading, and malnutrition continues to be a serious problem. In the 1970s the cost of control programs increased with the price of pesticides. And development itself causes new problems; for example, new irrigation channels enlarge the habitat of snails that carry schistosomiasis.

Improvements in water supply and waste disposal are important for long-run success. But they are expensive and must be accompanied by better hygienic practices. Once installed, new water systems must be maintained. Fortunately, some measures are simple and inexpensive—e.g., oral rehydration to replace body fluids lost in diarrhea attacks.

Health care outlays in LDCs are comparatively low. For example, Bangladesh spends $2 per person on health care, compared with $700 for Germany. The contrast in health conditions in the two countries is stark (see Table 2.3).

Improving basic health conditions is costly, slow, and difficult. However, one promising and cost-effective method is primary health care, a concept first developed in the 1970s and sponsored by the World Health Organization (WHO) and U.N. Children's Fund (UNICEF). It is an integrated approach to health, food production, water, and sanitation which emphasizes self-reliance and partnership between communities and the government. It uses community health workers with limited training to provide front-line service in midwifery, family planning, treatment of injuries, and referring seriously sick and wounded persons to medical centers. They are similar to China's barefoot doctors, who number 1.6 million, or one per 600 persons. Unfortunately, many poorer countries have no primary health care or give health expenditures low priority.

In many countries the private sector plays an important role in improving the quality of health care for the poor and lower middle class. In fact, in countries where public clinics have no incentive to provide quality care, the poor generally prefer private clinics.

Low-income countries would be well advised to place renewed emphasis on basic schooling for girls and strengthening of public health programs. Support for public financing of essential clinical services should be at the top of the policy agenda. Reducing public subsidies for middle-class services would also yield large benefits and should therefore be a key element of policy change.

The best prevention against many types of illness is better nutrition and more sensible ways of living. Government policy and private-sector activity can be combined to combat malnutrition. Better nutrition and education are also closely intertwined: poor schooling means people are less able to determine what foods are best for them.

Nutrition

Malnutrition is concentrated in the low-income countries of Africa and South Asia, and is common among lower income groups in most other LDCs except China. There are no precise estimates of the number of malnourished people; numbers range from 340 million to 730 million, of which four-fifths live in low-income countries. The proportion of people with inadequate diets probably declined in the 1970s, but population growth increased the total number of underfed people. Some 500 million suffer from blood loss and a shortage of iron, which causes anemia.

Young children suffer most from undernourishment, followed by pregnant and nursing women. The more children a woman has, the greater the probability of anemia, thus completing the cycle of poverty, high fertility, and low rates of child survival. Girls suffer more than boys, especially in South Asia and the Middle East, because of maldistribution of food within the family. Malnutrition of children stunts their growth and may retard their mental development. Studies show that malnutrition directly affects physical productivity and depresses earnings. We see here a vicious circle, as in so many other aspects of underdevelopment: poverty causes undernourishment, and under-nourishment aggravates and prolongs poverty.

Malnutrition is commonly caused by a general shortage of food, not just an imbalance between calories and protein, as was thought in earlier years, and the critical cause of malnutrition is low income and poverty. Other underlying factors are ignorance of good nutrition practices and the inequitable distribution of food within the family. Provision of food helps in the short run, but it does not solve the problem. Where there is slow income growth in the poorest nations, it is likely that malnutrition will also persist. The most effective way to deal with malnutrition is to accelerate income growth.

Paradoxically, the great famines in Asia and Africa were not caused by lack of food. Famines are a consequence of low incomes. Droughts so depress farmers' income that they cannot buy food from nonaffected areas. The observation that poverty or decline in income is the primary cause of hunger and malnutrition has consequences for both national and international policy. If global income were distributed differently, the present output of grain alone could supply every man, woman, and child with more than 3,000 calories and 65 grams of protein per day, far more than even the highest estimates of nutritional requirements. Eliminating malnutrition would require redirecting only about 2 percent of the world's grain output to the mouths that need it.[10]

If such a relatively small redirection of grain supply would solve the problem of large-scale malnutrition, why does so much suffering persist? The answer lies partly with poor education. In the individual family, where the battle must be won, lack of money is compounded by poor nutritional practices—e.g., by shortening the weaning period. Studies show that better educated parents have better nourished children. Education may also help to improve the distribution of food within the family. In most LDCs adult women receive less nutrition than men, and girls are less well fed than boys.

The central policy for eradicating malnutrition is to raise the income of the poor and to boost production of what the poor eat and grow. Several other measures must be taken, and each country will have to sort out its own priorities among them. These include nutrition education, which should be part of general education; stimulation of production of food eaten by the poor; and various kinds of subsidization.

Practical possibilities, the success of antipoverty action, and the availability of resources for strengthening education, health, and nutrition will be greatly enhanced by a slowdown in population growth. Effective development policies must include comprehensive efforts to reduce the growth of population, a topic that deserves to be discussed in some detail.

SLOWING POPULATION GROWTH

Poverty reduction and slowing population growth go hand in glove. Improvement in education and health, so crucial in eradicating poverty, will also help to slow population growth.[11]

Growth of population in LDCs peaked in the mid-1960s at about 2.4 percent per annum and has since been brought down to 2 percent. The difference in these rates may seem little, but it has enormous consequences for the year-to-year increase in the numbers to be fed, housed, and educated. The slowing of population growth has been brought about by changing socioeconomic conditions in many countries, as well as by family planning. Policies that encourage lower birthrates are an important element in efforts to reduce future populations. However, some of the methods employed under these policies raise critical moral issues for certain religious communities, which are further discussed at the end of this chapter.

Countries with official policies to reduce population growth make up more than three-fourths of the population of developing countries. Inclusion of countries with family-planning programs for health and welfare reasons brings the total population with population programs to over 90 percent of the population of developing countries.

We first focus on critical trends, especially the decline in the growth of population in China and India, and on what makes the demographics of many LDCs today so much more difficult than the situation the industrialized countries faced in the nineteenth century. Next we discuss the impact of the economic development process on population. Finally, we consider how economic policies influence population and what role external assistance can play.

Critical Trends

Since 1965 birthrates in both China and India have been coming down. The annual decline in population growth rates in the developing countries taken together is now faster than what occurred during the demographic transition in the United States and other industrialized countries in the nineteenth century. In most middle-income LDCs, widespread education and growing acceptance of family planning have begun to pay off in lower population growth. But most low-income countries, other than China and India, continue to have high fertility and high population growth rates.

The fertility differences among countries can be explained primarily by the socioeconomic environment. The poor have limited access to health care services, education for children and women, old-age insurance, and the consumer goods and social opportunities that compete with childbearing. For individual poor families, children are an investment that pays off in terms of earnings and in care for the parents in old age.

In historical perspective, the world population is now increasing at an unprecedented rate of 25 percent per decade, as against only 1 percent in the centuries leading up to 1800.

The nineteenth-century industrialized countries were far better off than the developing world of today. During the industrial revolution, both agricultural and manufacturing output grew in *geometric* proportions, and the population growth rates never reached the levels maintained in the developing countries today. The population growth rate of France and England was below 1.5 percent in the nineteenth century. Moreover, population increase was mitigated by emigration (some 20 percent of Europe's population increase in 1881–1910). Japan's population also increased slowly. The rural population in Europe grew by less than 1 percent, as against over 2 percent in Asia and Africa today. The U.S. population increased by more than 2 percent, but slowed down after 1900.

The Links with Economic Development

Progress in economic development and population growth are interrelated in many ways. Slow population growth has its own disadvantages; for example, care for the elderly is more burdensome with a slowly growing workforce. But the overwhelming evidence is that high population growth holds back development. At the family level, many children reduce the amount of time and money that can be devoted to each child's development. At the societal level, high fertility makes it harder to finance the investment in education and infrastructure that ensure sustained economic growth. Slower population growth will quickly reduce pressure on education facilities, but unfortunately, its effect in slowing the growth of the workforce will only be felt after fifteen to twenty years.

The LDCs that now enjoy relatively higher income and better infrastructure facilities also have achieved lower population growth rates, as for example in Korea and other countries in East Asia. But in Brazil, which has large untapped natural resources, the high population growth rate reduces the possibilities of educating and training the managers needed to exploit these resources. Agricultural and manufacturing expansion in low-income countries like Egypt and India require costly investments, which are harder to finance if population growth rates remain high.

As population increases, more capital, in the form of infrastructure and social investment like education, is needed to accommodate larger numbers of people. This "widening" of capital merely keeps up the amount of capital per person. At lower population growth rates, investable resources can be released to enable countries to increase capital per capita, a process of capital "deepening" which increases the amount of machinery available to industry workers and improves education.

High population growth has a powerful effect on the future growth of the labor force. High fertility in Nigeria in the 1970s meant that the labor force in the year 2000 will be double that in 1984. For China, the corresponding increase is only 45 percent. In the process of development, an increasing proportion of the labor force will become urban as workers move from low-productivity jobs in the rural sector to better urban jobs. A larger labor force needs a corresponding increase in capital, but an improvement in incomes requires a further increase in capital per worker. The rural workforce is increasing rapidly in many African countries today, hence it is harder to bring down its share in the total labor force. By contrast, the rural population of nineteenth-century Europe increased by only 1 percent per annum or less, so that the transfer of labor toward more productive urban jobs was much easier to accomplish.

High fertility puts the poorest countries at a disadvantage because it exerts pressure on land resources and food supplies. It is true that projections of global food production suggest that total grain output may double in the next two decades; barring a severe intensification of droughts, the supply of food will be sufficient to meet the needs of a rapidly expanding world population. But a favorable food supply does not help the poorest countries, where high fertility is putting pressure on the land. These countries suffer from shortages of agricultural land and of water for irrigation. In India rural households increased by 66 percent during the 1950s and 1960s, but the cultivated area expanded by only 2 percent. Though irrigated areas doubled in the 1960s and 1970s, now India—along with several other areas, such as the Nile basin, the North-East of Brazil, and Pakistan—has run out of land that can be irrigated at acceptable cost. The water constraint can be eased to some extent by improved management, multiple cropping, and raising yields, especially in Africa. But these possibilities are limited in some countries such as Egypt, where yields are already high.

Demographic Change

The demographic transition in the developing countries started with the decline in mortality in the 1920s. Longer lifespan increases the population, but the very conditions that bring it about, higher income and better education and health, also reduce fertility. Together with more effective family planning, these conditions slow the rate of population growth. This transition from lower mortality to lower fertility and lower population growth must still be completed in several African and other poor countries.

The demographic scene in the developing countries has some key characteristics:

- The post-WW II rate of population growth in the developing countries is without historical precedent. In only one year, the world population increases by 80 million, of which 73 million are in the developing countries.

- The population in the developing countries is much younger than in the developed countries. In the LDCs 40 percent of the population is aged fifteen years or younger; in the developed countries this figure is 23 percent.

- Internal, like international, migration now provides only minor relief. Despite rural-urban migration, most of the urban population increase is from births and the rural population is increasing by 2 percent or more. At growth rates currently projected, Mexico City will be the world's largest city by 2000 with a population of 31 million, followed by Sao Paulo with 26 million. London, the world's second largest city in 1950, will not even be among the top twenty-five cities.

Looking to the future, a further increase in life expectancy seems to depend crucially on improvements in living conditions, education for women, and health care for the poor. Projections show that population growth in 2000–2050 will depend critically on what happens to fertility in the next two decades. The standard projections for declines in fertility and mortality assume a continuation of ongoing trends. The projections with rapid declines in fertility and mortality rates assume that most countries will have the same favorable experience in bringing down birth rates that Colombia, Korea, and Thailand have had, and that in particular fertility will start coming down in Africa and Bangladesh. However, even assuming rapid declines in fertility and mortality, the projections indicate that total LDC population will double to 6.7 billion by 2050. For the prospect of world poverty conditions, it is significant that most of the increase in population will occur in the low-income countries other than China. In this large group of countries, population will increase from 1.3 billion in 1982 to 2.8 billion in 2050. The increase is highlighted by the population projections for selected countries:

- India will double to 1.4 billion by 2050, practically pulling even with China.
- Bangladesh will more than double from 93 million to 230 million in 2050, and more than triple to 357 million if the standard projection comes true.
- Kenya will increase from 18 million in 1982 to 73 million by 2050 and an even higher 120 million on the standard assumption.

Population Policy

Population policy has numerous components, ranging from setting tentative growth targets, providing pertinent information, health assistance, and contraception to special taxation and housing policies (as in China, where small families receive preference in the allocation of apartments). Both governments and private agencies can play a role in population policy and particularly in reducing fertility. Families consider the number of children they get from their individual vantage points, but do not weigh the effects on society. On the other hand, governments and private agencies of all kinds can take into account the interests of society as a whole and weigh the interests of the family against those of society. Health and education measures, crucial in reducing fertility, are often subsidized by the public sector. Governments can provide information on family planning, the health benefits of lower fertility, health care, and family-planning assistance. In many countries religious institutions, following their own moral guidelines, can also make an important contribution—for example, by providing encouragement, advice, and essential information.

As development proceeds, higher income levels and better conditions of health and education, especially of women, will induce and enable parents to have fewer children. But improvements in the standard of living take time. Hence it is important that governments take early and more direct action to reduce mortality and to improve education and the opportunities for women, so as to sustain a decline in fertility over the longer term.

A sane population policy does not absorb large financial resources, domestic or foreign. Most of the policies required to meet the population challenge call for suitable design and orientation. Population spending per se is at present less than 1 percent of government budgets. Governments could satisfy the large unmet demands for contraception of some 65 million couples by a 60 percent increase in population program expenditures. To reach the standard decline in fertility would require a 5 percent increase in real terms over two decades. The rapid decline in fertility would necessitate a quadrupling of funds. If all expenditures were to be financed with external funds, foreign aid would have to rise by at most $2 billion (or only 5 percent of all aid programs in 1982 and an even smaller percentage of capital inflows in the early 1990s). These would probably be highly cost-effective expenditures, since the ensuing development benefits would be huge.

EXTERNAL ASSISTANCE

Population policy assistance has been but a small portion of external aid. Yet outside help can make a vital technical contribution and play an important role in furthering population programs. The driving force behind reduction of population growth must come from *domestic* economics, politics, religion, and culture. Most of the effort must be organized and financed with the country's own resources. External assistance can, however, give supplementary support. It has a role to play, especially in providing policy advice as well as technical and financial help for schools, nutrition, and health services.

External assistance can become more sharply focused on poverty alleviation. There is also considerable scope for finding ways in which private capital can be put to use in fighting poverty; making the poor productive in a responsible and enlightened way should be profitable from a private point of view. Furthermore, the scarcity of external assistance draws attention to the role of indigenous ways to reduce poverty.

The external finance community now faces the urgency of stepping up antipoverty lending, including loans for improving basic conditions through strengthening primary education, sanitation, health, nutrition, and lowering population growth. After fifty years of external assistance, the number of people living in deep poverty, with per capita incomes of less than a dollar per day, continues to be more than one billion. Many countries suffer poverty rates between 25 and 50 percent of their populations. Poverty conditions have persisted, even though there have been important improvements in social indicators such as life expectancy, infant mortality, access to safe water, primary school enrollment, and immunization. Even where poverty rates have remained constant, infant mortality has gone down because of greater access to health services, and more children are attending primary school because of the spread of free public education.

Structural adjustment lending in the 1980s was designed to help middle-income countries reform their policies to overcome adverse conditions in the world economy and instability at home. In many of the poorest countries, especially in Africa, structural adjustment programs did not work well because these countries lacked the institutional capacity for policy reform and did not have sufficient supply response. Moreover, the poor, especially in urban areas, suffered from cutbacks in social expenditures and from increases in the prices of food and imports as subsidies were removed and exchange rates set at more realistic levels.

With structural adjustment lending aggravating poverty conditions in some countries, more attention began to be paid to poverty issues. For example, the World Bank placed poverty reduction in the center of its operations, following guidelines developed in its World Development Report, 1990.[12]

Decisions on external aid for poverty eradication are governed by economic, financial, and political considerations. Yet they also have a strong moral base.

A number of religious groups have criticized the World Bank's poverty alleviation programs. They have sought to increase popular participation in projects and to make external lenders more sensitive to local conditions. In response to these criticisms, the Bank has taken a number of steps to enhance local participation in its projects and to improve the procedures for hearing complaints and taking corrective action. As a result, the Bank has become a different institution from what it was ten to fifteen years ago.[13]

Several conservative analysts oppose foreign aid of any kind. For example, Milton Friedman believes that aid strengthens tyrannical governments and increases poverty. He points to the bad experience with Tanzania and urges that, instead of providing foreign assistance, we rely on the workings of the free market which did so well by the "four tigers," Korea, Taiwan, Hong Kong, and Singapore. However, what worked in these four countries may not succeed in Africa. Friedman and the authors to whom he refers—Bauer (1981) and Krauss (1983)—pay little attention to the effectiveness of the multilateral development banks. Aid, when well administered, can make the poor more productive by giving them the tools to lift themselves out of destitution.

In the future, external assistance will need to address the disintegration of entire societies and economies, such as some in Africa. It will also have to support ongoing reconstruction efforts in Eastern Europe and Russia and seek to help all countries to adopt a sane environmental policy. And it will be imperative that a significant share of international assistance be directed to population policy; primary education, especially for girls; and adult literacy. In addition, external capital must help to reverse the slowdown in food output through assistance to agriculture, reforestation, soil conservation, and agricultural research (Brown and Kane, 1994, ch. 16). Given a reasonable effort in these areas, what is the outlook for poverty in the developing countries?

THE OUTLOOK FOR POVERTY ERADICATION

The world suffers from a widespread feeling of uncertainty, making any discussion of the outlook for world poverty risky and tentative.

However, generally speaking, reduction of world poverty hinges on the creation of sufficient employment for the poor, through the pursuit of effective labor-intensive growth policies, and the provision of social services, especially primary education, basic health care, and family planning. A favorable external environment—vigorous growth in industrialized countries—would of course facilitate poverty-alleviation policies in the Third World.

Based on favorable assumptions, there could be considerable progress in the next couple of decades, with possible declines in poverty rates in China and India, which today account for a large share of world poverty. But progress may be slow in sub-Saharan Africa, where the poverty rate could remain well above 40 percent and the absolute number of poor even increase. And prospects could easily turn sour with adverse developments—some of which are already in evidence.[14]

Region-by-region analysis of the prospects for poverty yields at best a mixed picture. Over a period of two or three decades there have been widespread and substantial improvements, especially in East Asia, where the poor may well continue to improve their lot. The prospects for renewed improvement are particularly uncertain in Africa. Latin America, on the other hand, has made major strides toward democratic government and better economic management. In most countries, improvement in poverty conditions will depend on success in making their economies more efficient. But in reality, the necessary cutbacks in state power are difficult to bring about and often require a painful transition. Moreover, a number of factors could retard poverty reduction.

Factors Slowing Progress

Concrete action on a number of fronts can bring early improvement. The prospect is not one of despair, although basic conditions must change in Africa before fertility will start to turn down and the fruits of rising incomes will be felt widely. Financing the necessary programs may be hard at times, but it is not the central issue. The costs are relatively modest and the potential benefits are high. Moreover, external finance and technical aid can assist the measures that should be taken in education, health, and family planning.

These observations apply to the elimination of absolute poverty of the African or Bangladeshi type, as well as the pockets of poverty in India, Brazil, and other semiindustrialized countries. But progress will face difficulties all along the way. Social structures obstruct rapid progress. The rich have much at stake and are well entrenched. They have their own reasons to set themselves apart, as they face large numbers of poor and uneducated. They often control the political processes and may have a decisive influence. Furthermore, most present fiscal policies do not favor a reduction of prevailing inequalities. The income tax, a progressive tax which when well administered weighs most heavily on the rich, is usually the weakest element in the fiscal system. Most public expenditures actually benefit the rich more than the poor.

The various plans and policies that have been discussed must be put into operation in many different economic and social sectors. Along the way they are bound to face controversy and opposition.

Implementation of Antipoverty Programs

Much of the discussion in this chapter concerns the economics of fighting poverty. The sources are mainly economists or public health specialists, and their underlying assumption seems to be that government must undertake whatever action or initiative is needed. But that is wrong. All must play a role, not just government but the poor themselves, as well as the private sector, business, churches, and NGOs. Where the private sector is weak, as in some African countries, government and external assistance may help to strengthen it through policy measures, technical help, and financial assistance such as aid to local development banks.

Many but not all of the services rendered to the poor are provided by the government free of charge. And government agencies tend to act in a remote and bureaucratic way. The recipients themselves play a key role in the design, provision, and utilization of services to the poor; their participation enhances the chance that the expenditures will actually result in better education, health, and nutrition, and reduce the size of families.

Where feasible, the provision of services in both infrastructure and the social area should be carried out on a commercial basis. Competition among providers enhances efficiency and effectiveness. Household surveys show that poorer families often prefer private clinics, even though they are more expensive, for public clinics may have little incentive to give better service. The principle of competition may be a novel idea in some developing countries, but in the interest of better service it should be tried. In the end it is the poor who should benefit most, not the institutions that render the service.

THE ETHICAL DIMENSION

The economic analysis of poverty in the developing countries points to three essential issues, each with its own ethical and moral implications.

First, the world is deeply divided between rich and poor. Against this the Bible shows an overwhelming concern with the poor and teaches that all people are equal. This equality extends to all aspects of our lives, material as well as spiritual. Yet the blacks and other minorities in the United States and the peoples of the developing countries suffer more than their share of poverty. The fights against poverty and for racial equality go hand in hand wherever we see injustice.

Second, vast numbers of people live in hunger and misery. Over one billion people, one out of every five human beings, live at so low a level of nutrition, education, housing, and access to land and credit that normal productive life as we know it is impossible. Poverty of that severity depresses the life of the individual and destroys the fabric of the community. Against this situation the Christian and Jewish faiths hold that God has given the earth sufficient resources so all can live in dignity in terms of social as well as economic status.

Third, a critical step toward reducing poverty is a slowdown in population growth. Economic analysis shows that slowing population growth is a central factor in countries' ability to improve conditions for the poor. Reducing the number of children per family releases resources for education and enables countries to increase spending per student. It also facilitates the transformation from a traditional rural to a modern urban economy and strengthens a country's ability to free up markets and enhance employment opportunities.

Economic and social development will by itself reduce the growth of population but, given the reality in the poorest countries, special measures over and above stimulating economic growth are needed to stem their high fertility.

Birth control measures, however, have been opposed on ethical grounds by the Catholic Church and Fundamentalist groups in the United States. Their opposition has been directed primarily to abortion, but in reality they oppose all forms of birth control other than abstention from sexual intercourse. Few will deny that abortion is a highly undesirable practice. It is hard to disagree with the view that abortion entails infanticide to be avoided wherever possible. In this connection one should also recall that the Catholic Church not only speaks for life in theory; it has made strenuous efforts to operate major school systems and to educate children with many different social backgrounds.

Abortion is also defended on the ground that women must be free to choose. But free choice is always subject to a moral rule. From the moral viewpoint of the Catholic Church and Fundamentalist groups, abortion is a poor ground for defending the freedom of women to choose.[15]

A way to combat abortion is to make better birth control techniques more widely known and available, and to bolster research on improved methods. As long as the opposition is focused on a particular way of controlling the number of babies, in this case abortion, some important issues are swept under the rug. Reducing population growth is an undeniable feature of eliminating poverty in the developing countries. One must search for the best way of realizing this objective and improve education on population policy.

Though the mainline Protestants don't object to the use of contraceptives and have not taken an outright pro-life stand on abortion, some of them have expressed reservations about abortion—e.g., the Methodists in 1984 and the Lutherans in 1991—and they do not approve of its use as a method of birth control.

Looking beyond the question of how to reduce birthrates, the Catholic and the mainline Protestant churches recognize the Bible's central concern with the poor and have directed attention to the problems of poverty in the LDCs. They make a strong ethical case for the fight against poverty. Though their statements deal with poverty in the United States, their arguments extend equally to poverty in the Third World. Moreover, the Catholic Church has issued two major pastorals focusing on the problems of developing countries and the deeper meaning of development: *Populorum Progressio* (Development of People, 1967) and *Solicitudo Rei Socialis* (On Social Concerns, 1987). Pope John Paul II considers himself as heading the Church of the Poor and has on many occasions spoken about the efforts to overcome poverty. The American Catholic bishops have likewise spoken in favor of development assistance and devoted a chapter in their 1986 pastoral ("Economic Justice for All") to U.S. policies toward the developing countries (see ch. 10).

Deep and pervasive poverty and a lack of dynamic progress toward a better life for the poorest stands in the way of global stability and peace, and the reality of widespread and persistent poverty underlines the urgency of attention to its issues in both theology and economic policy. In this post-cold-war era, we can turn our attention to liberating the world from the shackles of poverty, while at the same time helping the Eastern European countries and the former Soviet republics in their transition toward a freer economic system. These two tasks make up an ambitious agenda, and one should not be pursued at the expense of the other.

A major factor in the success of antipoverty action is the degree of popular support and the contribution and commitment of communities and private parties. Concerted action is needed through cooperation of the central and local government, business, and religious and civic organizations. And it is also important to recognize that the informal sector makes its own efficient contribution to employment creation and growth (Oxford Declaration, 1990, par. 48).

Churches, synagogues, and religious groups in general can play a critical role in the fight against worldwide poverty. They can call for concrete steps toward a more caring, less selfish society, broaden political and popular support for antipoverty campaigns in the developing countries, and influence the level and direction of all forms of help. This role is of course especially important where the church has a large and influential membership as, for example, the Catholic Church in Latin America and the United States and the Fundamentalist churches in our Southern states. Refusal to take a position against poverty would deny an essential part of the Christian message.

In the end, it is encouraging to know that countries and people can work themselves out of poverty. Regardless of their social philosophy, they can pursue essential and effective policies, often supported by technical and financial assistance from outside. In addition, they can help themselves through improvements in education, health, and nutrition and can put in place essential support systems. But to be successful, they must have faith in themselves and their future. And here the churches can play an obvious role by contributing directly to a country's educational and social efforts, by helping to strengthen the lives of its individuals, and by drawing attention to the urgency of a renewed worldwide campaign against poverty.

*   *   *

The foregoing analysis has alluded on several occasions to the special role of women in the development process, particularly in education and the reduction of fertility. Women in both developing and industrialized countries are often at the short end of progress. The role of women in the struggle against poverty is the subject of the next chapter.

3
Women: The Poor of the World

The discussion so far has been neutral as to gender. We have looked at the conditions of the poor and at the measures, strategies, and policies which must be pursued to combat poverty. We have not looked at how women and men are differently affected by poverty, which has both economic and moral consequences.

Wherever we look, we find that women are poorer than men, more poorly educated, more poorly paid, and more constrained in their productive activities. In more ways than one, women are the poor of the world. These basic observations are confirmed by an overview of the economic position of women in the global economy and by a look at the role of women in both developing and developed countries. The pervasive unequal treatment of women is, of course, in direct conflict with the moral view that all people are equal. But, as discussed in "The Ethical Dimension" at the end of this chapter, the writings of theologians do not give unequivocal support to the equality of women, nor have some religious communities fully come to accept this position. The Bible itself is often murky on this issue, although in essence it teaches that all are created in the image of God, the Mosaic laws were fairer to women than the practices of nations surrounding Israel in ancient times, and Jesus stood apart from contemporaneous tradition in his even-handed dealings with the other sex.

Economists have assembled a mass of statistics on discrimination against women in all strata. This work was accelerated during the decade of the 1980s, the United Nations Decade of Women, which organized international conferences focusing on the plight of women, and was further broadened and intensified at the 1995 United Nations Fourth World Conference on Women in Beijing.

New research has produced abundant evidence of the extent and consequences of the poverty of women. It is amazing that standard texts and theories of development have ignored the plight of women for so long. Take, for example, the theory of the surplus labor economy

71

first formulated by the Nobel Laureate Arthur Lewis. The theory envisages that as the rural, agricultural sector is modernized, low-paid rural workers will move to the modern urban sector. There economic activities, especially manufacturing, first benefit from the low rural "subsistence" wages these new workers are paid, and the resulting extra profits earned by enterprises help to pay for new investment. Once substantial numbers of workers have moved to the city, labor in the rural sector becomes scarcer, and wages everywhere rise to a "commercial" level where marginal cost equals marginal output. Nowhere did Sir Arthur and his successors explore the human consequences of these changes (Fei and Ranis, 1964).

In Africa, where this kind of modernization is still in process, the men move to the city and begin to receive higher pay, which they may or may not send home. Women stay behind, raise children, and care for the family; they continue to raise food for the home in a traditional way and hence do not reap the benefits of modernization. In contrast, when men stay at home they may start using new production methods in agriculture; but here again, men ride the tractors or use modern techniques to raise cash crops for exports, while women carry on in the traditional manner.

The Danish agricultural economist Ester Boserup pioneered the analysis of women's role in the developing economy in her "Women's Role in Economic Development." Though the book broke new ground in 1970, it was largely ignored in the development community, and a standard development economics textbook like Gillis (1987) neither mentions Boserup's seminal work nor takes up the subject of women in development.

Low pay and the care of large families by unwed or deserted mothers are key factors in the impoverishment of women. The feminization of poverty has spread to both advanced and developing nations. Women everywhere share a deep sense of inequality of opportunity and the injustice of the traditionally imposed second place. Throughout the world, more women than men are poor, and their numbers are growing. In the United States, two out of three adults below the poverty level are women; one elderly woman in six is poor.

Discrimination against women in the marketplace, the factory, the family, health, and nutrition comes at a very high cost. One of the reasons for sluggish long-term development in, for example, South Asia and parts of Africa could be the persistent and widespread mistreatment of women. They are not merely up against economic facts and phenomena, but face deepseated and unjustifiable cultural attitudes as well. It is hard to conceive that countries will experience genuine development if they do not enable women to work effectively as full partners in a common enterprise. Making women more productive economically will make everybody better off—men, children, indeed the entire economy, albeit poor or developed.

In most situations women suffer a natural handicap: they face severe strains and social objections when they combine raising children with a job outside the home. If they are to do so successfully, they need all the help they can get from society, their families, and friends. Both parents must shoulder the tasks of raising children. The more domestic chores are shared between husband and wife, the better for the family and the economy.

WOMEN IN THE GLOBAL ECONOMY

In the past few decades the number of women in the global workforce has risen dramatically in all regions except the Middle East.[1] One woman in two between the ages of fifteen and sixty-four is in the paid workforce. But most of the expansion of jobs has been in a few segregated categories where women receive low pay and little training. Technological advances in the developing countries have begun to benefit male workers, but have so far bypassed most women. They continue in traditional agriculture or work long hours at menial jobs. And while school enrollment of women is up, this education often does not prepare them for highly paying technical work (Boserup, 1970; Sivard, 1985).

A disproportionate number of women are unemployed or underemployed. Their share of part-time employment in the industrialized countries is inordinately high: 64 percent in Italy, 70 percent in the United States, and 94 percent in Germany and the United Kingdom. And women are highly concentrated in a narrow range of fields and jobs requiring only low responsibility or skill, where the pay is low. For example, in Austria 63 percent of women are concentrated in six out of seventy-five occupations. In Sweden over 40 percent of women are in five out of 270 job categories: secretaries, nurses' aides, sales workers, cleaners, and children's nurses. The predominantly female occupations attract but few men.

Concentration in a few jobs is associated with unfavorable work conditions: lower wages, lower status, longer hours, and lack of fringe benefits and job security. Women simply do not have parity in wages and salaries. Overall, women's hourly earnings in manufacturing average less than three-fourths of men's. In LDCs the wage gap is larger than in industrialized countries. In industrialized countries the highest female-to-male pay ratio has been achieved in Sweden (90 percent), while Japan suffers the lowest ratio, with females earning only 43 percent as much as males. In addition, women face discrimination in recruitment, training, and promotion policies, all of which tend to favor men.

The salary structure in industry is strongly influenced by the percentage of women in each employment category: the higher the ratio of female workers, the lower the pay. Work at home or part-time, seasonal, or temporary work, in which females are the majority, are low in pay, low in benefits, and less likely to provide training or career development.

Despite some improvement, women still fill comparatively few management positions. Women are identified with caring and supportive roles in school and home, and this attitude carries over into the marketplace. They choose jobs which are compatible with family responsibilities and have to accept work which is repetitive, dull, and demanding.

But change is possible. Improvement in child care facilities is enabling women better to combine jobs outside the home with their position in the family. Legislation can help to limit sex discrimination and provide for support in terms of hours worked, parental leave, and child care. In 1994 President Clinton signed a parental leave bill. But while essential, laws are not enough. In the industrialized countries what is needed is realistic affirmative attitudes in the job market and support for training and guidance to help women break away from technical illiteracy.

WOMEN IN DEVELOPING COUNTRIES

In the developing countries women face numerous obstacles, often associated with the process of change. Agriculture provides about two-thirds of paid jobs, with industry and services sharing equally in the remaining one-third. Women are in dead-end jobs without skills or training. Where women are employed in raising cash crops, they do the backbreaking work of planting, weeding, and harvesting, while men operate the mechanical equipment. In the service sector women do menial labor as domestics, or in the informal sector they sell food and home-grown produce. In industry women are low-paid assembly line operators in textiles, apparel, and electronic products. They are employed for a few years in routine operations, and when they become less efficient in the tedious work they are replaced by a new crop of young women. The "older" women in their mid or late twenties are sent home without skills that they can use in their communities. Is the only alternative to low-skilled manufacturing jobs for women to stay in poverty at home or become prostitutes? Why can't the manufacturers act like good citizens by providing their employees with training and by helping them find outside employment after they can no longer work in their factories? Is this too much to expect from large companies that often operate on a global scale?

Women are discriminated against in ways other than job segregation. With the same skills and education, they earn less than men or have less access to nonfarm employment, a high-return activity. Low earnings give them low status in and out of the family, which in turn intensifies discrimination. In Tanzania, even with secondary education a woman has half the chance a man does of finding a job. Nonagricultural labor markets have a large government component, but governments hire relatively few women.

Women in rural areas of the less developed countries (LDCs) are the most disadvantaged. They work eighteen-hour days. With too many children to nurse and care for, they are overworked, undertrained, undernourished, and illiterate. They have little chance to make it in the cash economy. Yet they account for more than half of the food produced in the Third World and 90 percent of the family food supply in Africa. The roles of men and women in traditional agriculture were well-defined and more equal before "development" dawned. But women were bypassed by modern labor-saving techniques. The commercialization of agriculture increased women's workload and reduced their opportunity of earning cash incomes from their produce. As a result, women have become more dependent on market conditions and the remittances of husbands who have migrated to the city.

Development Policies

The prevalence of female-headed families has far-reaching implications for development policy, particularly in Africa. While rural women raise food for the families they head, the men who have gone to the cities do not always send money home. If they stay in the agricultural sector, men have most ready access to the most important assets: land, livestock, and cash crops like coffee. Where women originally held land rights, they reverted to male ownership when the rights were marketed. Urban families are mostly headed by males (Collier, 1988; Schultz, 1989). Overall, men have more access to modern technology, jobs with high productivity, and credit. Women have inferior claims to assets and are more restricted in job opportunities. Female-headed households are poorer than those headed by males.

Problems in obtaining domestic credit further weaken the position of women. While women raise food on small plots, they own no marketable land rights and no collateral on which they can borrow. Formal credit programs are based on earnings from nonfood crops, in which men specialize. Subordinated in their own households, women have a hard time establishing independent creditworthiness. Typically, credit bridges the temporary periods of lower earnings and higher expenditures, but it does not function in this way to lighten the costs of human reproduction.

There is great need for public credit programs directed to households headed by women. The programs can be based on the financial assets which they own independently or in groups. Women have banded together in savings clubs which possess their own liquidity and have the capacity to finance investment or obtain credit. This is a fertile field for innovation by domestic financial institutions or international agencies like the World Bank, which has been active in furthering domestic credit programs for over three decades.

But until recently the special needs of women were mostly ignored by the development programs and policies sponsored or encouraged by external aid agencies. Planning tended to be male-oriented, assuming social structures based on the man as household head and primary producer. The U.S. Agency of International Development (USAID) spent very little of its total program on women in development activities. In 1987, after a slow start, the World Bank organized a special division for women in development which, with encouragement from its president's office, has published a few in-depth country studies and explored the operational implications of their economic findings (World Bank, 1988a; 1990 a and b). The United Nations Development Programme (UNDP), with the Netherlands, Norway, and

Sweden, lent assistance in this effort. The World Bank also cosponsored an international initiative for safe motherhood, together with the UNDP and other United Nations agencies. Moreover, the bank gives specific assistance to women in development in its lending for education, health, nutrition, population control, agricultural extension, and credit for female entrepreneurs.

Many government policies, such as those adopted under structural adjustment programs sponsored by the World Bank, emphasize export promotion or economic import substitution of manufactured products. The policy tools used are devaluation of the currency or rationalization of protective tariffs, which promote export production in the agricultural sector or factories, where men are the principal workers. Governments directly improve the economic position of women by hiring more of them and providing more services that directly benefit them.

Health and Education

In developing countries women are more likely than men to be malnourished, poor, and illiterate; to carry a heavier workload; and to have less access to medical facilities. In Africa and Asia, females are held in low social esteem. For example, in India and Bangladesh better care for boys and female infanticide are responsible for a large difference in mortality: female mortality between ages one and five ranges as much as 30–50 percent above that of males. Females are discriminated against in their own families. In the Indian family, for example, men eat first and the females get what is left over. The upgrading of women's health services and education assists women and their children, and ultimately society at large, mainly through a reduction in the birthrate.

Females in general have longer life expectancy than men, except in the most vulnerable ages of early childhood and childbearing. Repeated childbearing, short birth intervals, and pregnancy at an early age pose serious health risks to women. Maternal mortality accounts for one-fourth to one-half of all deaths of women in the childbearing age. Each year there are half a million maternal deaths, of which 99 percent are in LDCs. Industrialized countries have two to nine maternal deaths per 100,000 live births. In LDCs the figure is 300–1,000, and some 25–50 percent of these deaths are caused by illegal abortions from unwanted pregnancies, because women do not have access to the family-planning services they want and to safe medical procedures. In addition, millions of women are permanently disabled by pregnancy and often ostracized by their families and communities. For every death, ten to fifteen women are disabled by giving birth because they are poor and neglected. One important social factor is the early age at which women get married (for example, 70 percent of women age fifteen to nineteen are married in West Africa; only 7 percent in Europe).

Maternal mortality can be reduced at relatively low cost by improvement in prenatal care, basic health, and first-referral services. In addition, family planning has broad benefits for women: they can enjoy better health and control their lives, enlarge the choices open to them, become better educated, improve the opportunities for their children, and increase their participation in economic development. The adverse cultural conditions holding women down may lessen as economic conditions improve and specific health measures take effect.

The education of women has what economists call a high return on investment, both for the individual and for society at large. Educated women are more able to care for the health and nutrition of their children, to find work outside the home, and to plan their families. There has been substantial improvement in education in the past three or four decades, but an enormous task lies ahead, especially in Africa.[2] Illiteracy remains at intolerable levels, and there is no space in primary schools for large numbers of girls.

Female enrollment in primary education quadrupled from 95 million to 390 million in 1950–1985. More recent data show a further increase in the percentage of females enrolled in primary education. However, despite enormous expansion, school systems are not equipped to accommodate the rising numbers of school-age children. In Africa, four out of ten eligible children cannot be accommodated. The shortage of educational facilities affects girls more than boys. In LDCs girls are more likely to be left out than boys; 60 percent of girls aged five to nineteen are not in school.

Low school-enrollment rates and discrimination are reflected in higher illiteracy rates for women, especially in sub-Saharan Africa. Adult literacy for all LDCs was only 50 percent for women, as opposed to 68 percent for men. In sub-Saharan Africa the figures were 34 to 53 percent. As might be expected, most illiterates live in poor countries. Sixty percent of illiterate women live in countries with per capita income below $300; in low-income Africa and South Asia, four out of five women over twenty-five never had any schooling. Despite widespread legislation for universal enrollment, the poorer countries are still far from that goal.

Finally, education for girls seldom prepares them for good jobs in technical fields. Girls are expected to be passive and obedient; boys to be active, competitive, and combative. In most developing countries, teaching materials tend to reflect a cultural prejudice against women. Segregation within the school system retards any change in established patterns. Women teachers cluster in lower grades and ranks, teach the softer subjects, and get lower pay than men in equivalent positions. In higher education few women hold professorial rank, and they typically account for less than 10 percent of total academic positions, with very few in mathematics and technical subjects. Textbook stereotypes become self-fulfilling prophecies as women select subjects that conform to their cultural image. Women seek positions in the humanities, education, and the fine arts, while men go into more technical and more highly paid fields: law, engineering, and medicine.

The economic and social obstacles to be overcome in developing countries are in many ways more formidable than those faced in the United States and other industrialized countries. Yet in these latter countries, the situation is far from simple.

WOMEN IN THE UNITED STATES

When we compare per capita incomes, and even more when we look at the position of women in relation to men, we find that women in the United States and other industrialized countries are much better off than those in developing countries. Real wages in the United States have risen dramatically in this century, and though women get paid 25 to 35 percent less than men, both their pay and their participation in the workforce have risen steadily and sharply. But we still find deep and widespread poverty among American women. Hundreds of thousands are divorced or have been deserted and must care for their children without adequate earnings. Welfare assistance for these women has been inadequate and demeaning. The work they can get is often low-paying and leaves them with the expense of daytime child care (Bergmann, 1986).

Many American women work not out of choice, but out of necessity. Many work because they lack child support, but even in other circumstances women must work simply to make ends meet.

The United States faces a wide and difficult agenda for policy reform, of which we can only give a brief overview. What has happened to women in the labor force? Why are women's wages still substantially lower than men's? What can be done through affirmative action, and what are the basis and prospects of pay equity? What is the economic plight of housewives? How deep and widespread is the poverty of single mothers, and what can be done to help them? And what are the priorities for action?

Ten years ago Barbara Bergmann pointed to the profound changes in the economic role of women in industrial society. She drew attention to the passing of the old system under which men had access to money making and mature women were restricted to the home. The forces behind the release of women from obligatory domesticity have been at work for many years and are far from spent. The move of women into paid work started modestly more than a century ago and is bound to progress further. Barring some economic or Fundamentalist-inspired upheaval, women are unlikely to retreat back into domesticity. On the contrary, we can expect an acceleration of the emergence of women into fuller participation in the economy (Bergmann, 1986, p. 3).

Despite this optimistic assessment, millions of single mothers still struggle to support themselves and their children with their own meager earnings. They need jobs with wages that will enable them and their children to live decently. As a realistic goal, should we not expect that women and men will have equal economic opportunities? Should not policies aim at getting rid of the habits and institutions that are sources of injustice or are out of line with new realities?

Productivity and Social Factors

Rising productivity and progress since the industrial revolution 200 years ago have caused women's wages to more than quadruple in real terms from 1890 to 1984. They have, in fact, risen to the point that many women's time has become too valuable to be spent entirely at home. Participation of women under sixty-five in the labor force passed the 50 percent mark in 1970 and is now two-thirds. At the same time, women with children stayed longer and longer on the job. At first they quit their jobs with the first pregnancy, but now they stay away from work for as short a time as possible. In the nineteenth century women from the most prestigious families stayed home; today they are in the most prestigious professions.

The economic environment itself provides the impetus for women's participation in the workforce. There has been a steady rise in jobs suitable for women. Periods of inflation or flat earnings of males raise the need for higher family income, and in many industries men's wages have not kept pace with prices. The high cost of labor-saving devices, new consumer items, and not least housing are all reasons behind women entering the workforce. It is unlikely that this momentum will reverse itself. Social changes—lower birth rates, improved education, and higher divorce rates—reinforce the purely economic factors.

The number of children per white woman in the United States has declined from seven in 1800 to less than two now. Rural birthrates are higher, but the rural workforce itself has declined drastically (from 53 percent in 1870 to 3 percent now). Birth control has become more feasible since oral contraception and sterilization became widespread in the 1960s. In the 1980s, in 41 percent of families wanting to prevent new births, either the wife or the husband underwent sterilization; the male was sterilized in 38 percent of these cases.

Supporting these developments were significant changes in law affecting the freedom of people to plan their lives. The Supreme Court struck down the laws restricting use of contraceptive devices by married couples in 1965, and abortion restrictions were struck down in 1973 in Roe v. Wade. Women can now carry out plans for their lives in a way not possible before.

The fewer young children a woman has, the more likely she is to participate in paid work. Her ability to earn a good salary has been strengthened by improvements in education: the number of women earning bachelors degrees rose from 100,000 (or 32 percent of men earning degrees) in 1950 to 500,000 (or 95 percent) in the 1980s. But despite improvement in professional training, women still lag significantly in such fields as medicine, dentistry, law, and especially engineering.

The increase in numbers of unmarried or divorced women is, of course, another factor underlying the greater number of women entering the job market. Besides the increase in divorce, more women now stay unmarried altogether (around 40 percent, compared with less than 30 percent in 1965). About 80 percent of divorced women with child custody are in the job market; alimony is too low or unreliable, though in recent years some improvements have been brought about by legal pressure on delinquent fathers. Most divorcees in effect have the option to be poor, be on welfare, or go to work.

Affirmative Action

Affirmative action and public persuasion can be instrumental—and may indeed be indispensable—in opening new segments of the job market to women and overcoming male domination in several sectors. It is necessary to understand how the job market works in most industrialized countries.

Segregation of the job market is the fundamental cause of women's pay being lower than men's: some jobs are reserved for women, while others with higher pay are off limits. Women are, in effect, crowded into a female job ghetto where wages are pressed down. They are prevented from moving into better male jobs by employers' prejudice, alleged difficulties of mixing males and females, and the belief that certain jobs are unsuitable for women.

As their numbers in the workforce have risen, women have taken over jobs, especially clerical and sales fields, once dominated by males. Thus in 1900 about one-fourth of clerical positions were held by women; by now this has risen to 80 percent. Women had 17 percent of sales jobs in 1900, almost half now. However, when women enter male occupations, their wages stay relatively low. As shown by Chris de Vries, in these situations women's and men's wages converge, but at a lower level, and men's wages fall relative to those in other occupations. The entrance of a large number of women pulls the earnings of all workers in that occupation down (C.M. de Vries, 1984). As long as most women are in a job ghetto, all women's pay will be subject to downward pressure. Pay differences persist as women enter professional fields, but they are more subtle.

Treating women equally benefits the entire economy because all workers are able to utilize their full productivity. Conversely, job segregation forces women to be less productive than they could be in open markets. Likewise, men's fields would be exploited more fully if productive women were permitted to enter freely.

Getting women to enter new and more rewarding job categories is a long process intimately related to economic and social change in society at large. One may well ask: Can legal action speed up the process? More specifically, what can affirmative action do to improve the economic position of women? They have been able to exercise their rights under Title VII of the Civil Rights Act of 1967, which ruled out discrimination on account of race or sex. Under the law women were able to seek to get equal pay for work of "comparable worth," but the reality is that affirmative action has had only a limited impact on wage equality.

The Civil Rights Act of 1964 outlawed discrimination against minorities and women. The act declared it unlawful to "deprive any individual of employment opportunities or otherwise adversely affect his status as an employee, because of such individual's race, color, religion, sex or national origin." Moreover, President Johnson's Executive Order 11246 of September 1965 required companies that contracted with the federal government "to act affirmatively," to guarantee that employees were not treated differently because of their race. (Sex was added a couple of years later.) Despite objections to affirmative action by presidents Reagan and Bush, this executive order was never rescinded. In 1970 President Nixon's labor secretary George P. Shultz created the first "quota" plan, under which building contractors in Philadelphia who received federal funds had to hire minorities, especially blacks. The ensuing regulations specifically called for goals and timetables.

Under this legal regime the government vigorously pursued affirmative action, often with the objective of promoting greater diversity in the workforce and without careful demonstration of the extent and nature of past discrimination. Women and minorities made considerable gains in a workforce that was becoming increasingly diversified as a result of socioeconomic as well as legal factors. Affirmative action was initially needed to assure all people a place at the table. In its practical application, people accepted the rules of fair treatment for everyone. But affirmative action also resulted in reverse discrimination, with white workers resenting the idea that they had to fight hard to make a living in a harsh environment, while black workers would get preferential treatment and some minority operators got rich from the favored treatment they received under the law. In some situations the Supreme Court ruled against affirmative action on the ground that all people must be treated equal.

In the political arena, the Democrats have not actively pursued affirmative action, while Republican administrations have been outright hostile to it. A few days before the 1990 fall elections, President

Bush vetoed the Civil Rights Act of 1990, which was designed in part to make it easier for women to go to court to get equal pay.

In 1995 the Supreme Court brought an end to the regime that had been in effect for some thirty years by ruling in favor of a contractor whose low bid had been refused in favor of a more costly Hispanic contractor (Adarand Constructors v. Pena). As a consequence, most past affirmative action decisions were invalidated. Henceforth plans to bring diversity or to end societal discrimination, rather than to remedy past discrimination against specific groups, would not qualify. Action will have to be justified by in-depth study of particular situations and must specify why certain groups are to be favored. Simple set-aside programs first started by the Philadelphia plan will not meet the test.

Under past legal action, women had in some respect received more favorable treatment than male minorities. In general, judges were less sensitive to sex discrimination than to race discrimination, and applied laxer standards in judging action in favor of women. In legal terminology, their approval was based on evidence that was "important" rather than "compelling."

Since the 1967 Civil Rights Act, women have made some improvements in relative pay. But even after thirty years of legal action, women still typically receive less pay than men in comparable jobs. Moreover, the disparity women suffer gets worse with age. The pay gap has declined since the early 1980s, but part of the reason is the fall in men's real earnings. In 1995 white women's wages were on average 27 percent less than men's, compared with 39 percent in 1967. In professional jobs the gap is smaller: women with comparable duties earn 5–15 percent less than men. Black women have also gained, but in recent years the pace of their progress has slackened; in 1995 black women's wages were on average 63 percent of white men's wages.[3]

The modest improvements in women's pay may cover up major improvements in individual cases and categories. It is striking, moreover, that black women have made substantially more progress than white women, although their pay is still lowest. In the private sector, the law has moved action from individual employers to the government, and for that reason affirmative action has been accepted by the larger corporations which find diversity in the interest of a more peaceful world: barring blacks from jobs increases crime.

The government has had a hard time placing women in jobs where management questions the advisability or where the public at large, including many women, is opposed. Yet after thirty years affirmative action has had considerable impact. Women have made progress in many businesses as well as government, and have demonstrated that they can make a valuable contribution and are at least as able, despite the prevalence of the glass ceiling. It is possible that women can continue to advance in the private sector without the government's overt encouragement. But prejudice and barriers continue in many quarters. On the other hand, the number of men in responsible positions who have qualified wives or daughters who face these problems is already quite large and will increase over time. This could well contribute to an improvement in the work environment for women.

Some will argue that in practice society is always choosing among imperfect alternatives: if affirmative action succeeds, one would expect that the new situation will entail less harm overall than the old one. In reality, to overcome the scourge of poverty caused by discrimination, we must do more than proclaim the case for equal treatment. We must prepare the ground for greater economic equality through education, training, job opportunities, and investment in human resources. In this way we will be able to act affirmatively by focusing on the poor and giving those below a certain income level an advantage in getting started in better paying jobs.

Pay Equity

Closely related to the objectives of affirmative action is the establishment of pay equity for women (that is, equal pay in jobs of "comparable worth"), but this too presents many practical and conceptual problems. To determine comparable worth requires in practice technical comparisons and calculations which are not easy to make. Through professional evaluation, jobs receive a score based on requirements, each with proper weights, such as skills, mental demands like problem solving, and the exercise of independent judgment. But in practice, evaluations are based on job clusters of predominantly female and male jobs, each cluster anchored on a job with a market-determined wage, such as secretary for women and truck driver for men. The female anchor begins with lower pay than the male anchor, and hence the whole cluster of female jobs tends to receive lower pay.

To be effective, pay equity action will need help from many quarters, including the judicial system, labor unions, and government. The government can help by establishing guidelines for minimum wages, or specifying wage ratios for groups of male and female employees. However, many businesses and business-oriented politicians would react vigorously against any government "interference."

An example of the difficulties encountered is the failure of nurses in Denver to improve their equity. They took judicial action under the Equal Pay Act of 1963. However, this act has been given a very narrow interpretation: equal pay for the identical work for the same employer. Nurses employed by the city of Denver got paid less than tree trimmers, even though trimmers did not even need a high school diploma, while nurses needed far more extensive job training and experience. The judge reviewing the nurses' complaint extolled the workings of the free market and threw out the complaint; his ruling was upheld on appeal.

Some claim that the economy cannot afford pay equity. However, Bergmann has calculated that the gap between male and female pay adds up to 5 percent of the GNP. If the gap were to be removed all at once, it would cause a shock and exert inflationary pressure. But in practice, pay equity would be put into effect gradually and the economy could handle it. Some opponents feel that pay equity action interferes with the workings of the market. But the aim here is indeed to interfere because market operators exercise discrimination. Others have argued that higher wages for women will shrink their market or cause them to be replaced by males. In practice, such effects are often minimal, especially since changes come gradually and are accompanied by many other shifts in the economy. Affirmative action allows women to have access to jobs that they can enjoy and be good at.

A ray of hope comes from Ontario's Pay Equity Act, which became law in January 1988. "Ontario is the first, and still in 1990, the only jurisdiction that requires public and private employers to identify undervalued female-dominated jobs and to raise the pay so that women are paid comparably to men for similar jobs. One of the most significant parts of the Ontario plan is that it puts the burden on employers, rather than having the process be driven by employees' complaints."[4]

The Housewife's Job

An important category of women is entirely outside the sphere of affirmative action and pay equity and largely outside the organized job market, yet of great importance to the role of women in our economy. One-third of women over sixteen (about 33 million) are full-time homemakers. Their problems are different from the concerns of those holding paying jobs, but are in no way less important. The role of housewives, when it is based on love and caring, is far more attractive than the economics of the "job." The cost of being a housewife is considerable: she foregoes monetary earnings and often works in lonely circumstances. The husband may control the family's money tightly; he can leave her, even though she doesn't have the skills or job experience needed to be able to make a decent living. In some respects, housewifely duties are like those of a servant or a slave: seven days a week of work, her economic security hostage to the personal whims of her husband, the money earner. Moreover, she could be in harm's way; 14 million women are battered in the home each year. The housewife cannot easily move to a similar job, or build a cash reserve for contingencies.

The value of a housewife's job can, of course, be calculated from the market prices of the services she renders. But actual pay for housewives is controversial, and the feminist movement has not succeeded in getting it off the ground. One version of housewife pay is maternity leave, though forced maternity leave may keep women from highly paying jobs. It may be more effective to have work-reduction schemes for both spouses: each could work half time, or they could take off alternately.[5]

Finally, severe problems are faced by the displaced homemaker. One-half of current marriages will end in divorce. When the divorcing couple has children, the woman suffers a precipitous decline in income, while most men get off pretty cheaply. Women receive little if any reward for their past sacrifices in raising their families. Only a fraction, less than one-fifth, of women are awarded alimony, most only for a limited period, and the average alimony pay is only a small share of the family's previous income. No wonder many observers consider the treatment of displaced homemakers a crucial social issue.

Poverty and the Single Parent

Displaced homemakers are in a broader category of women who face often serious poverty: those who must shoulder the responsibility of parenthood without adequate support from the father. Both social and economic forces have greatly increased the number of single parents. In 1960 only 7 percent of families with children were headed by deserted or unmarried mothers; this share has risen to 25 percent.

Decline in traditional values and institutions, birth control, better opportunities in the labor market, and government support for single mothers have all contributed to the breakup of the traditional family. The ability of women to get a job gives men less guilt about leaving their children, and marriages are more apt to break up.

The general rise in wages has made it possible for a larger percentage of single parents to live above the poverty line, but in practice many women working full time are not earning enough to pay for day care for one child and still live above the poverty line. This should be clear from the low earnings of unmarried mothers; on average, they earn little more than one-third of working married couples.

Welfare (in the past "Aid to Families with Dependent Children," AFDC) did come to the aid of single mothers, but the inadequate payments kept recipients in poverty. For example, Pennsylvania welfare provides only about three-fourths of the poverty threshold. Until 1968, welfare was designed to assist single women tending to their children; it assumed that they had no job. Welfare could not be given if there was a man in the house. Unfortunately, the working single mother is often worse off than the welfare mother, since her average earnings are small in relation to Medicaid and welfare receipts. This anomaly is reinforced by the payments working mothers make for child care. There are, of course, many other objections against this kind of welfare, not least that it discourages responsible behavior on the part of some recipients.

About half of unwed mothers are living in poverty, and their children make up a rising percentage of the total number of children in poverty. Over half of all black children live with mothers who are not currently married. Should we acquiesce in a life of poverty for unwed mothers, even if they were immoral or unwise? And do their children deserve a life of deprivation?

Present conditions calling for corrective action led to the welfare "reform" enacted in 1996 (see ch. 13). The objective should be to reduce poverty among single mothers and assure reasonable prospects for their children. Higher and more regular child support payments from fathers are essential; until recently, less than a quarter of mothers received the full amounts that were awarded to them, and these amounts were commonly inadequate from the start. Steps have been taken to assure that deadbeat fathers who avoid child support live up to their obligations. In addition, measures are needed to secure child care and medical aid to unwed mothers.

Priorities for Action

In the face of the many reform measures called for to strengthen the economic position of women, there is an obvious need to define carefully the priorities of action by the community and the body politic. Society faces a formidable agenda to assure women an equal position in the family, the workplace, and the marketplace. There must be active public discussion, with participation of both women and men, on the key issues of fairness in the workplace, a system for helping single parents, and a better sharing of household and child care tasks. In addition, basic cultural and religious issues, some of which are taken up under "The Ethical Dimension," must be addressed.

It is not easy to summarize an agenda for priority action, but the following points were among the priorities set forth ten years ago by Barbara Bergmann (1986, ch. 13) and may still be used as benchmarks against the progress made in the intervening years and to explore the need and feasibility of further action.

1. Improve enforcement of fairness in placement and promotions. The Equal Employment Opportunity Commission does not have an enforcement mechanism like, say, the Internal Revenue Service. At present many firms lag behind the objectives of the law. They either hire no college-trained women, or they put these women in clerical jobs; no women are placed where they supervise men; and they are kept out of training programs. It should be possible to monitor companies that sell to the federal government, and businesses should receive help and guidance in developing policies that conform to the law. Setting guidelines is different from imposing new regulations. They can work only if the executive branch of government is in sympathy with improving the role of women in business.

2. Realign male and female wages. Some state governments are already doing this, and the federal government should not fall behind. The government can set wage guidelines for important sectors, and government contractors should be encouraged to realign the wages they pay. Government action will affect the private sector.

3. End sex segregation in vocational and engineering education and in union-run apprenticeship programs. One school that has led the way is the Massachusetts Institute of Technology.

Since its beginning, in contrast to Harvard, MIT opened its doors to women in both faculty and student body, and over the years has made no distinction between men and women in its education and in career assistance.[6]

4. End discrimination against part-time and temporary workers. Treating part-time workers better will benefit women, since 20 percent of employed women work part-time, as against only 5 percent for men. Universities should adjust their pay scales to give fairer treatment to female teachers.

5. Continue the campaign against sexual harassment.

6. Introduce a national system of deduction-based uniform child support, such as has already been adopted by Wisconsin. Women deserve more regular and higher child support payments from biological fathers who have left their family. Under the Wisconsin plan, awards would be 50 percent above current levels and total child support would quadruple; it would not diminish if the mother takes a job.

7. Set up a high-quality child care system, funded from both private and public resources. This should be available to single parents in particular need, for example, when changing jobs. Since the early 1980s many more child care centers have been set up, but the costs remain high, especially for single mothers.

These measures should help to lift women out of poverty, although the impact will be less direct for some than for others. Obviously, many other desirable steps can be taken, some economic, others social. Decreasing the hours worked so parents can spend more time with their children would be desirable, but would run contrary to current trends in the labor market. Some important changes would fall in the realm of moral and social attitudes. Thus, there is ample room for a new work ethic of sharing family care more equitably between men and women.

It will take work to introduce and implement a comprehensive program of action, and satisfactory results will depend on leadership in government and cooperation from the private sector and individuals. A broad and ambitious program can only be realized if both men and women make a personal commitment to work toward a world of greater equality, less selfishness, and less poverty. This effort extends well beyond the realm of economics and law, and it deserves the full consideration and cooperation of the religious community, to which we now turn.

THE ETHICAL DIMENSION

The economic and social differences between women and men manifest themselves in numerous ways in both industrialized and developing countries. While the number of women in the workforce has greatly increased, they continue to suffer from unequal treatment. In the developing countries they find themselves in an unequal legal position, suffer more than men from inadequate educational facilities, are treated in an inferior way at home and in the marketplace, and have fallen behind the pace of technological progress. In the United States women's pay and job opportunities lag behind those of men, despite affirmative action and pay equity legislation; housewives are in an unjust economic position, and half of single women are in poverty.

The inequalities in economic and social status place women at a severe disadvantage in the struggle to overcome poverty and raise pervasive questions about what is just. How does the inequality between women and men measure up to the standards of God's order? Is the world's economic and social reality in conflict with the moral and ethical values taught by the Bible? Are these values shared by different groups of believers? To what extent must religious communities themselves overcome prejudices? To answer these questions, we first explore biblical and theological perceptions of the status of women.

Visions from the Bible

What does the Bible have to say about the plight of women in our society? We must keep in mind that the biblical message was delivered against the background of a patriarchal society, which in many ways reflected the inhumanity of man against woman. The economic emergence of women in our society obviously far outstrips the social and economic circumstances of women in the Bible. Nevertheless, in the final analysis the essence of the biblical message comes through loud and clear: both women and men are created by God in His image and both receive salvation in Christ.

In the view of some commentators, women are shown in an unfavorable light right from the very start of the biblical story when Adam accuses Eve. He excuses himself to God: "The woman you gave me made me eat this apple." It is useful to look at the Genesis story as seen through the eyes of Eve (Milne, 1989). Early Christian writers depicted Eve as subordinated and inferior to Adam, arguing that she was created after and from him; they saw her as weak, seductive, and evil, the cause of Adam's disobedience. Eve was "the mother of all living things," but also the paradigm of evil as inherent in all women. This view is reflected in early church traditions. Women were prohibited from speaking in the assembly as early as the first book of Timothy. Thomas Aquinas significantly extended the argument *against* women in the thirteenth century, claiming that women were defective in nature, "misbegotten males." The consequences of this thinking can be found in fifteenth-century writings such as *Malleus Maleficarum (Hammer against Witches)*, which provided the Inquisition with the theological justification for the witch hunts in which many women were executed.

The themes of inferiority, evil, and seductiveness continue in the writings of Luther, Calvin, and Knox, and have remained prominent in the twentieth-century voices of TV Fundamentalists. The learned fathers of yesterday and the TV preachers of today show their own sinfulness in the way they approach women. Today there are still men who use the story of Eve's eating the forbidden fruit and then having Adam do the same (Genesis 3) to justify their right to physically discipline a wife who is not properly subordinate; and there are battered women who accept such treatment on biblical grounds. These people have read or heard only part of the Bible and have barely reflected on what they were told.

Dietrich Bonhoeffer, the German theologian-martyr, is a notable exception among theologians: he gives us the spiritual significance of the Genesis story and does not present Eve, the companion of Adam, in an inferior manner. In his view, the story of the creation and fall shows us the spiritual meaning of man's relation to woman and of both man and woman to God. He explains the meaning for our lives of the tree of life in the biblical story of the tree of knowledge of good and evil, and of the creation of Eve as a companion to Adam. In his description of the fall, he makes no distinction between the acts of man and woman; they act as one and fall as one. According to Bonhoeffer, the Bible depicts in its first chapters the deepest predicaments of our life. It describes how woman and man are both directly involved and equally concerned, each playing an individual role. In his explanation of this story, Bonhoeffer describes the essential role of woman and the meaning of what could be called healthy relationships between man and woman (Bonhoeffer, 1959 and 1965, pp. 51–59).

Some women reject the creation story outright, and more generally display deep bitterness at the way women are treated in the Bible, so bitter indeed that they have a hard time accepting the message of salvation. Mary Daly (1973) rejects God the Father and Jesus Christ because they are male or depicted as male. One can argue that God need not be depicted like Michelangelo's old man of the Sistine Chapel ceiling, but does that deny the entire story of salvation?

Other female theologians have sought to give a new interpretation, among them an early pioneer, Elizabeth Cady Stanton (1815–1902). An extensive reinterpretation was undertaken in the 1970s by Phyllis Trible of Union Theological Seminary (Milne, 1989). She found that the problem was not the text itself, but instead centuries of accrued sexist context. None of the patriarchal claims are altogether accurate, most are simply not present in the text, and some actually violate the rhetoric. For example, from Gen. 2:22, woman is regarded as inferior because she is created last. But humans are not regarded as inferior to animals, even though they were created after them (Gen. 1:27). If later is better, then the creation of woman is the crowning achievement. Also, the serpent speaks only to Eve, perhaps because she is the more intelligent of the two, with better understanding of God's command and greater independence. By contrast, Adam is silent, bland, passive, and belly-oriented. Eve is created as a helper, a helpmate, but "companion" is a better translation. The implied relationship between the two is beneficial and does not connote inferiority, but rather mutuality and equality.

The Bible returns often to the role of women. Mosaic law places women in an inferior position by treating them as chattel. For example, when someone damages one's property the perpetrator must be punished, even when the damage is done to a daughter's virginity. If the property (a woman) is unfaithful or runs off, it must be stoned (Deut. 22: 13–29). On the other hand, the Mosaic law itself gave women certain rights; Mosaic divorce provisions were more humane than those in contemporary cultures. The Bible also gives an important role to some women. Proverbs 31 vividly portrays an enterprising and capable wife, although understandably not including work outside the home. Deborah, a judge, ruled over her nation before the kings took over. Ruth, a woman with genuine character, became the gentile ancestor of David and hence an ancestor of Jesus Christ, the son of David. And Esther, the beautiful Jewish refugee, became a Persian queen and at great personal risk warded off what would have been an earlier holocaust; she was a true savior of her people. In a spiritual sense, Queen Esther is an image and forerunner of Christ the Savior.

Jesus goes far beyond the law of Moses in his relations with women. In Jesus' entourage we find several women besides his mother Mary. For example, his close friends Martha and Mary, the sisters of Lazarus whom he restored to life. His disciples were surprised when they saw him talk to a Samaritan woman at the well, someone who had had a checkered history as a wife to many different men. His understanding attitude is also clear from his reaction to the demand that a woman "caught in the act" should be stoned; his answer is simple but stunning: let him who is without sin throw the first stone. Women attended Jesus as he was dying, and they saw to his burial. Mary of Magdala, who washed Jesus' feet at a banquet in gratitude for her conversion from sin, also was among the very first to witness the resurrection.

In his treatment of women, Jesus Christ differs sharply from his contemporary environment. "Women did not count in society at that time and had to avoid men's company in public. Contemporary Jewish sources are full of animosity toward women who, according to Josephus, are in every respect inferior to men. The legally and socially weak position of women in the society of that time was considerably upgraded by his prohibition of divorce, which had hitherto been possible only if the husband alone issued a writ of divorce" (Kung, 1976, pp. 266–67).

Many have also reacted against the inferior position Paul seems to assign to women in the church. In an early prescription for life in the church, we read: "Women should learn in silence and all humility. I do not allow women to teach or to have authority over men; they must keep quiet" (1 Tim. 2: 11 and 12). However, these views most likely reflect those of early church leaders rather than Paul himself. Paul was a basic thinker who probed the deep meanings for our personal lives of the presence of Christ. The churchmen who came after him reflected the attitudes of the surrounding Roman society and the Jewish law. In his discussion of behavior in the church, Paul assumes that both men and women participate in the leadership of the church. Thus in 1 Cor.

11: 2–16 he discusses not whether but how women should address the congregation. There is also ample evidence in his letters that women were among the leaders of the early church, and indeed among Paul's closest associates in the ministry (e.g., Chloe, Euodia and Syntyche, Priscilla and Phoebe) (Furnish, 1979, pp. 101–09). In a number of passages Paul gives a deeper, spiritual meaning to his views. In 1 Cor. 7 he speaks explicitly about marriage and does not put women in an inferior position. In Eph. 5: 21–33, he compares the husband-wife relationship with that of Christ and the church. Christ loves the church and gives his life for the church. The church becomes Christ's own body. Paul asks men to love their wives as their own body and envisages a reciprocal relationship: submit yourselves to each other.

The biblical presentation of positions and issues touching on the status of women have been the subject of intense contemplation and debate in many religious quarters. Several religious communities have published commentaries on what the Bible says about women and presented their views on the problems of women in contemporary society. Some examples from Reform Judaism and various Christian churches follow.

Reform Judaism

The 1983 and 1984 meetings of the American Hebrew Congregations and the 1984 Convention of the Central Conference of American Rabbis, held at Grossinger, NY, noted that poverty in North America falls disproportionately on women, who have suffered many forms of discrimination and economic disadvantages. They called for support of the Equal Rights Amendment and legislation incorporating principles of economic equity for women in a wide range of issues and areas such as insurance, pension reform, social security, tax issues, day care and family assistance, regulatory reform, and enforcement of child support requirements. They also endorsed efforts to correct discriminatory practices in private industry and government. They called on congregants in their individual or corporate relationships to eliminate discriminatory practices against women.

The Roman Catholic Church

In their 1986 pastoral "Economic Justice for All" the American bishops gave a thorough analysis of economic relationships in the American economy. They dealt in depth with the economic plight of poor women and the causes of their poverty. The pastoral spoke of the poverty in female-headed families and of their children, a disproportionate share belonging to minorities. The bishops noted the wage discrimination against women and its impoverishing effects, and recognized the segregation of women into low-paying jobs with low status and little security. And they observed that though women have primary responsibility for the rearing of children, child support laws and enforcement are inadequate. They called for action to remove barriers against full and equal employment for women and minorities, and endorsed job training, affirmative action, and upgrading of poorly paying jobs.

In their treatment of social problems the bishops must, of course, observe the basic teachings of the church. The church does not ordain women as priests and does not give them positions of leadership.

The Mainline Protestant Churches

Certain themes recur in the testimony of the mainline Protestant churches. Generally, they call for full participation of women in church and society, equal rights for women, and an end to discrimination. This is reflected in several statements by the National Council of Churches of Christ (NCCC) which, starting in 1963, has given comprehensive support to a more meaningful role for women.[7] More specifically, the churches recognized the changing relationship between women and men, and the increasing role of women in society; advocated both legal and substantive action toward greater equality for women; protested discrimination against women and disapproved of the weakening of affirmative action in the 1980s; urged that people reverse past mistakes as did, for example, the Lutherans in their 1972 statement and the Methodists in 1984; and called for new worship forms and official language expressed in generic terms which clearly denotes humanity rather than gender, a practice that has now been adopted in the Catholic church and some Protestant denominations.[8]

The Evangelicals and Fundamentalists

While most mainline Protestant churches support greater equality of women on both theological and ethical grounds, the Evangelical and

Fundamentalist churches have either shied away from taking a position or come out negatively. Their emphasis on the traditional family fails to recognize that millions of married women who have to work outside the home need support for child care and against wage discrimination. Jerry Falwell opposed the ERA amendment, although he said he would join President Reagan in urging state governments to eliminate wage discrimination. Women play a subordinate role in Pat Robertson's Virginia Beach establishment. Timidity (if not backwardness) in dealing with the women's issues is also evident from the conservative Christian Reformed Church's refusal until recently to permit women members to become "elders." In this respect, it lagged well behind its Reformed sister churches in Europe.

What is perhaps most telling is the galvanizing effect of the abortion issue on the Fundamentalists, with their uncompromising "pro-life" stand. Opposition to abortion can be justified on humane grounds, for it is an awkward and often painful procedure, and in the view of many a form of infanticide. There are many preferable and more effective ways of reducing the number of children per family and preventing unwanted teenage motherhood: better education of women and wider availability and more effective use of contraceptives may well hold the clue, although some Fundamentalists also object to the latter. Their adamant opposition to abortion has given the Fundamentalists a smokescreen that hides their own unwillingness to treat women with equality and to work for a decline in population growth needed for human, environmental, development, and economic reasons.

*   *   *

To conclude, both men and women must be changed in Christ in the sense that they put the rule of love first in all their relationships. In this way Christ can change society in the marketplace, the government, and the family. The government becomes his instrument, and no employer who has accepted Christ in all his fullness can tolerate discrimination against women. In Christ there is no East nor West, and there is no distinction between women and men (Gal. 3: 27–28). Christ is the true foundation for the liberation of both women and men.

Understanding the mandate of the Bible requires a continuous search for meaning. The scripture often presents ideas and objectives that conflict with the values of contemporary society. It seems clear that the inequality between men and women stands in sharp contrast to the equality of all people before God.

What the Bible says applies to all countries. In practice, progress everywhere depends on changes in religious and cultural attitudes and on the example of change elsewhere. In many countries the greatest suffering among women occurs when the impact of poverty is aggravated by environmental degradation. We need to take a careful look at the linkage between environmental conditions and poverty, the topic of the next chapter.

4

Our Environment

Action against deterioration of the environment is important to improving the conditions of the poor, who have little defense against environmental degradation. Poor farmers suffer when their lands are overgrazed or their natural resources are depleted.

It is joyful to sing the praises of the beauty and bounty of the earth. Who is not stirred by the grandeur of mountains, oceans, and sky, the overwhelming variety of flowers, and all kinds of growth we see around us. But much of the beauty and resources of the earth are in danger; despite many improvements made in the United States, the land is dying, the water is polluted, and the air people breathe is poisoned in many other countries.

Concern for the earth's environment has come to the center of the fight against poverty. While poor people and nations may not be persuaded of the importance of environmental policies, they suffer from the deterioration of their own environment, much of it caused by human activity and excessive exploitation of natural resources.

"Our Common Future," the report of the World Commission on Environment and Development to the UN General Assembly, presented by Gro Harlem Brundtland, Prime Minister of Norway in October 1987, called for a new focus on sustainable development. Parallel with this report, Barber Conable, World Bank president (1986–1991), made the Bank give explicit attention to the environmental effects of its operations.

Concern for the environment has brought together prominent scientists and political and religious leaders. Prestigious scientists led by the late Carl Sagan, for many years an eminent scholar at Cornell University, issued an urgent appeal to religious leaders, stressing that only the full support of religious conviction could avert environmental disaster. As a U.S. Senator, Al Gore took the lead among U.S. politicians in drawing attention to environmental issues.

The seriousness of ecological issues underlines our moral obligation for a better environmental policy. The pursuit of a sane environmental policy calls for people who are deeply committed, have a right attitude toward their neighbors and their environment, and are prepared to adopt lifestyles compatible with ecological needs, love of nature, and a frugal use of the fruits of the earth. In this sense, as discussed in more detail at the end of the chapter, environmental policy must rest on a moral base.

The 1992 Earth Summit (The UN Conference on Environment and Development or UNCED) of representatives of 160 nations in Rio de Janeiro set a new global environmental agenda and focused world attention on the urgency of environmental protection and the links between growth and environmental health. UN conferences of this kind have been notorious for accentuating the split between North and South, the developed and the developing countries. But this time the international configuration had changed markedly, and the subject matter had become more urgent and specific: the communist block had disappeared, and the developing countries had to be counted as the possessors of many of the earth's remaining natural treasures and not as the principal sources of pollution.

Nongovernmental organizations (NGOs), in parallel meetings, strongly advocated environmental causes and put themselves on the world map as agents of change and influence in international policy. NGOs can enhance the impact of governmental policies through essential local initiative and action (Hackman, 1992). Furthermore, while the official conference stayed clear of population issues, so critical to environmental policy, the NGOs did take up questions of demography and pointed to the importance of controlling the growth of population. The UN Conference provided an incentive for international institutions like the World Bank, NGOs, and religious organizations to focus on environmental questions and prepare themselves for proenvironment activities in their own fields.

In the fight against poverty, environmental and economic policy are closely intertwined:

- The depletion of the ozone layer and the related "greenhouse effect" has been accelerated by industrial growth, urban concentration, and increased energy needs. Industrial waste, the burning of fossil fuels, unrestricted deforestation, the use of certain types of herbicides, coolants, and propellants are all known to harm the atmosphere and the environment. The consequences range from damage to health to the possible submersion of low-lying lands, many populated by the poorest people of the world.

- Delicate ecological balances are upset by the uncontrolled destruction of animal and plant life and by reckless exploitation of natural resources.

- Solutions to ecological problems cannot be found solely at the national level, since their effects transcend national borders. International instruments and policies will need to be adapted to the new tasks at hand, even though international action does not lessen the responsibility of individual countries. Within their own territories countries must prevent the destruction of the atmosphere and biosphere and, among other things, monitor the impact of new technological and scientific advances.[1]

- Al Gore's proposals for international action contained several interlinking policies, such as stabilization of world population, development of environmentally appropriate technologies, formulation and application of economic concepts that make allowance for environmental effects, and negotiation of new institutional agreements for implementing global environmental plans (Gore, 1992, ch. 5).

Ecological balance, a crucial objective of environmental policy, cannot be found without addressing the root causes of poverty. Rural poverty and unjust land distribution have led to subsistence farming and the exhaustion of the soil. Once their lands yield no more, many farmers move on to clear new land, thus accelerating uncontrolled deforestation, or they settle in urban centers, which lack the infrastructure to receive them. In some countries the push for export expansion may aggravate ecological imbalances.[2]

This chapter takes a look at environmental phenomena that have a direct bearing on poverty issues: degradation of the land, turning fertile fields into barren desert, salinization of irrigated lands, and the causes and effects of deforestation; the deterioration of the earth's atmosphere, caused mainly by the industrialized countries; the prospects of global food production in the light of environmental and climate changes; changes in economic analysis that are necessary when explicit attention is given to environmental factors; and the compatibility of environmental policies with economic growth. "The Ethical

Dimension" at the end of the chapter highlights the economic findings that call for moral action and commitment, and discusses the ethical response to the economic challenges.

DEGRADATION OF THE LAND

When the land is spoiled and soils lose their integrity and fertility, farmers are robbed of the foundation of their livelihood. Droughts, their impact made more severe by deforestation, further deepen the farmers' misfortune. Some may remember the Okies of the 1930s, families uprooted by the effects of drought and land erosion in Oklahoma. Today millions of poor farmers are affected by drought conditions and degradation of their lands. They are seeking their fortune elsewhere, often with very little lasting success, and their suffering demonstrates the consequences of environmental crisis.

Much of the world's agricultural land is sapped of its productive potential by overuse, lack of care, or unwise treatment, which turns good land into desert. Each year desertification claims 6 million hectares, a land area twice the size of Belgium. An additional area, more than six times the size of Belgium (20 million hectares) is so impoverished that it becomes unprofitable to farm or graze.[3] More than one-third of the earth's land surface (4.5 billion hectares) is threatened by desertification, most visibly in Africa, where more than half of the world's livestock-dependent people live. But erosion is also a serious problem in India and China. The Ganges and Brahmaputra rivers on the Indian subcontinent transport 3 billion tons of sediment to the Bay of Bengal each year, far more than any other river system in the world. Unless it takes urgent measures, China will lose a land area twice the size of Taiwan to desertification by the year 2000. Behind the numbers lies a deteriorating relationship between people and the land that supports them, a tragic situation in which the dwellers on the land are both cause and victim.

The Causes of Degradation

The principal causes of land degradation—overgrazing of range lands, overcultivation of crop lands, waterlogging and salinization of irrigated lands, erosion, and deforestation—stem from excessive population pressure or poor land management.

Poor practices have degraded many of the irrigated lands where one-third of the world's food is raised. These lands typically yield two to three times more than rain-fed fields. Over time, seepage from canals and overwatering cause the underlying water table to rise. In the absence of adequate drainage, water eventually enters the root zone and damages crops. In addition, in dry regions salinization usually accompanies waterlogging as moisture near the surface evaporates, leaving behind a layer of salt that is toxic to plants. The UN Environmental Programme (UNEP) estimates total salinization at some 40 million hectares, about half of it in India and Pakistan, while other regions are the Tigris and Euphrates basins, the San Joaquin Valley and the Colorado River basin in the United States, China's North Plain, and Soviet Central Asia.

A major cause of land degradation is deforestation which, by accelerating soil erosion and reducing the soil's water-absorbing capacity, often accentuates the effects of overcultivation and overgrazing. Forest clearing may result in a net decline in the productivity of the land. Having lost its inherent fertility, the land can no longer support intensive agriculture. Large areas of pasture and cropland that replaced tropical forests in the Brazilian Amazon have been abandoned. National land policies in Brazil and Indonesia have long sponsored resettlement programs that encourage clearing of tropical forests, even though the newly cleared land can support cropping for only a few years.

Behind the direct causes of degradation is a complex web of cultural and economic relationships that underlie the process of decline. A major concern is the rapid increase in populations that occupy poorly endowed lands. In India, degradation of more than half its forests is caused by excessive demand for fuelwood.

Unequal distribution of land in some countries forces many peasants onto marginal lands, where they observe unsustainable management practices. Settlers in the Amazon region are pushed off their farms by the rich 1 percent of landowners who own 60 percent of the land in Brazil. In the Philippines, indigenous farmers who had previously pursued sustainable methods were moved to steep hillsides, where they produced lower yields and soon exhausted the soil. Similar scenarios are played out on the "Bantu homelands" of South Africa. In the absence of more equal land-distribution patterns, the number of smallholder and landless families worldwide is bound to grow further.

Lack of secure land tenure means farmers cannot use land as collateral for credits to make improvements. In Thailand, only one-fifth of the land has secure titles, and some 500,000 farm families are landless. China has made progress in land rehabilitation by improving tenure and decontrolling farm prices.

Long-lasting corrective action against degradation is a crucial component in overcoming the causes of poverty. But the many causal factors, economic and social as well as cultural, suggest that no single remedy will work by itself and that the corrective policies to be pursued must have broad support and remain in place for a long time.

Fighting Degradation: Reforestation and Other Measures

Trends in the reduction of the earth's tree coverage are alarming. Many developing countries remain tightly wedded to wood as a primary source of energy, in its raw form or after conversion to charcoal. Population pressures have made the use of wood for fuel an unsustainable practice. In addition, industrialized countries' appetite for tropical hardwood has encouraged many LDC governments to "mine" their forests to earn vital foreign exchange. Loggers do not fell just the desirable trees, often less than 5 percent of the area cut, but the unwanted trees as well. The human and ecological costs of wood scarcity are high. In rural parts of the Himalayas and the African Sahel, women and children spend between 100 and 300 days each year gathering fuelwood. Where fuelwood is critically scarce, people have no choice but to divert dried dung and crop residues from fields to cooking stoves, a practice that diminishes soil fertilty and depresses crop yields. A successful strategy to meet people's fuelwood needs must include increasing the productivity of natural forests; making better use of wood now wasted, including logging residues and trees cleared for cropland; raising the efficiency with which wood is now burned, and planting more trees.

Forests also have a vital ecological function; they stabilize soils, conserve nutrients, and regulate water supplies. Loss of tree cover on steep slopes can lead to large losses of topsoil. Where overgrazing or poor cropping practices occur, soils compact and lose some of their ability to absorb rainwater. Perhaps nowhere are the destructive effects of flooding and silting more evident than in the heavily populated plains of the Ganges and Brahmaputra rivers.

Degradation can be overcome through changes in the use and management of land. Certain types of corrective action are feasible, even in the poorest countries. Tree planting has been combined with improving crop yields in several places, as for example China's Loess Plateau, Sudan, and Senegal. Increased use of mulch may also be possible, as has for instance been shown in Nigeria.

Land rehabilitation calls for terrace construction, planting of trees, and improvement in maintenance. Battling desertification requires crossing disciplinary and bureaucratic boundaries (for example, agriculture, forestry, water management, and pastoralism).

Reforestation of large areas that have been laid barren has turned the tide of environmental decline in some regions. It calls for a major effort and deserves special attention. The problems of erosion, drought, and flooding, can often be traced to the ill effects of deforestation. Much new tree planting has been commercially motivated, increasing the supply of forest products that yield economic benefits: marketable timber, pulp, and fuelwood for cities. By contrast, reforestation for noncommercial reasons has not received sufficient attention.[4]

Reforestation must be made a top development priority. It will require popular participation, political leadership, and close cooperation between NGOs and official agencies, as well as finance. Around the world thousands of voluntary groups, women's organizations, peasant collectives, and church bodies have taken up tree planting. Larger amounts of external assistance could usefully be put to work against the onslaught of the desert. In recent years only $170 million per year was provided by donor agencies for field-level work in the Sahel, much below the $4.5 billion per year estimated by UNEP to be needed to bring desertification under control over a twenty-year period.

China's experience shows what is possible through determined government efforts, but it also brings out the difficulties that countries face. It planted some 33 million hectares and greatly expanded its tree cover from 8.6 to 12.7 percent of its land in 1948–1978. But the increased demand for wood products in the wake of China's economic reforms after 1979 outstripped the supply, even with annual planting of 4 million acres, so that the government had to double new planting.

The late prime minister of India Rajiv Gandhi recognized that deforestation had brought his country "face to face with a major ecological and socioeconomic crisis." He assigned forestry a central place in his development agenda and made funds for tree planting and nurseries directly available to local organizations.

The positive effect of Ghandi's political leadership could be multiplied by increased attention to basic forest research. An effort similar

to that of the Green Revolution of the 1960s may be necessary to promote indigenous tree species and diversify agroforestry, with direct
benefits to the marginalized and landless.

Large-scale reforestation could also make a significant contribution to improving the quality of the earth's atmosphere. Deforestation
adds greatly to carbon in the atmosphere, perhaps as much as one-
fourth to one-half of the amount that is produced by the burning of
fossil fuels by automobiles.[5] Atmospheric deterioration poses major
issues of environmental policy. While corrective action against degradation of the land is a crucial task facing poor countries, the industrialized countries apply more technology and management to counteract
spoilage of their agricultural resources. But they contribute to the
destruction of the ozone layer and global warming.

DETERIORATION OF THE ATMOSPHERE:
THE OZONE LAYER AND GLOBAL WARMING

Excessive and widespread use of certain chemicals in industrialized
countries has reduced the ozone layer in the earth's atmosphere, with
possible serious consequences for human health. Control of the underlying causes will require an entirely new type of international cooperation, which has only just begun.

In September 1987, after years of negotiations, twenty-four countries signed the Montreal Protocol on Substances that Deplete the
Ozone Layer. The agreement limited production of chlorofluorocar-
bons (CFCs) and dichlorodifluoromethane (Halon), widely used chemicals that are harmful to the ozone layer and cause an increase in
ultraviolet radiation reaching the earth's surface to dangerous levels.[6]
Ozone absorbs much of the ultraviolet radiation that the sun emits in
wavelengths harmful to humans, animals, and plants. The decline in
the ozone layer may well be causing an increase in certain types of
cancer and have other effects in nature.

By 1993 it had become clear that the Montreal treaty and associated public pressure had started to produce results in a marked slowdown in the growth in CFC use. Scientists could now anticipate
eventual rebuilding of the ozone layer; in 1994 the latest scientific estimates suggested that the ozone layer will start getting slowly thicker
by the year 2000 and thereafter.

Global warming is caused by the increase in emission of carbon
dioxide and other "greenhouse" gases. The best available estimates

indicate that the average global temperature has risen about one-half to one degree Fahrenheit in the past 100 years.[7] Scientific evidence of global warming was again confirmed by an international expert group in 1996. The changes in atmospheric conditions and other environmental factors may have repercussions for the world's food supply, itself a vital parameter influencing conditions of the poor.

THE ENVIRONMENT AND THE PROSPECTS FOR WORLD FOOD PRODUCTION

Degradation of the land and erosion, aggravated by droughts, adversely affect the growth in world food output. Developments since the mid-1980s may have signified a break in the steady increase in grain production of the previous forty years, caused by the much-reduced availability of new unused agricultural lands, lower use of fertilizer, and a reduction in irrigation possibilities.[8]

Since the mid-1980s, both grain production and the growth of areas under irrigation have turned down. Use of fertilizers, which had expanded rapidly for over three decades, declined in the wake of weakening agricultural prices and cutbacks in fertilizer subsidies. The transition in the former Soviet republics has cut into all kinds of new investment, including irrigation works. While they and the Eastern European countries had been able to reduce their dependence on grain imports, further progress depends on the success of reform in agricultural policies.

The depletion of aquifers and the water table in the United States, China, India, and the former Soviet Union has brought an end to the era of rapid increase in irrigation. There are still opportunities for further moderate increases in India, the former Soviet Union, and some of the smaller developing countries (e.g., Thailand and the Philippines).

In the mid-1980s, some populous countries (China, India, Indonesia, and Mexico) seemed to have reached a plateau in their grain production. India tripled her wheat harvests in 1965–1983 as a result of the green revolution, but since then there has been no further increase. Japan, Korea, and Taiwan have also experienced declines in grain production since they reached a peak in the late 1970s. China has been importing an increasing proportion of its food requirements, and if this trend continues its imports will soon surpass those of Japan and the former Soviet Union, making it a major factor in the world market.

Over the longer term, food prospects may be improved by the application of new technologies, as for example biotechnology. Western Europe has demonstrated the possibility of progress through more advanced technologies, combined with favorable support prices and low population growth. The developing countries, on their part, can go some way in raising their productivity to the level of the industrialized countries.

The global market is bound to adjust to shifts in resources, supplies, and production technologies. Prices may rise, sometimes markedly, to the disadvantage of the poor. Food habits will also adapt to new supplies, and most likely people will spend more on food.

Many other changes could, of course, contribute to greater grain supplies, as for example improvements in storage facilities, reduction in the consumption of meat, or cutbacks in grain use for nonfood purposes (e.g., ethanol). But in the end it may be the poor, rural landless and low-income urban residents (who already spend 70 percent of their income on food), who will suffer most of the consequences. Even today some 900 million people fail to get enough calories to maintain a normal level of activity, while 36 percent of schoolchildren in LDCs are below normal weight for their age.

These observations once again point to the importance of slowing population growth. External assistance can help to increase aid for improved agricultural production, reforestation, agricultural research, and conservation (Brown and Kane, 1994, ch. 15 and 16). The prospects of food production depend critically on rehabilitation of degraded land and improved land management. Decisions and deliberations leading to essential changes and initiatives will involve economic analyses, often of a new kind and undertaken with new objectives.

ECONOMICS AND THE ENVIRONMENT

Recognition of environmental factors has a major impact on economic thinking and the measures taken to encourage growth and development. It is important to see how conventional economics must change in response to environmental concerns.

The Greening of Policy

Taxation and price incentives, the growth and composition of exports and the prospects of individual export crops, the cost of investment, and the limits of agricultural growth are directly affected by environmental considerations. Incentive policies executed through price or fiscal measures can have an important impact on environmental degradation.[9] Yet although economists are increasingly aware of the links between overall country analysis and environmental questions, much remains to be done to make environmental concerns an integral part of economic policy thinking.

Much of conventional economic analysis deals with questions that are of obvious concern to environmentalists, such as the consequences of slash-and-burn agriculture, the long-run cost and benefits of projects, and demographic issues. But their treatment often does not touch on environmental issues, as is clear from a development economics college text like Gillis (1987), which discussed these topics but nowhere mentioned the environment. Herman Daly sought to correct for past shortcomings by placing traditional economics in a broader framework of ecology (Daly and Cobb, 1989).

Recognition of environmental factors is especially important in the national accounts, which are commonly used in measuring growth and economic planning. But the widely applied UN system of national accounts did not allow for the environmental effects of production or consumption, and are now being "greened." Unless properly revised, they give the wrong signals for policy making. Omitting environmental considerations may have made sense in the past, when natural resources were regarded as abundant and costless "free gifts of nature." Further, expenditures made to defend the environment, as for example abatement of industrial pollution, were conventionally treated as a productive activity, but are merely offsets to adverse environmental effects, quite different from new equipment or consumer goods.

Conventional national accounting allowed for depletion of plants and equipment, but not for depletion of nonrenewable resources, deforestation, erosion, or land degradation. When a country is exhausting its resources, conventional calculation overstates the country's current income or the true value of its exports of natural assets. The cost of erosion is another offset to economic production not normally reflected in the national accounts.[10]

The adverse effects of subsidization present a strong case against undue deviation from free-market pricing. Irrigation water provided below cost—often as much as 90–95 percent—encourages excessive use of water, which in turn may cause logging and salinization.

Overbuilding of irrigation works caused by subsidization may displace whole communities. Subsidization of pesticides and fertilizers, achieved through tax concessions, low interest rates, and other financial means, may be bad for the structure and productivity of the soil. Subsidies often favor chemical fertilizers and discourage the use of organic manure. While chemical fertilizers supplement organic materials, organic fertilizer protects soil productivity and reduces erosion by preserving desirable physical and biological properties of the soil. In developed countries, chemical runoff is widely recognized as a source of water pollution.

Prices of farm machinery, kept low through subsidization, encourage uneconomic use of equipment at the expense of employment. The resulting overuse of machinery can lead to excessive forest clearance and unnecessary disturbance of the soil.

New investment, which plays an important role in environmental policy, can be justified on both financial and economic grounds. Consumers are usually willing to pay for improved water supply and sanitation projects. Safe drinking water can be supplied through appropriately designed community systems, often at one-tenth the cost that slum dwellers without such systems now pay to water carriers and vendors.

Policy reform stressing greater reliance on market forces is generally conducive to sound environmental management. But regulation is sometimes necessary to resolve environmental problems in an efficient or equitable manner. Some activities, like livestock and forestry, may have to be taxed rather than subsidized. Measures to avoid flooding might include incentives for industrial or residential relocation to less damage-prone areas. Increases in rates for electric power and municipal water, justified to cover environmental costs, present politically charged problems in Latin American and other developing countries. [11]

Alan S. Blinder, the eminent Princeton University economist and vice-chairman on the Federal Reserve in the early 1990s, and others have argued that market-based controls of environmental pollution impose smaller costs on industry and work more effectively than the direct controls frequently used in the United States. Emission permits, sold at a price, or emission taxes place the decision as to how to reduce effluence in the hands of the manufacturer. This lets the company act out of self-interest rather than being subject to inspection and regulations (Blinder, 1987, p. 159). In his 1996 "State of the World" report,

Lester Brown, head of the Worldwatch Institute, likewise called for fiscal charges on polluting activities. While little use has been made of economic incentives so far, recent legislation in the United States and other industrialized countries has begun to make greater use of them (The *Washington Post*, Aug. 24, 1994).

Making economic policies compatible with environmental objectives imposes on governments and politicians alike a demanding task, which reaches into many facets of policy. But do the various measures taken fit in with a growth-oriented policy? The compatibility of growth and environmental policies is of strategic importance to fighting poverty.

Is Environmental Policy Compatible with Growth?

In the United States environmentalists have been in conflict with advocates of growth, but the dilemmas posed in the debate are often false. Timbermen oppose protection of the spotted owl on the ground it would endanger jobs and profits, yet all but 15 percent of the old-growth forests in which the owl thrives has already been cut, and most of what remains is on public lands. The timber industry and loggers will be better off looking for new fields of activity, facing up to the need for economic diversification and job retraining. Attention to environmental factors can create new jobs and new areas of growth. Environmental protection equipment makes up a new growth industry. After two decades of cleaning up dirty air, unsafe water, and toxic waste, the environmental services industry counts nearly 70,000 businesses, well over a million workers, and an income of $130 billion in 1991 in the United States, with export earnings of $6–8 billion. The global market for environmental goods and services is estimated to range from $200 to $370 billion per year, of which $50 billion enters international trade. Germany's commitment to reduce carbon dioxide output by 25 percent by 2005 is spurring innovation and export promotion (Wirth, 1992). With sales well over $11 billion, it has shown that its tough pollution control and recycling laws actually enhance productivity and competitive strength. Along with Italy and the Netherlands, it allocates about 10 percent of its research and development budget to new environmental technologies. Japan is also mounting a major effort in this field.

In the developing countries, land degradation threatens sustained economic growth. Even today's income levels may be difficult to maintain, especially in many of the poorest countries with their dwindling resource base and rapidly expanding populations. It is essential that projects be found that satisfy the twin objectives of economic growth and environmental protection.[12]

Governments of poor countries feel compelled to give top priority to immediate budgetary and balance of payments problems, and to delay action on future needs. Poverty may be a cause of both environmental degradation and lessened ability to take action. It is essential to devise growth-oriented policies with special emphasis on improving the incomes of the poor.

Even where environmental and growth objectives are compatible, governments face politically difficult choices. The urgency of current needs, the uncertainty about the future, and the short-term perspective of many decision makers underline the importance of political commitment to shape and pursue an effective environmental policy. If it is to be translated into effective action, commitment must be supported by broad public understanding of the urgency of the problems and the need for remedial action.

Many of these points have been spelled out in greater detail in the World Development Report (WDR) 1992, written by a World Bank team headed by Andrew Steer. The report showed that environmental policies are a central element in a comprehensive strategy of fighting poverty. The poorest groups can be helped by improved agricultural practices, education, sanitation, and the provision of clean drinking water. The often-high cost of environmental protection is justified by a favorable payoff over the longer term. Industrialized countries should assist, especially where they are the beneficiaries of better environmental policies in the developing countries. Growth, an essential ingredient of success, can be compatible with the objectives of a healthy environment, provided market-related policies are judiciously combined with direct intervention.[13] Somewhat unusual for a World Bank study, the 1992 WDR considers fighting poverty through better environmental policies a moral imperative. The thrust of the report is a suitable starting point for the discussion of the ethics of environmental policies.

THE ETHICAL DIMENSION

Environmental degradation does great harm to the poorest countries and people, the disadvantaged, the poor, less educated, and politically less powerful elements of society. The urban poor, living in unsanitary conditions without safe drinking water, are hurt by noise, flooding, and water pollution, and cannot afford to pay for better services or to defend themselves against damage. The rural poor, farming flood-prone valleys and swiftly eroding hillsides, cannot afford to invest in conservation measures, grow crops which take a long time to mature, and move to more productive lands. Deforestation has made the plains of Bangladesh subject to flooding, which endangers the lives and livelihood of millions. Overgrazing of African lands has worsened the prospects of poor farmers and calls for careful remedial action.

Often conditions in the poorest countries damage the health of the environment, even though the industrialized countries are still the most significant source of global pollution. Broad-based action, both national and international, is needed to counteract environmentally destructive forces. The various changes called for in policy action and community commitment have profound ethical implications.

It should come as no surprise that we look at environmental policy from an ethical perspective. Environmentalism in the United States is itself close to a religion. It has a pantheon with widely admired people—Henry David Thoreau, Ralph Waldo Emerson, Aldo Leopold, John Muir, Rachel Carson, and others. Its heroes are the fighters for conservation and the national parks, led by progressive leaders like Teddy Roosevelt and Harold Ickes, FDR's secretary of the interior. In the view of nature lovers and conservationists, our national parks are holy ground, and they walk their trails with reverence.

Equally powerful is the Christian commitment to love of nature. Some environmentalists accuse the Christian faith of being exclusively human-centered and inherently indifferent or hostile toward nature. Worse, they accuse Christians of advocating wanton domination of nature. The Bible's view of the environment is that God created all of nature, humans as well as other creatures on land, in the air, and in the sea. All creatures have their reason for being here in the eyes of their maker. When God commanded us to have dominion over nature, He did not mean for us to dominate it, even less to destroy it, but to govern it with love. "Dominion" theory is not of biblical origin, but instead has utilitarian roots going back to Francis Bacon. Utilitarians manage nature for profit, but Christian farmers must love their animals and seek to restore rather than deplete the soil. The same is true for Jewish farmers, as is abundantly clear from the agricultural and conservation practices in Israel. In their daily life, Christians and Jews are called to embody lifestyles and cultural attitudes that are relevant to present ecological needs and serve as signs of the Reign of Love. They must love and care for both people and natural resources, and be frugal in their use of the fruits of nature.

The dominion over creation which God gave human beings (Gen. 1:30) does not give them license to abuse creation. Human beings, created in the image of God, cannot ravish creation but, like God, must sustain it. And they are an image of God not as isolated individuals, but as a community (Gen. 1:28). Hence they are to exercise dominion in a way that is responsive to the needs of the total human family, including future generations. Human dominion in the biblical sense consists of the twofold task of tilling and taking care of the garden. Economic systems must be shaped so that a healthy ecological system is maintained over time (Oxford Declaration on Christian Faith and Economics, 1990, par. 5–7). A similar view was expressed by the 1990 Seoul convention of the World Council of Churches and the U.S. Catholic bishops' pastoral "Renewing the Earth" (1991).

In his challenging exploration "Loving Nature," James A. Nash of Wesley Theological Seminary urges that on environmental issues we should address ethical virtues of restraint and frugality, recognize the reality of human interdependence, and extend the principle of solidarity to the whole biosphere (Nash, 1991, pp. 64–67). From an ethical point of view, excessive emphasis on growth and high standards of consumption in the industrialized countries are incompatible with a global solidarity through which the poor countries must improve their levels of living. Nash also recognizes the role growth must play in meeting developing countries' basic needs for food, energy, health care, housing, education, transportation, etc. (op. cit., p. 202). The industrialized countries must curtail their consumption so the earth may breathe again and the poor countries may be able to raise their living standards. The pattern of U.S. growth may have to change, become less energy-intensive, economize through large-scale recycling, emphasize educational and cultural development, and generally have less stress on purely material welfare.

It seems plausible that scarcity pricing in the industrialized countries will bring about needed shifts in consumption, which can be encouraged by technology and taxation. Shifts in consumption can of course be induced by more progressive income taxation and levies on luxury items. Nash also points out that the developing countries need more production, education, and health services as part of a broader reform for better treatment of the earth.

Views in Different Religious Communities

In many places the Bible proclaims the beauty of God's creation, the intimate link between God and his creation, and the role human beings must play. A central message of the Bible is that when human beings turn against God, they become alienated from themselves and hostile to their environment. Only when they become new beings, live in a new relation with God and themselves, can they attain a new and right attitude to themselves and to their environment. Thus environmental policy, with its many economic implications, must have a moral base to succeed.

Very early in its testimony, the Bible sees the breaching of social justice in conjunction with damage to the environment. "The idea of social justice is inextricably linked in the Scripture with ecology. In passage after passage, environmental degradation and social injustice go hand in hand. Indeed, the first instance of "pollution" in the Bible occurs when Cain slays Abel and his blood falls on the ground, rendering it fallow. According to Genesis, after the murder when Cain asks, "Am I my brother's keeper?" the Lord replies: "Your brother's blood calls out to me from the ground. What have you done?" God then tells Cain that his brother's blood has defiled the ground and that as a result, "no longer will it yield crops for you, even if you toil on it forever" (Gen. 4: 10–12) (Gore, 1992, p. 247).

Many religious groups have expressed views on the environment: Judaism, the Vatican and the U.S. Catholic bishops, diverse Protestant groups who prepared the 1990 Oxford Declaration on Christian Faith and Economics, and the 1990 Seoul Convocation of the World Council of Churches, as well as some individual mainline churches.

The *Union of American Hebrew Congregations* ("Union") is unique in that its statements are directed to specific policy issues and make but few general ethical observations (see ch. 8). In 1965 it found that "America, in thoughtlessly abusing its natural resources, has disregarded the Biblical injunction to conserve God's creation for the good of all" and called on government to extend its leadership in conserving and developing America's natural resources. "Development of nuclear power resources, improved irrigation, flood control, desalination and increased water power, tapping new natural resources while preserving the old, are all part of the vision for a better society." In 1969 the Union pointed out that Judaism inherits "a tradition which is marked by a reverence for life and must preserve the earth and all its varied life for our own sake and for generations yet unborn." The Union called for government and the private sector to take action to remove or ameliorate the growing threats to environmental pollution and to afford protection to the environment.

The Union commended the Carter administration for taking the initiative on developing a comprehensive national energy policy (1978). Its decisions were based on "the principles of our Jewish tradition that stress mankind's responsibility to care for God's earth and to safeguard its resources, thus fulfilling our trust to generations yet unborn." A comprehensive national energy program must be spearheaded by appropriate and responsible government policy, with energy efficiency and conservation encouraged by economic incentives. "Strict standards must be imposed on the development and use of all energy sources in order to minimize both further harm to health and further degradation of the environment." An energy policy must define the responsibility of all Americans and assure that the burden it imposes will be equitably shared by all segments of society. These and other principles of social justice were reaffirmed in a 1979 pronouncement which underlined the importance of conservation, increased oil exploration, and help to relieve the burdens of the poor. It urged the government to develop its own database on energy sources and not be dependent on private industry for this purpose. A 1983 resolution of the Union dealt with issues of toxic substances. The 1990 Central Conference of American Rabbis stressed the importance of recycling and based its recommendations on an environmental ethic which commands us to preserve and not destroy God's world.

The *Pope's message* of January 1, 1990, for the celebration of the World Day of Peace dealt exclusively with the theology and policy of the environment, starting out with the observation that God saw that what He had made was very good. While Adam and Eve were to have exercised their dominion over the earth with wisdom and love, they destroyed the existing harmony by going deliberately against the Creator's plan, by choosing to sin. This resulted not only in the alienation of human beings against themselves, but also in the earth's rebellion against them. The theological argument proceeds from the creation story to Paul's observation: "All of creation became subject to futility, waiting in a mysterious way to be set free and to obtain the glorious liberty together with all the children of God" (Rom. 8:20–21). Creation is made new in Christ, who made peace with God by the blood of his cross.

Creation has received new life, while "we wait for new heavens and a new earth in which righteousness dwells" (2 Pt. 3:13). "These biblical considerations help us to understand better the relationship between human activity and the whole creation. When man turns his back on the Creator's plan, he provokes a disorder which has inevitable repercussions on the rest of the created order. If men and women are not at peace with God, the earth itself cannot be at peace: "Therefore the land mourns and all who dwell in it languish, and also the beasts of the field and the birds of the air and even the fish of the sea are taken away" (Hos. 4:3) (John Paul II, 1990, p. 5).

The Pope's message brings out two elements which are not found as explicitly in the statements by secular policy advocates and international bodies. First, the seriousness of the ecological issue lays bare the depth of our moral crisis. This crisis finds its origin in the interconnectedness of all elements of nature and of human society, both national and international. Human beings cannot take any action if they do not take account of the consequences for other creatures or for plant life. "We cannot interfere in one area of the ecosystem without paying due attention both to the consequences of such interference in other areas and to the well-being of future generations." "Respect for life, and above all for the dignity of the human person, is the ultimate guiding norm for any sound economic, industrial or scientific progress" (op. cit., p. 6).

And secondly, modern society will find no solution to the ecological problems unless it takes a serious look at its lifestyle. "Simplicity, moderation and discipline, as well as a spirit of sacrifice, must become a part of everyday life, lest all suffer the negative consequences of the careless habits of the few" (op. cit., p. 7).

The *U.S. Catholic bishops' pastoral message "Renewing the Earth"* (1991) focuses on ethics and appears to have left environmental policy issues until later. It stresses the central role of Christian love in environmental policy, and calls on various groups to get involved in environmental action. Its principal themes echo some of the ecological virtues expressed by Nash:

- We must basically be humble toward nature, based on faith in God and respect for people and animals;
- The poor suffer more from environmental degradation than the rich;
- We must consume with greater constraint, so as to relax pressure on limited resources;
- Ecological concerns have highlighted our awareness of just how interdependent the world is;
- Development is constrained by concern for our natural resources; and
- We must tackle the population problem.

These points highlight the importance of constraint in our personal and corporate behavior, supplemented by investment and production processes that are environmentally sensitive.

The *Oxford Declaration on Christian Faith and Economics*, prepared by various Protestant groups (1990), sets forth the biblical base for environmental stewardship as part of a broader analysis of what Christians think about economic issues, confirming that God, the creator and redeemer, is the ultimate owner of the world's resources. Human beings, responsible for the earth on God's behalf, have been thoughtless, greedy, and violent, and have damaged God's good creation and produced a number of ecological problems and conflicts. All things—human beings and their environment—are "for God" (Rom. 11:36, 1 Cor. 8:6, Col. 1:16) (See also Gore, 1992, p. 244). Christian hope for the future includes an entirely new creation (Rom. 8:21). The views of the Oxford Declaration were confirmed by Ron Sider (1991) of the Evangelicals for Social Action; he also deals with specific issues like disposal of hazardous waste and energy policy.

The *World Council of Churches* Convocation on Justice, Peace and the Integrity of Creation (Seoul, South Korea, March 1990) concluded with a number of affirmations concerning the broad spectrum of social concerns of the churches, including poverty, racial equality, equality between women and men ("both are created in the image of God"), dedication to truth and peace, participation of young Christians in church affairs, and environmental policy. The affirmations on the environment ("Creation is beloved of God" and "The Earth is the Lord's"), drafted in quite general terms, rejected the view that humans can exploit the earth's resources in a destructive manner, and joins in solidarity with indigenous communities struggling for their cultures, spirituality, and rights to land and sea; and peasants and poor farmers seeking land reform, who "await the fulfilment of the promise for the meek to inherit the earth. When there is justice in the land, the field and the forests and every living thing will dance and sing for joy" (Ps. 96:11–12).

The *Presbyterian* statement "Restoring Creation for Ecology and Justice" (1990), which deals with both "eco-theology" and policy issues, urges attention to energy policy, hunger, and economic justice; and calls for action on sustainable agriculture, water quality, wildlife and wildlands, and waste management. The broadly cast report was a suitable preparation for the 1992 Earth Summit.

Environmental issues have now joined the earlier, more conventional, justice and peace issues in the advocacy of the churches.[14] Environmental concerns are not on the periphery of the peace and justice agenda, but a central part of it. As the U.S. Catholic bishops remind us: "Francis of Assisi, the patron saint of the environmental movement, tamed wolves and preached to the birds only after a long novitiate in which he ministered to outcasts and lepers."[15]

Making general moral pronouncements about the environment is, of course, easier than the execution of pro-environment measures which also make sense from an economic viewpoint. Environmental policies may be costly to particular industries or may run against the interests of some wealthy groups. The going gets rough when these groups are opposed in the interest of the whole community. Faced with the complexities of environmental issues, the religious community has a clear and important role to persuade people of their moral obligation to join the fight for a more sensible environmental policy. It has a unique role to give a coherent picture of God's work in creation and our human response to it. It can also make a vital contribution by calling for restraint in consumption in the richer countries and for larger assistance to environmental policies of benefit to the poor.

The churches' central message is that we must nurture and love nature, rather than rob, exploit, and destroy. Of all the violence against nature and the environment, none is worse than the damage inflicted by war. War likewise is in conflict with the struggle against poverty, as reviewed in more detail in the next chapter.

5

Our Military Burden

Military expenditures raise many difficult issues on both moral and economic grounds. Jewish and Christian ethicists are foremost in stressing the importance of peace in the behavior of individuals, as well as in the relations between communities and nations. They have long raised fundamental objections against many forms of war. There are likewise many economic reasons against high levels of military expenditures. They are in fact a principal enemy of antipoverty action, since they divert resources from modernizing and rebuilding infrastructure and social services for the poor. Moreover, the emphasis on manufacturing for the military weakens the competitiveness and efficiency of the overall economy, and hence its capacity to fight poverty. Developing countries that have high military programs suffer from lower growth, lower savings, and a reduced capacity to tackle the many problems of the poor.

The interaction between the military and the civilian economy in the United States is the first item for our attention. We focus on the drain of resources from poverty programs and then on the impact the military has on the efficiency of industry. We also review the changes in the U.S. economy since the end of the Cold War. Next we discuss the effect of large military programs on developing countries. Our economic analysis of the consequences of military expenditures in the United States and the developing countries leads up to a consideration of the many ethical issues that throw doubt on the justification of military programs.

Now is a unique time for taking stock of the consequences of the military for the fight against poverty. There has been a widely shared conviction that the end of the Cold War has brought us to a historic crossroads from which a new start is possible. The demise of the Soviet Union has made possible a substantial downsizing of our military establishment. But our defense effort faces new challenges in many trouble spots around the globe. The former Yugoslavia, Iraq, and other

Middle Eastern countries come to mind. The economic upheavals in the former Soviet Union could explode into new critical situations, even though the threat to us may be less concentrated than in the past.

Further progress toward reductions in military expenditures may well be slow. We can expect resistance from the military themselves and from their supplier industries. Many believe there is a continuing need for development of technologically advanced weapons. The unemployment effects of military contraction also caution against proceeding too rapidly.

THE MILITARY AND THE CIVILIAN ECONOMY IN THE UNITED STATES

At the end of the Cold War, the size of the American armed forces and its supporting military–industrial complex was beyond the comprehension of most lay persons. Military hardware was technologically the most sophisticated available. An annual defense budget of say $300 billion overwhelms the needs of our civilian economy. (It was $282 billion in 1987 and rose further thereafter; after 1990, total outlays started to fall, except of course for the cost of the 1990–1991 Gulf War.) The number of people employed by the military in peacetime, directly and indirectly, was some 7 million: over 2 million in the services, 1 million civilians working for the Pentagon, and some 4 million civilians working for military contractors. Some estimates put the total direct and indirect jobs in the military much higher. There is no doubt that the total number of people affected by downsizing our defense has been enormous; the unavoidable layoffs were bound to add considerably to our unemployment problem in the short run.[1]

On the question of how big our military program should be, opinions vary widely with people's perception of the objectives of our government and the strength of our adversary. With hindsight, many would say that President Truman's decision to counteract Soviet aggression was correct. Our subsequent courage to stay this course was also correct, but one may well ask whether our military effort was too large or too small, or whether containment should have been more political and less military. President Eisenhower believed the buildup of the military–industrial complex presented a threat to our civilian economy. And this legitimate concern raises the question which we address here: How much damage did our military effort inflict on the economic base of our freedom? We will see the answer is twofold.

TABLE 5.1   Military Expenditures, 1944–1987

	$ Billions	% Federal Outlays	% GNP
1944	79.1	86.6	39.2
1948	9.1	30.5	3.7
1952	46.1	68.1	13.4
1960	48.1	52.2	9.5
1968	82	32.6	6.2
1972	79	34.3	6.9
1976	90	24.1	5.3
1980	134	22.7	5.0
1987	282	28.4	6.3

Source: Office of Management and Budget,
Historical Tables, Fiscal Year 1987.

First, military expenditures take away from rising civilian needs. Second, they may affect adversely the efficiency and growth of the civilian economy.

Diversion of Resources

A simple way of judging the impact of our military effort is to compare the military budget with total federal outlays or the GNP. In the years before the demise of the Soviet Union, military expenditures were about 27 percent of federal outlays and 6 percent of the GNP. So out of every federal dollar more than a quarter went for the military, not a negligible proportion in peacetime. Yet of every $100 we produced as a nation, only $6 went for the military, so why be concerned?

Over the post-World War II years, military expenditures have gone up and down with the ebb and flow of troubles abroad and threats of war (see Table 5.1). In 1944 the World War II effort took up 87 percent of federal outlays and almost 40 percent of the GNP. After World War II, defense expenditures were first rapidly reduced, then again increased during the Truman (1944–1952) buildup against communist threats in Korea and Europe. At the start of the Eisenhower administration in 1952, they were 68 percent of federal outlays and 13 percent of the GNP.

During the 1950s, the United States built up its nuclear arsenal and strengthened its bases in Europe and the Pacific. Eisenhower kept military expenditures at a fairly steady level in absolute terms, although he reduced them in relation to total federal outlays and GNP—52 and 9.5 percent—respectively, but still high even by Reagan standards. After the Eisenhower administration, military expenditures showed a declining trend, except for the Vietnam War bulge.

In 1980 military outlays were lower in relation to the federal budget or the American economy than they had been at any time since 1948. This was one of the factors motivating President Reagan to more than double expenditures from $134 billion in 1980 to $282 billion in 1987, outspending any previous peacetime president—quite a record for someone who said he wanted to shrink the size of government.

But what do military expenditures mean for the prosperity and productivity of the civilian economy and its ability to reduce poverty?[2] True, military expenditures are counted as part of the total GNP; as they rise, so does the GNP. But they don't buy consumer satisfaction or economically useful goods and, equally important, they don't provide the means for improving private productivity. They provide jobs for people who otherwise might be poor, but they may not provide the infrastructure, such as schools or urban rehabilitation, that the poor need over the longer term.

In the 1930s and 1940s it was widely believed that war expenditures would take up the slack in the economy, reflected in 18 million unemployed and underemployed in 1939. After four years of war, unemployment was gone, but the U.S. plant had become rundown. After the war new investments were necessary in plant and equipment, as well as infrastructure, and while massive new construction went forward and urban and suburban development changed the face of the land, military outlays also took up a large share of our resources. In fact, in thirty years after World War II (1946–1975), the military spent a total of $1,500 billion.

The eminent student of the effects of the military on the civilian economy, Columbia University professor Seymour Melman, calculated that military expenditures in this period (1946–1975) were equivalent to the total value of all residential and commercial structures in 1975. A more recent estimate puts military spending from World War II to 1988 at $9.6 trillion in 1982 dollars, about $1.5 trillion more than the estimated value of the country's tangible assets, except for the land itself. "At present the stock of military "machinery"—weapons—is valued at two-fifths of all industrial equipment, while over one-third of U.S. engineers and scientists work for the military" (Ullmann, 1991, p. 57).

Writing at a time of increasing concern with decay in our inner cities, Melman found that the military budget was sufficient to meet the total cost of urban restructuring. He and others made calculations of what the resources spent on the military could have accomplished in various areas of civilian needs. Here are some examples:

- The 1986 Cuomo plan for *low-income housing* for New York City, $4 billion, was half of the funding for additions to the stock of U.S. nuclear warheads (already a mere 37,000 units in total);

- The 1986 reduction proposed in the *AMTRAK budget* and the modernization of the Northeast rail corridor, $741 million, equaled the cost of 26 Navy aircushion landing craft (Melman, 1985, ch. 8);

- The $1 million cost of a one-year supply of *nutritional supplements* for 5,000 pregnant women at risk is the same as that of two infantry combat vehicles; and

- The cost of a five-year program for *universal child immunization* against six deadly diseases, preventing 1 million deaths each year, is the same as that of one Trident submarine ($1.436 billion) (Sivard, 1987, p. 35).

As military outlays were reduced in the 1960s and 1970s, the federal government was able to increase antipoverty programs. However, with greater emphasis on the military during the Vietnam war, antipoverty action had to be scaled back. While poverty declined from around 22 percent of the population in 1960 to 11 percent in 1972, it rose thereafter, reaching 15 percent in 1983 (Sawhill, 1988; ch. 1, ftn. 7).

The military also influenced the direction of *industrial research* to the detriment of civilian industries. They could in effect pursue their own industrial policy by dominating government assistance to industry. Military research accounted for 1–1.5 percent of the gross domestic product (GDP), equivalent to half of total industrial research. It was concentrated on technologically highly complex products, which are of little use to the civilian market and did not induce growth in productivity. Manufacturing has benefited much more from research that concentrated on civilian technology such as in France, Germany, and Japan (De Grasse, 1984, p. 14).

The disparity between government assistance to military and civilian research continued in the 1980s when the U.S. government devoted well over twice as much money to weapons as to all other research, including energy, health, education, and food. Only one-fourth of government-sponsored research was directed to products for the civilian market, as against 70 percent in Europe. The impact on education was especially serious: "In the competition for public finances, U.S. education has taken second place to military programs, starving resources needed to train and maintain a high-quality, skilled workforce. Currently U.S. expenditures on education are barely three-fourths of military expenditures; West Germany by comparison spends 40 percent more on public education than on military defense, Japan five times more" (Sivard, 1987, p. 14 and p. 39).

Reduction in Industrial Efficiency

High defense expenditures also tended to reduce the efficiency of military industries and, as a consequence, the productivity of the entire economy. This becomes clear when one takes a closer look at the many firms that make military hardware. At the time of Defense Secretary McNamara (1961–1968), the Pentagon was served by some 20,000 firms, which in turn were aided by some 100,000 subcontractors. During the 1980s many smaller companies closed shop, while bigger firms consolidated and diversified their operations.

The critical difference between military and civilian firms is that the former do not seek to minimize costs, while the latter are forced to do so by market pressures. Management in the military industries does not make crucial production decisions, which are left to the Pentagon. Unlike civilian industries, military industry has no incentive to keep costs low, since the Pentagon normally stands ready to cover cost increases. The principle of cost-plus calculation applied by the Pentagon leads to higher rather than lower costs. Under the rules of military procurement, producers have until recently been prohibited from using procedures under which each item is broken down into its components, that in turn are priced according to competitive market standards. Cost estimates for military product items instead had to be based on historical data, with past price records used as a guide, including an allowance for price escalation permitted under McNamara's procedures. In practice, past price data could, however, be inflated, resulting in higher costs and considerable cost overruns, as much as four times the original estimate in the case of one plane (Melman, 1985, pp. 30–32).

Thus military procurement tended to push up the cost structure in supplier industries. For example:

- *Overhead* and the number of engineers employed in military industries are higher than those in civilian industry or even comparable European military industries. The French employed fifty design draftsmen for the Mirage II, compared with 240 just to monitor the design of the U.S. Air Force F-15.

- *Capital* is provided by the Pentagon, often in the form of progress payments which can earn interest in bank accounts.

- The wages of *production workers* are higher than those in civilian industries.

Communities that are heavily dependent on defense expenditures live at a standard that is higher than can be justified by civilian economic considerations.

Military expenditures crowd out productive investment with consequent adverse effects on industrial productivity and growth. The emphasis on the military tended to reduce infrastructure expenditures, with the resulting deterioration in the quality of rail, commuter, and intercity transport symptomatic of the weakening of the civilian economy as a whole. The decline in American industrial efficiency contrasts sharply with the rising competitiveness of Japan and Germany, which spent much less on defense. As far back as 1971, defense expenditures were equivalent to 52 percent of gross domestic investment in the United States, compared with 14 percent in Germany and only 2 percent in Japan. The difference in industrial performance can be seen from the comparison in Table 5.2.

The impact of high military expenditures on economic growth is not easy to demonstrate statistically. As the military absorbed a relatively small share of our resources in the 1960s, U.S. industrial growth and productivity were healthier than in the years of the peacetime military buildup. When military programs took up a greater proportion of our economic and technological resources, the international position of American industry deteriorated persistently, as became evident in the 1970s when U.S. industry lost one-third of its world share, while its share of the home market also went down. The cost to the U.S. economy was the loss of $125 billion of production and 2 million jobs. In analyzing the causes of our industrial decline, observers pointed to rising labor costs, short-sighted management, social spending, and

TABLE 5.2 Military Spending and Industrial Performance

	Military Spending, % of GNP 1980	*Growth in manufactured output per man-hour 1975–1980*
U.S.	5.5	1.7
Germany	3.3	4.3
Japan	0.9	8.0

Source: Melman, 1985, ch. 4.

regulation, but few identified the military as a cause of the troubles in our manufacturing industries in the 1970s. The continuing deterioration of our industry in the 1980s ran parallel with the military buildup. Adding further to the weakening of our economy, the government permitted much of the technological knowledge from U.S. inventions, especially semiconductors, to slip to the Japanese and other competing nations (Tolchin, 1992).

The decline in American productivity in the 1960s and 1970s contrasts sharply with earlier developments. In 1965–1980 the United States trailed Europe by 60 percent and Japan by 70 percent, but in 1870–1950 U.S. productivity growth had exceeded that in Europe and Japan by substantial margins. This turnaround in productivity growth is exemplified by what happened in the machinery industry. Over long periods the fall in the cost of machinery in the United States relative to labor had encouraged the use of more sophisticated techniques in manufacturing. But after the 1960s the decline in productivity in the U.S. machinery industry and the corresponding rise in machinery prices discouraged investment in modern technology at a time of deep changes in the world economy.

The important changes in the U.S. economy that began in the 1990s will go some way in redressing these imbalances. As military expenditures were scaled back to 4 percent of the GDP, there was a growing awareness of the needs of our schools. But concerns with overall budgetary constraints, a desire to limit the federal government's social responsibilities, and renewed interest in strengthening the military may once again put a damper on meeting civilian needs, especially those of the poorest amongst us. These trends hold important lessons for the future.

The adverse impact which programs have had on our economic productivity and efficiency points to the opportunities that are opened up by a scaledown in military expenditures. As the influence of the Pentagon becomes less dominant, new funds must be raised for reconstruction of our infrastructure, strengthening civilian manufacturing, and for concentrating our scientific and technological efforts on raising the productivity and quality of our manufacturing. Industrial restructuring and the scaledown of the military have involved shifts in the employment of millions. This process can be accommodated best in an environment of sound growth. While the free market will go far in facilitating many aspects of the changes in industry and the labor force, some consequences call for attention of the public sector, in particular the reemployment of many types of workers—professional and technical as well as skilled—in areas that have been heavily dependent on defense contracts or are affected by industrial restructuring. Yet government's ability to help has been limited by its budgetary constraints. It will be useful to see to what extent U.S. society has met these challenges since the end of the Cold War.

THE U.S. ECONOMY AFTER THE COLD WAR

Has the demise of the Soviet system brought our economic policies closer in tune with ethical standards? To what extent has there been a fulfillment of the ancient prophesy: "They shall beat their swords into plowshares, and their spears into pruning hooks" (Is. 2:4, KJV)?

The "peace dividend" could have been applied to badly needed improvement in infrastructure to make up for some of the decline in public investment, which had fallen to one-third of its level in the 1960s (in relation to GNP). A number of key developments in the economy had a major impact on the actual pattern of American production and the prospects of the poor.

The reductions in defense were not as large as some had expected. Vested interests, the threat of layoffs, trouble in several foreign countries, and the need to keep modernizing the military services combined to keep military outlays from falling as much or as rapidly as had been envisaged by some who had kept an eye on the needs of the civilian economy.

The sizable deficit in the federal budget that emerged from the Cold War could not be erased merely by cutting military expenditures, nor could it be dealt with exclusively by raising taxes in an atmosphere of tax-weariness. As a result, there was a significant shortfall in new resources for infrastructure and urban renewal that are of interest in improving conditions for the poor. Rebuilding infrastructure would have opened up sizable civilian markets.[3]

Much of the political debate has been focused on major domestic issues, many of them concerning the poor—in particular, the reform of welfare and the health insurance system (Medicare and Medicaid). These changes were motivated in part by the conservative desire to encourage personal responsibility among welfare recipients. But equally strong was the need to put the health insurance system on a sounder footing and bring the rise in federal outlays under control.

Few of the government's actions have been directed to the modernization of civilian industry, contrary to the hopes of some industrial engineers that the peace dividend would be applied to public sector help for modernization of manufacturing.[4] The shift from military to civilian production should, however, in itself enhance the overall efficiency of the American economy. The restructuring and modernization of manufacturing has been left to private initiative as government, and particularly the conservatives in Congress gave little thought to any advance planning for the industrial changes that had to take place in the wake of the Cold War. Talk of such planning might be found in academic journals or periodicals with an engineering slant like MIT's *Technology Review*. Most observers, and especially conservative economists like Murray Weidenbaum, a former chairman of the Council of Economic Advisers, argue that the emphasis on private markets has successfully led to a stronger and more competitive U.S. economy. Much of this success has, however, occurred initially at the expense of high levels of unemployment in the regions most directly affected and a widespread feeling of insecurity about future prospects in large segments of the middle class.

Parallel with restructuring in civilian industry, there has been major reorganization in the defense industry, with many smaller firms dropping out and a few large companies consolidating their position through mergers and otherwise. There are, however, but limited opportunities for military firms to make products for the civilian economy.[5] On the other hand, companies specializing in information technology are bound to benefit from the rising Pentagon desire for computerization of its operations.

Growth in the post-Cold War years has been a rather low 2.5 percent. Most economists feared that higher growth would funnel inflation. When growth did rise above 2.5 percent in 1994, the Federal Reserve raised interest rates to forestall the alleged inflationary consequences of more rapid growth. In pursuing such a policy, the Fed also reduced the opportunities for marginalized people to enjoy the fruits of a more vigorously growing economy.[6] On the other hand, the long stretch of U.S. growth in the 1990s combined with declining unemployment and relatively stable prices has been the envy of the industrialized world.

As military expenditures are cut and procurement put on a more commercial basis, the greater efficiency of civilian industry will be a tonic for the economy, to the benefit of all. Some may justify the burdens imposed by the military in rich industrialized countries as follies only the rich can afford. That cannot be done in many developing countries, where military regimes have cut deeply into resources for lifting the poor into a better life.

ARMS AND THE POOR: THE DEVELOPING COUNTRIES

Both economic and moral arguments against military expenditures are even stronger in countries with much lower standards of living than the United States. The military burden in the poor countries is not any lower than in the industrialized countries, and in some it is much heavier. The end of the Cold War and the lessening of international tension also offer considerable opportunities for the developing countries to reduce their military spending and make available more resources for the eradication of poverty.

Unfortunately, developing countries on average spend more on the military than industrialized countries. For the world as a whole, the military absorbed some 5 percent of total resources from 1972 to 1988, and 2.8 percent in 1991–1995. This percentage was slightly lower in the Western industrialized countries, but in the former Soviet Union the military took up substantially more than the world average.

In the developing countries, military expenditures accounted for about 5.5 percent of the GDP in 1972–1988 and 3.0 percent in 1991–1995 (Hewitt, 1991). But there are marked differences among the developing countries themselves. In some up to one-fourth of the GDP and as much as one-half of central government expenditure are allocated to the military. The rich oil producers in the Middle East are among the countries with the highest military outlays. On the other hand, the small low-income countries and those heavily burdened by foreign debt have military expenditures (in relation to GDP) at about half the global average. The wide variation among different countries is evident from Table 5.3:

TABLE 5.3   Military Expenditures in Selected Countries

| | Percentage of GDP | |
	1972–1979	1980–1988
Brazil	1.3	1.2
China	12.2	6.3
France	3.8	4.0
India	3.4	3.8
Japan	0.9	1.0
Netherlands	3.1	3.1
Nigeria	3.8	1.9
UK	4.7	4.9
USSR	11.3	12.0
US	5.6	6.2

Source: IMF Working Paper 91/54, Table 8.

High levels of military expenditures contribute to low growth and domestic economic hardships by diverting resources from social programs, development projects, and the private sector.[7]

One hopeful sign is the decline in military expenditures in relation to GDP since the mid-1970s and in real absolute terms since the mid-1980s. The decline in absolute figures is partly related to the democratization of a number of Latin American and Asian countries. The external debt problems of the 1980s imposed additional constraints on military spending in some countries.

The experience of individual countries made for large changes in the military burden over time. The high levels of military outlays in (South) Korea and Taiwan in the 1950s and 1960s were associated with authoritarian governments and high levels of foreign military assistance. Democratization and economic growth in these countries caused a steady decline in military expenditures during the 1980s.

The Middle Eastern oil-producing (OPEC) countries, an example of industrialization led by the military, have high relative military burdens, averaging around 10 percent of GDP and one-third of central government expenditures, and are heavily dependent on imports of foreign technology. There is considerable pressure to maintain or even increase military spending, with relief obviously depending on improved trust in the region.

Several of the low- or middle-income semiindustrial countries (like Argentina, Brazil, Chile, India, or Pakistan) have technology-intensive military sectors that buy or produce expensive weapons systems. However, military spending per soldier and as a share of GDP or central government spending is much lower than for the OPEC countries, while civilian manufacturing is much more significant. Considerable political pressure for military spending arises from domestic instability, external threats (India and Pakistan), and the political role of the military. But important political constituencies may make themselves felt during periods of democratic rule. On the other hand, there are considerable technological pressures to sustain high levels of military spending. Advanced weapons systems are very important symbolically, for defining a particular branch of the military or demonstrating commitment to defend national sovereignty. In these countries, increases in the share of GDP devoted to military spending seem to be correlated with slow growth rates. Increases in military spending tend to depress savings and lead to a reduction in overall investment.

Similar to the U.S. experience, absorption of a military–technological style may have hampered the competitiveness of civilian manufacturing in developing countries. In some poor African and Central American countries, policy changes adopted under structural adjustment, discussed in the next chapter, were accompanied by increased military spending. But in most cases, military spending in the low-income primary producing countries has fallen in real terms, even in situations of continuing violence, such as in Peru and the Philippines (Kaldor, 1991, pp. 9 and 10).

China deserves special attention because of the drastic fall in military spending (from 12 percent of GDP in 1972–1979 to 6 percent in 1980–1988) and the contribution of military industries to civilian production. The structure of the military sector has shifted from a labor-intensive people's army to a smaller, more technology-intensive and professional army; technology has been developed indigenously and does not correspond to the Western model. The reduction in arms spending was accompanied by a dramatic increase in arms exports and production of civilian goods and services by the army and the military industries. The commercial output of the military industries increased by 20 percent annually in the 1980s, twice the rate of overall growth. While the dramatic reduction in military spending was presumably intended to release resources for China's program of economic liberalization, it was not accompanied by political liberalization. And a disturbing feature of the conversion program is the extension of control by the military industries over the civilian economy.

One of the problems associated with reductions in military spending has been increased *pressure to export armaments*, for example in Brazil, Chile, and India, as well as Eastern Europe, China, and some other semiindustrial countries. Efforts to introduce multilateral schemes for the control of the arms trade have been largely unsuccessful. Unilateral constraint has worked better, as for example shown by Sweden, Germany, and Japan refusing to supply arms to countries in conflict or with repressive regimes. Their existence does constitute a restraint, although the rules are sometimes broken. Economic constraints have also helped to reduce the purchase of arms in the 1980s.

Adverse Economic Effects

There has been considerable debate about the implications of the military for development. Some have justified military spending by claiming it can contribute to economic development. A controversial 1973 study by Columbia University professor Emile Benoit found that higher spending was positively associated with economic growth. This and subsequent studies argued that military spending can have positive spinoff effects, such as fostering technological development, training personnel who later move into civilian work, providing employment opportunities, building domestic institutions, stimulating a country's tax effort, and promoting more intensive use of existing resources. Furthermore, military industries can be a focus of industrialization activities.

But these positive effects appear to be more than offset by the long-term negative impact of military spending. The most basic criticism is the diversion of scarce resources from more productive civilian uses. Moreover, the military has typically been the sector most protected from spending cuts. Growth of military spending during the 1950s and 1960s significantly reduced overall investment, agricultural production, and economic growth. Studies have also found a negative correlation between military spending and spending for social development (including education and health) and between military spending and savings. Critics of military spending have argued that the

spinoff effects are overstated—for example, that the linkages with
civilian industries are weak or that the benefits of military training to
the civilian economy are few in countries with professional armed
forces. Moreover, defense spending often has a high import content,
and payment for military imports can add considerably to balance-of-
payments problems and the debt burden. In sum, evidence increasingly points to high military spending as contributing to fiscal and
debt crises, complicating stabilization and adjustment, and negatively
affecting economic growth and development. Whatever benefits might
arise from such spending must be carefully weighed against these
heavy costs.[8]

The adverse impact of military expenditures in developing countries is
now widely recognized. The basic message from a 1991 IMF staff
study is that support of the military has considerable opportunity
costs, in that it diverts resources from social and economic services.
Countries that allocate a large proportion of expenditures to the military often spend more on defense than on development or capital formation, and in some cases more than on food or housing. While some
have argued that military expenditures enhance economic growth,
there are much more efficient means of using resources that provide
greater benefits to the economy. Hence, justification for military expenditures must be based on security needs, not on incidental economic-
growth benefits. For these reasons, military outlays above the basic
threshold of security can be designated as "unproductive expenditure" (Hewitt, 1991).

The high cost of military expenditure to development has caused
a number of observers to recommend that international development
assistance be tied to cuts in the defense programs of the recipient
countries. For example, the "Independent Group on Financial Flows to
Developing Countries," chaired by former German chancellor Helmut
Schmidt, suggested that countries with military expenditures below 2
percent of GDP receive special consideration in the allocation of aid.
The case for this kind of tying is strengthened by the possibility of
diversion of civilian development aid to military purposes. But linking
of development assistance to cuts in military programs may be difficult to achieve, since countries regard military security as their own
prerogative. Yet it is encouraging to see that greater attention is being
given to the ill effects of the military on development and what can be
done about it (McNamara, 1991).

In the reduction of military spending, economic and political
measures supported by effective international institutions can play a

useful role. Overcoming political resistance to military cuts requires a new approach to security thinking, in which military force is not seen as an answer to instability or to regional dictators. New ways of managing conflicts require support for democratization processes, an emphasis on dialogue and diplomacy, and an effort to ensure a greater representativeness and accountability of international institutions, such as the United Nations, the European Community, or the International Monetary Fund. Action through multilateral institutions can give poor countries greater political weight. The economic implications of such an approach could be considerable if it would cut military spending and arms sales. But it would also mean military spending, along with economic policy improvements, would be regarded as important in attacking the sources of instability.

Conversion from military to civilian production can provide major benefits for broad layers of the population, especially the poor. The process of change may, however, also impose costs on people and communities where military cutbacks cause a loss of jobs. There are obvious limits to the reduction in military spending, since the military serves an essential function of maintaining order and security in troubled regions. Yet military programs produce and deploy weapons of destruction and death that can easily be misused. At the root of these deliberations are ethical questions that must be carefully considered.

THE ETHICAL DIMENSION

Our economic analysis shows that military programs divert resources from fighting poverty. They weaken the efficiency of civilian industry and hence the economic base for antipoverty action. These adverse effects are felt everywhere, but worst of all in the poorest nations. The impact of military programs on the poor is worsened by the human and environmental consequences of war. They raise many ethical questions.

When the Prince of Peace speaks, where love rules, the guns of war fall silent. All wars are bad, most in their motivation, all in their impact on the environment, the poor, and the people who live in occupied territories. Defense is the only good motive, but defense sometimes means going after the aggressor and can easily turn into reprisal. Any ethical discussion must start with the biblical message of love, reconciliation, and salvation. True, some of the heroes in the Bible are great warriors, and just like people in the Bible, modern people must come to grips with war and violence in their lives and society. But our attitude must be determined by the universal message of love and peace, not by hatred and hostility.

In practice, our attitude toward the military is governed by our views of the merits of particular wars. The overwhelming majority of our people supported World War II, the "good" war against Nazi Germany and Japan, and millions enlisted voluntarily. There was much criticism of the influence politicians exercised over the conduct of the Vietnam War, but little reaction against the military per se. The 1991 Gulf War was a triumph of military leadership, but the churches were divided on the merits of the war. The National Council of Churches and the mainline Protestant churches were opposed, but some Evangelicals came out in support of President Bush's decision. Evangelist Billy Graham and Richard John Neuhaus, a prominent ethicist, gave their blessing. Neuhaus argued that the Gulf War was a just war, and he had to adopt scholastic reasoning to make his case. They were willing to overlook the more than 100,000 Iraqis killed in the war and the fact that our military decision was closely tied to the lack of an effective energy policy and our consequent dependence on Arab oil.

In their "Lines in the Sand: Justice and the Gulf War" (1992) Alan Geyer, a professor of ethics at the Wesley Theological Seminary in Washington, DC, and Barbara G. Green, a Presbyterian theologian, raise many questions about the justification of the Persian Gulf War. They point to the enormity of the Iraqi casualties, environmental disaster, and seductive exhibitionism of high-tech weaponry, as well as the broader issues of our own unrestrained consumption of oil and the disparagement of the UN's security role. They question the validity of the "Just War Theory" insofar as it is not an ethic of war and peace that calls us to consider moral principles by which to weigh war and its alternatives.[9]

The lines were more clearly drawn when it came to the issues posed by the use of nuclear weapons of destruction as a bargaining chip in our relations with the Soviet empire.

Condemnation of Nuclear Arms

The arguments against the nuclear arms race are worth recalling, for they go to the heart of religious thinking about war in general. It is no wonder that many churches and synagogues have spoken out against the arms race on both theological and economic grounds. The churches, almost universally, spoke out against nuclear war and deterrence. The Cold War was not to be regarded as a simple war of good against evil. Peacekeeping had to be seen in the context of peace-building. Some churches also took cognizance of the adverse economic consequences of war expenditures.

Reform Judaism took a position against the nuclear arms race in a 1969 statement "Priorities for Peace" by the National Federation of Temple Sisterhoods. It reaffirmed its commitment to peaceful international cooperation, arms limitation and control, deescalation of the war in Vietnam, and the development of economic and technical resources for the achievement of human welfare, and it appealed "to all peoples, and particularly to the Congress of the United States, to reduce military expenditures so that more funds can be made promptly available for the fulfillment of essential human needs, both at home and abroad."

The National Council of Churches of Christ in the USA (NCCC) issued a number of pronouncements warning against the threat of nuclear war. The Council made a strong ethical case against excessive armament, while also recognizing the many technical and economic details and dangers of nuclear preparation. The 1951 pronouncement "International Regulation and Reduction of Armaments" points out that "pending the acceptance by all nations of a trustworthy system whereby all armaments, including atomic weapons, can be placed under international control, it is unavoidable that the United States should strengthen its military defenses. Our recognition of this fact, however, must not be construed to mean that we are ignorant of, or indifferent to, the dire consequences that may befall our own and other nations unless the race in arms now under way can be stopped." When this pronouncement was published, it was still possible to be optimistic. The United States, it is noted, is ready to participate "in arrangements that would bring the armaments of the nations under international control. President Truman added (November 7, 1951) that once the burden of armaments is lifted, "new energies and resources would be liberated for greatly enlarged programs of reconstruction and development." As the United States expanded its military and space programs, the NCCC statements became more urgent and frequent, as is evident from pronouncements made in 1957, 1958, and 1968. The 1968 policy statement "Defense and Disarmament: New Requirements for Security" underlined the importance of a non-proliferation treaty, the control of nuclear weapons, and greater reliance on the United Nations as a peacekeeping and peacemaking agency. It also stated its basic theological beliefs: a) "Man's responsibility for the created order is a responsibility to preserve and develop it, not to abuse and destroy it"; b) "God's sovereignty places limits on the moral autonomy of any aspect of the political order"; and c) "God's reconciling act in Christ denies the ultimacy of the parochial community and affirms that the "enemy" is the brother for whom Christ died" (NCCC, 1968).

As the United States and the Soviet Union began to make progress in arms-reduction talks, the NCCC statements expressed new hope for the future (1986, 1987, and 1988). Throughout the post-World War II period the NCCC pronouncements supported the role of the United Nations in arms control and peaceful settlement of international disputes, in which they were joined by most other churches. Geyer and Green (1992) also urge a more effective United Nations for "global governance."

Evangelical groups have likewise expressed opposition to nuclear armament, for example in the 1973 Chicago Declaration and the 1978 "Call to Faithfulness" (see ch. 12). However, the vast majority of Evangelicals, polled in 1983 by the National Association of Evangelicals, approved of Reagan's way of dealing with the nuclear situation.

The Theology of Condemning Nuclear Warfare

The Reformed Church in America (RCA) articulated a theology of opposing nuclear armament in "Christian Faith and the Nuclear Arms Race: A Reformed Perspective" (Cook, pp. 165–81). It considers the nuclear arms race first and foremost a false religion, based on the illusion that true security can be guaranteed by strategic superiority. The religious character of the arms race is seen, first, in its appeal to the human longing for security or, more precisely, its manipulation of that longing. The quest for false security was condemned by Isaiah, who chided the people of Israel who, in their struggle with Egypt, relied on horses and chariots instead of the living Lord (Isa. 31:1). Ultimate security is not to be found in this world, but in God who transcends the world while making himself known to his people in it. Moreover, the *"just war"* theory formulated by Augustine sees war as a defensive response to unjustified aggression. Its goal is peace with the enemy, and war is to be conducted with restraint in a spirit of love rather than hate or vengeance. A just war requires careful discrimination between soldiers and noncombatants, protection of civilian populations, and humane treatment of prisoners. *"Nuclear war and the preparations for it violate every code by which historic Christianity has determined a war to be just"* (our ital.). *Reliance on nuclear arms is pure idolatry,* in that it places its trust in "gods made with human hands."

Christ has set people free from personal sin and guilt, but also from bondage to the corporate powers of the age. Christ assures victory over these powers and enables his followers to see these powers in their proper place (Col. 2:13–15) (Berkhof, 1963). Consistent with this theology, the Reformed Church has urged action against nuclear armament on a number of occasions.[10] Through these various actions the RCA has practiced the Reformed tradition of expressing witness on questions of social responsibility and civic righteousness.

The reasons why the churches opposed nuclear weapons continue to be important in the post-Soviet world. The churches regard trust in nuclear weapons as reliance on false gods, which impedes the reign of love by which concern for our neighbor is put into practice. The nuclear arms race allegedly is over because the Soviets have crumbled, but we must recognize that it was wrong to begin with.

Opposition by Lutherans and Methodists

The Lutherans have historically adopted an ethical framework that seeks to restrain both the entry into and the conduct of war. The Lutheran Church in America made a clear theological statement in "Peace and Politics" (1984), but in the end it shied away from an oversimplified presentation of the Cold War conflict. It rejected the notion that the conflict between the nuclear superpowers was an apocalyptic struggle between the absolute Good and the absolute Evil, and that a particular nation-state could pridefully presume a historic calling to "save" the world from political, social, or religious "error" and make the world over into its own likeness. Likewise, it did not believe that any nation can isolate itself behind walls of military might and economic protectionism, and it condemned the misappropriation of valuable resources for "an escalating arms race that impairs our financial ability to foster economic and political justice at home and abroad." The Lutheran church did not regard nuclear deterrence as acceptable from a Christian standpoint, and its position against deterrence is clearer than that of the Catholic bishops. "It is an outrage that under present conditions, the United States and the Soviet Union, with their allies, must confront each other with the possibility of mass slaughter.

Yet that is precisely the situation of the two superpowers today. We hold therefore that nuclear deterrence involves us all in a sinful situation from which none are exempt" (ALC, 1982, pp. 6 and 7). It stressed, moreover, the need for peacebuilding, and in that connection stressed *the importance of working through international institutions.* Peacekeeping must be seen in the context of peacebuilding. Peacebuilding is a constructive enterprise involving such diverse elements as negotiations between nations, mediation, cultural and humanitarian exchange, trade, and international travel.

The United Methodists likewise took a strong stand against nuclear deterrence: "We say a clear and unconditional No to nuclear war and to any use of nuclear weapons. We conclude that nuclear deterrence is a position that cannot receive the church's blessing. We state our complete lack of confidence in proposed "defenses" against nuclear attack and are convinced that the enormous cost of developing such defenses is one more witness to the obvious fact that the arms race is a social justice issue, not only a war and peace issue" (Bishops' Pastoral Letter, 1986). The United Methodist bishops' pastoral letter also saw the nuclear issue in the broader context of justice: "We urge a renewed commitment to building the institutional foundations of common security, economic justice, human rights, and environmental conservation. And we make appeal for peace research, studies and training at all levels of education." The bishops' letter was supported by strong and substantial arguments in an accompanying Foundation Document.

The Catholic Position

The 1983 pastoral letter of the U.S. Catholic bishops "The Challenge of Peace," dealing primarily with the ethics of the nuclear arms race and the prevention of nuclear war, condemned the race in no uncertain terms: "The arms race is one of the greatest curses on the human race; it is to be condemned as a danger, an act of aggression against the poor, and a folly which does not provide the security it promises" (p. *v*).

Some compromise crept into the Catholic bishops' discussion of nuclear deterrence. They considered it as a step toward progressive disarmament, and in that sense could be judged as acceptable. But this acceptance is strictly conditional, since killing the innocent is not morally right. Hence deterrence is not an adequate strategy as a long-term basis for peace. Good ends like defending one's country and protecting freedom cannot justify immoral means (pp. 69–76).

The crisis of nuclear threat "arises from the fact that nuclear war threatens the existence of our planet; this is a more menacing threat than the world has ever known. It is neither tolerable nor necessary that human beings live under this threat. But removing it will require a major effort of intelligence, courage and faith. As Pope John Paul II said at Hiroshima in 1981: "From now on it is only through a conscious choice and through a deliberate policy that humanity can survive."

Besides making the ethical case against the arms race, some churches also recognized the *economic distortions caused by the military*. In the mid-1980s the *Presbyterian Church (USA)* summarized the ill effects of our military program. Though the program could not "buy" security, it nevertheless absorbed 40–50 percent of general tax revenue (excluding social security taxes). The church called for a rollback of military expenditures to the level of the mid-1970s, before the then-current buildup began (Presbyterian Church, 1985).

The 12th General Synod of the *United Church of Christ* (UCC) (1979) emphatically called for a reversal of the arms race. The 1987 UCC study paper "Christian Faith and Economic Life" also drew attention to the adverse economic effects of our military buildup (par. 229–39).

In brief, the churches made a strong ethical case against the nuclear arms race and general warfare that endangers civilian life. Some churches and Jewish organizations took cognizance of the adverse economic impact of the military. They brought a central message of love to publish their opposition to war. And in this case, as in others, the rule of love and the economic interests of the community go hand in hand. But the Judeo–Christian ethical position often stood in sharp contrast to the military realities during the Cold War.

The adverse economic impact of war is most evident in countries with few resources. The decline in military expenditures in the past decade has released substantial resources for nonmilitary purposes, including antipoverty action and private investment. However, in the 1970s and 1980s the military in many developing countries borrowed heavily abroad to finance military hardware, often at the expense of their countries' ability to borrow for more worthwhile purposes and causing debt-servicing difficulties. There are many other causes of these debt problems, to which we now turn.

6
Poverty and Foreign Debt

The problems of servicing foreign debt are a consequence of the financial relations between the poorer debtor nations and the richer creditor countries. They present both serious economic and moral issues. When the smooth functioning of debt servicing is interrupted, the poorest segments of the population are bound to pay the highest price in terms of unemployment and lower living standards. Ethicists raise serious objections against creditors' insistence on debt payments by the poorest nations when such difficulties occur. The laws of ancient Israel cautioned against asking interest payments from one's poor brother. They understood that indebtedness can cause poverty, landlessness, and slavery, and that fundamental corrections had to be made when indebtedness becomes oppressive.

The debt crisis of the 1980s had disastrous implications for the fight against poverty. Sudden sharp decreases in the willingness of creditors to lend and lack of funds with which even to pay the interest on outstanding debt meant that heavily indebted developing countries were forced to take draconian measures that brought economic depression. Not only was the previous economic expansion of these countries, which had been accompanied by at least some poverty reduction, suddenly brought to an abrupt halt, but now living standards actually dropped, in some countries precipitously. In brief, poverty in heavily indebted countries worsened in what has been characterized as the lost decade of the 1980s. Only by the mid-1990s has the debt crisis been regarded as ended, and many developing countries are again expanding economically. However, by no means are all of them out of the woods. Many groups argue cogently that international institutions, such as the World Bank and the International Monetary Fund, which helped the poor countries during the debt crisis, ought to forgive all of the debts still owed by these countries to these institutions.

In order to understand why and how the debt crisis brought about increased poverty, we need to give some essential background. This chapter first describes why developing countries need to borrow from abroad and how much external debt they can safely incur. The chapter then relates why and how the debt crisis of the 1980s came about, what was done to help resolve it, and where we stand in the 1990s. "The Ethical Dimension" at the end of the chapter takes a closer look at the moral issues raised by debt accumulation and the position taken by Judeo–Christian ethicists.

The debt crisis highlighted many of the problems the developing countries face in the global economy: adverse external developments intensify the suffering of the poor; the dependence of poor countries on the international system of trade and payments; and the uncertainties these countries suffer as a result of shifts in the lending policies of foreign banks and changes in global markets.

The crisis caused a severe slowdown in economic growth of the major debtors, at enormous cost in production and investment opportunities foregone and aggravation of the conditions of poverty. Per capita income fell substantially in the countries suffering most from indebtedness, and by the late 1980s total output in these countries was more than a third below the trend line.[1]

Yet it is important to realize that the debt crisis is not exclusively responsible for the setbacks in Latin America, where most of the highly indebted countries were located. This seems evident when their performance is compared with that of other regions.

The total debt service relative to export earnings (debt service ratio) of the East Asian-Pacific (EAP) countries was lower and came down more quickly than that of the Latin American and Caribbean (LAC) countries (see Table 6.1).

The Pacific Rim countries were able to shake off the consequences of high indebtedness through rapid adjustment of domestic policies and investment plans, and through superb export performance.[2] The pull of the Japanese economy at the time greatly contributed to the success of many Pacific economies, but this alone does not explain their better performance in comparison with Latin America. The growth of India, a country that is more self-sufficient than most highly indebted countries, also accelerated in the 1980s. To understand the differences in country experiences, it is important to look at the interrelation between development and debt in a more general way.

TABLE 6.1.   Comparative Debt Service Ratios

	Debt Service Ratio (%)	
	EAP	LAC
1980	13.6	37.1
1986	24.3	43.7
1990	15.5	26.9
1992	12.9	29.8
1995*	12.2	29.5

*Projected.
Source: World Debt Tables, 1993–1994, pp. 178
and 186 (Washington, DC, The World Bank, 1993).

THE ROLE OF DEBT IN THE DEVELOPMENT PROCESS

In the 1960s it became clear that the debt service of developing countries was rising well above the levels with which bankers and policy
makers had been comfortable. As debt service started to climb higher
and higher, the question arose as to what level of debt would be compatible with the country's ability to meet its servicing obligations and
at the same time maintain a satisfactory rate of growth. The analysis
that sought to answer this question envisaged that countries pass
through different stages as they progress up the ladder of development and the buildup and eventual repayment of debt.

Accumulation of Debt

Developing countries are like growing business enterprises, which
have a natural need for using outside capital. External capital supplements countries' domestic savings in the financing of essential investments such as electric power, roads, and irrigation. Local savings
finance by far the greater part of investment in all but the poorest
countries, while external capital provides both finance and technical
and managerial assistance.

In the earliest stage of development, countries are poor and able
to grow only slowly with their own technical and financial resources
(Avramovic and Assoc., 1965; Barend A. de Vries, 1971). They receive
relatively little foreign capital, and external assistance is likely to be on
soft terms—i.e., in grant form or at interest rates below the market. In

this early stage, countries have little debt and the debt service poses no problem. In the 1950s and 1960s, many African countries found themselves in this position.

Development itself improves the ability of countries to prepare and execute more and better investments—transportation, electric power, social infrastructure, education, and health facilities. As the pace of development quickens and growth improves, the country's creditworthiness for external loans also strengthens. However, countries' ability to use external capital for sound investment often improves more rapidly than their domestic savings, which are low since large parts of the population remain very poor, even while other parts of the economy surge forward and upward. External capital is contracted to cover the shortfall in domestic savings below sound investment levels, so that the country can proceed more rapidly than if it had to rely entirely on its own resources.

The economic case for borrowing abroad rests on the high return achieved on new investment financed by external capital and the ability of countries to translate investment into higher output and exports. The increasing net inflow of capital and the corresponding increase in debt service payments (interest and amortization) are supported by the countries' ability to meet these debt obligations with higher savings and exports. In the 1960s and 1970s some African countries like Cameroun and Cote d'Ivoire and many Latin American and Pacific Rim countries made effective use of foreign capital to supplement their domestic resources.

In a later phase of development, savings will eventually overtake investments so that the countries will no longer need to receive a net inflow of external capital. This stage was reached by a number of countries, such as Finland and Greece, in the 1970s. Even then countries need to continue borrowing abroad for some years to cover interest payments on outstanding debt. Countries must produce a large resource surplus—an excess of exports over imports of goods and services—over a period of years, before they can pay with their own resources for all their interest obligations. Only then can they live without any new foreign capital and start to reduce their external debt.

The rethinking of the role of debt in the development process also clarified the conditions under which the accumulation and subsequent repayment of debt can proceed smoothly. When these conditions are not met, a debt crisis is bound to ensue.

Causes of Debt Crises

Two conditions are critical to ensure that the buildup of debt is accompanied by an even more rapid improvement in countries' ability to service the debt:

1. The rate of return on the investment financed must be favorable, in fact higher than the (interest) cost of the external loans. If capital is not used effectively, the return on investment will be too low in relation to the subsequent debt service, and the project's or country's ability to service the debt is in danger.
2. The growth of the borrowing economy and, in particular, of its exports must exceed the interest rate on new external capital. If the interest rate on new debt exceeds the borrowing country's export growth rate, the country's debt burden will rise to excessive levels where the debt-servicing process breaks down, and it must ask for some kind of rearrangement of its debt.[3]

A third and broader condition is that borrowing countries must instill confidence in both domestic and foreign investors, so they will not take their capital out of the country and precipitate a crisis that is detrimental to growth and antipoverty action.

These conditions point to some of the realities that debtor countries face in seeking finance for their development. For one, if a country is able to grow but slowly, or carries out investments with low economic return that do not produce rapid increases in output, it will need low-interest loans to avoid debt-servicing difficulties. This reasoning provided the justification for grants or low-interest loans by the International Development Association (IDA) of the World Bank and many bilateral government aid programs for poor African countries and other countries like Bangladesh, Bolivia, or Haiti.

Further, when after a period of heavy borrowing (such as took place in the 1970s) countries simultaneously face a sharp rise in interest rates and a decline in export growth, the second condition breaks down. This happened in 1982, and as a result debt-servicing difficulties occurred on a wide scale. Countries had begun to suffer from a "debt overhang," an excess of debt they cannot service without cutting sharply into their essential investments and social expenditures. Eventually difficult measures must be taken to reduce the level of debt-service payments or to strengthen the economic base for servicing additional debts. Following the debt crisis of the early 1980s, debtor

TABLE 6.2   The Cost of Adverse External Developments

	(billions of dollars)
Oil price increase in excess of U.S. inflation, 1974–1982:	260
Increase in real interest rates in 1981 and 1982 over the 1961–1980 average:	41
Terms of trade loss (increase in import prices relative to export prices) in 1981 and 1982:	79
Loss in export value caused by world recession:	21
Total cost	401

Source: William R. Cline (1984, p. 13); John T. Cuddington gives a more detailed discussion of this topic in ch. 1 of "Dealing with the Debt Crisis," The World Bank, 1989.

and creditor countries had to take drastic steps to reduce the debts outstanding. The debtor countries also had to make sometimes painful adjustments to strengthen their economies and earnings of foreign exchange. These measures had to be taken in a rapidly changing external economic environment facing these countries.

THE ORIGINS OF THE DEBT CRISIS

The debt crisis had its origin in the turmoil of the world economy in the 1970s associated with several interrelated events, including a rapid increase in commodity prices, the breakdown of the Bretton Woods system of fixed exchange rates established after World War II, the devaluation of the U.S. dollar, and the sharp rise in oil prices.[4]

The quadrupling of oil prices in 1973 produced large cash surpluses for the oil-exporting countries, but caused severe hardships for oil-importing developing countries. The "recycling" of these surpluses, mostly to the LDCs, put the international banks in center stage and made them the most important creditors of the major LDC borrowers.[5]

Following the 1973 oil price increase, the world economy became considerably more unstable. Adverse external developments weighed heavily on the borrowing countries, as is evident from the cost of exogenous shocks facing the nonoil LDCs after the rise in oil prices (see Table 6.2). The total cost of the adverse shocks, some $400 billion, may

TABLE 6.3   External Debt of Developing Countries

	Long-term Debt (US$ billion)				
	LDCs	HICS	D/X	DSR(%)	% Var. Rate
1970	66	31	77.8	12.1	3.9
1980	437	205	87.6	17.4	55.4
1982	562	279	175.0*	23.4*	66.9*
1987	996	457	272.0	24.5	66.0

* 1983

be compared with an increase in debt of $482 billion in 1973–1982. But clearly external factors were not solely responsible for the buildup of debt and the post-1982 difficulties. Mexico and Nigeria, for example, enjoyed significant increases in oil-export earnings, but they nevertheless ran into serious debt troubles. These and other countries were poor managers of their temporary bonanza in the 1970s. They overspent, often on wasteful projects, and their oil booms were accompanied by increased rather than reduced external borrowing.

The external debt of all developing countries increased sharply and steadily during the 1970s (see Table 6.3).[6] At the same time, their exports also grew rapidly and interest rates were well below export growth rates: interest rates on commercial lending averaged 10.7 percent, while export earnings grew by 21 percent per annum. Hence, even though external debts increased, the debt burden (e.g., as measured by debt and debt service in relation to exports) did not rise in any alarming way between 1970 and 1980.

Once the highly indebted countries experienced debt-servicing difficulties in the early 1980s, their economic situation was aggravated by the cutback in net private flows of long-term capital. Stability of official lending was a plus factor, but it was insufficient to offset the fall in net lending by private creditors.

Many debtor countries undertook strenuous policy reforms that encouraged a resumption of growth, particularly of exports. But their debt burdens continued to be too high and the response of private investors was lagging. Obviously, deeper and more drastic measures were needed. It is useful to look at the behavior of the principal players in the debt drama, both creditors and debtors; their story could well hold lessons for the future.

THE PRINCIPAL PLAYERS IN THE DEBT DRAMA

The private banks were the prime movers in the 1970s and early 1980s, as the developing countries were borrowing heavily to keep up their economic growth. The major debtor countries were eager to take advantage of easy credit and used some of the foreign loans for non-productive purposes, including the financing of capital flight; after the crisis they had to undergo a difficult process of restructuring their policies and economies. The United States and the other industrialized countries, on their part, gave the private banks a free hand in the recycling of petrodollars in the 1970s, but once the situation had gotten out of hand, the creditor governments had to formulate new policies for managing international debt. The Bretton Woods institutions had taken little direct action in the recycling process, except for a special oil facility set up by the International Monetary Fund and a rapid increase in lending by the World Bank. After the problems developed, the IMF moved into the center of managing the debt crisis, while the World Bank continued to expand lending. Both Bretton Woods institutions started structural adjustment operations which tied new financing to necessary policy reform in the developing countries.

The Private Banks

Private long-term lending accelerated after 1973 as banks took on most of the recycling of the oil surpluses of the nonoil LDCs.[7] Net long-term lending from private banks to all LDCs increased almost four times *in real terms* during 1970–1981, a period of growing capital flows to developing countries from all sources.

But in their enlarged role the private banks did not apply strict standards of creditworthiness assessment, and they continued lending even after warnings of borrowing excesses were sounded by IMF management, World Bank country reports, and some reports of the commercial banks' own economists. Moreover, the banks usually did not lend for specific projects or programs and did not tie their operations to policy reform that was badly needed in most borrowing countries. The lax conditionality, preferred by the borrowers, weakened the ability of the World Bank and other official lenders to apply conditions that were of interest to the development of the borrowing countries.

After 1982 commercial banks refused to renew loans, and their strongly negative "lending" deprived the major borrowers of the resources they needed for growth and poverty eradication.[8] The total of outward transfers from the highly indebted countries to the banks ("financial markets") reached $150.6 billion in 1984–1990.[9] The sharp reduction in net lending was clearly against the long-run interests of the banks' customers, while the continuing high level of interest payments imposed an additional burden.

The U.S. government did little to alleviate the situation. The Baker initiative, named after James Baker, then U.S. Secretary of the Treasury, envisaged a net flow from the private banks of $7 billion per year in 1986–1988, in conjunction with the adoption of growth-oriented adjustment programs by the debtor countries. The initiative enabled the World Bank to increase its capital and lending operations, but it failed to induce the banks to raise their lending, and the net private resource drain on the debtor countries continued unabated.[10]

While the private banks were the prime movers in the years leading up to the debt crisis, the policies of the debtor countries were crucial in determining the outcome of their borrowing.

The Borrowing Countries

A critical question that must be addressed is whether borrowers made effective use of the loan funds. Some writers claim that the major borrowers used external funds well, pointing to the increase in both investment and savings during the 1970s (Cline, 1984). The World Bank also defended the record of the borrowers and the private lenders, but its analysis was rather superficial.[11] Others pointed out that the rise in nonproject lending under the aegis of the private banks was likely to increase the use of borrowed funds for consumption, which in fact did rise parallel with foreign borrowing. External loans used for consumption purposes do not result in an increase in output or exports, which are the foundation of countries' future debt repayment capacity.

External loans also financed substantial capital flight, a drain on national resources from which many Latin American countries and the Philippines have suffered for decades. Much capital movement is, of course, part of normal healthy economic intercourse, helping to finance trade and enabling investors to move their capital to where it can earn a higher return. But capital flight burdens and distorts normal patterns.[12]

The structure of incentives for resource allocation is a further important element of a country's ability to manage debt. A realistic exchange rate stimulates exports, a positive real interest rate encourages savings, and low and evenly spread import tariffs prevent concentration of resources in inefficient industries. Countries with rational incentives tend to have more efficient economies which are able to adjust more rapidly to external shocks.[13]

In the same vein, countries with open economies and outward orientation may be subject to larger external shocks, but are also able to adjust more quickly. These countries have price structures in line with the international economy and rational incentives which do not unduly favor any particular industry. They are able to adjust through rapid growth of export earnings, as can be seen in Korea and other Pacific economies, which throughout the 1980s and into the 1990s put in a strong performance. On the other hand, countries with inward orientation suffered from greater inefficiency in public investments and large public sector deficits. Characteristically, they had overvalued exchange rates which priced exports out of their markets, created unsettling expectation of devaluation, and fueled capital flight.[14] In brief, countries with outward orientation were by and large able to adjust more rapidly than those with inward orientation, and were also in a stronger position to work out agreements with the creditor countries and the Bretton Woods institutions.

The Creditor Countries and the Bretton Woods Institutions

Was there an alternative to the predominant role of the banks in the recycling process of the 1970s? The International Monetary Fund (IMF) sought to play a direct role in the recycling of petrodollars by setting up an oil facility under which it could borrow funds from the oil-exporting and other surplus countries for relending to the oil-importing countries. Compared with the large surpluses of the oil-exporting countries, the IMF oil facilities, set up in 1974 and 1975, were minuscule, a total of SDR 6.9 billion, of which SDR 4.3 billion was taken up by developed countries (including SDR 1 billion by the United Kingdom and SDR 1.45 billion by Italy) and only SDR 2.53 billion by developing countries. (An SDR is a unit of account linked to the major currencies; it was equivalent to about $1.20 at the time.) Despite their modest size, the establishment of these IMF facilities gave international recognition to the importance of counteracting the deflationary effects of the sudden oil price increase. But had the United States and other creditor countries actively cooperated with the IMF, the facility could have been larger and both lenders and borrowers induced to use recycled funds more effectively for the unavoidable adjustment of their economies.[15]

The extent and severity of the debt crisis was not at first generally recognized. Initial assistance efforts—in 1982–1984—were aimed at injecting sufficient liquidity into the LDCs concerned so that a general default and systemic crisis could be avoided. Under energetic IMF leadership, fresh liquidity was quickly provided, on a country-by-country basis, in conjunction with new ("concerted") bank lending and on condition that the recipient countries take unavoidable stabilization–adjustment measures. Had the IMF not acted so expeditiously, both creditors and debtors might have suffered more, and the commercial banks may have had to cut their losses sooner than they did. The actions initially taken by the IMF and creditor governments and their central banks saved the international financial system from chaos, but did not suffice to restore the economic health of the debtor countries (Volcker and Gyothen, 1992, ch. 7). On the other hand, by enabling the debtor countries to continue paying interest on their obligations to the banks, the IMF indirectly assisted the banks.

Steps to Reduce Debt

By 1987 a number of countries had defaulted on their debt obligations, but they did not do so in unison. Some tried to limit or stop interest payments, for example, Brazil and Peru. But left-leaning or populist governments, like Peru under President Alan Garcia, that stop or retard debt-service payments often also turn out to be poor economic managers, their stance on debt not backed up by disciplined economic management. Under pressure from the banks, Brazil resumed interest payments in June 1988 in conjunction with a package of new finance.[16]

When the default route was closed, cooperative action toward reduction of the debt outstanding came to be seen as the only viable option. In 1987 and increasingly in 1988, reduction of debts to the commercial banks was voluntarily achieved through a "menu" of market-based options, including debt-equity swaps and buyback of debt.[17]

In this environment, the *Brady initiative* of the United States emerged quite naturally in the spring of 1989. Riots in Venezuela and the fear that they might spread to other countries and undermine democratic governments gave the initiative a sense of urgency. For the first time the U.S. government gave official sanction to debt reduction and began pressing the banks to accept less than a dollar on their outstanding loans, often a greater discount than the banks were willing to provide on their own. The IMF and the World Bank were to make available some $10 billion each in support of reduction of debt or debt service by guaranteeing interest payments on new bank loans that replaced old ones at a discount. While a significant break with the past, the plan was initially criticized on the ground that the supporting resources of the IMF and the World Bank were too small.[18]

First to benefit from the Brady initiative were Costa Rica, Mexico, the Philippines, Uruguay, and Venezuela. The initiative helped to reduce their debt to the commercial banks by $20 billion, or some 25 percent. A major benefit of the debt reduction was the increased confidence of domestic investors. Moreover, a small group of countries (Chile, Mexico, and Venezuela) regained access to private capital markets, especially bonds. These countries also benefitted from a surge in foreign direct investment.[19] Foreign direct investment was of little benefit to the poorest countries and continued to be concentrated on a few countries mostly in East Asia and Latin America.

Mexico was the prime candidate for the Brady initiative. It was taking fargoing steps to diversify its exports, cut subsidies, restructure and privatize state enterprises, and reduce its structural government deficit. In addition, it joined the General Agreement on Tariffs and Trade (GATT) and laid the groundwork for joining the North American Free Trade Zone. It received some $5 billion in new financing from the IMF and the World Bank, provided in association with improvements in overall economic policies and policies in the financial sector, industry, and public enterprises. The commercial banks were reluctant partners, pressed to accept discounts on their old loans. In addition, large amounts of private capital (direct and portfolio investment) started flowing into Mexico. In all, net transfers once again became positive, and Mexico was able to increase growth in output and imports.[20] There was, of course, a danger that some of these new capital funds might move out again, as became painfully clear in early 1995. Moreover, Mexico's contractual debt has not been reduced significantly ($97 billion in 1990 as against $101 billion in 1986). However, interest payments became lower relative to growing export earnings; in 1990 interest payments in relation to exports were less than half what they had been in the mid-1980s.

While Mexico's economic measures met with high praise in the financial community, the stabilization efforts initially had adverse effects on employment conditions, which the government sought to cushion by a "solidarity program" of numerous small infrastructure projects, some $2.5 billion in 1995. Furthermore, Mexico's economic turnaround came at a considerable price for labor unions and the development of lagging areas like Chiapas, which came to world attention in 1994. In the past, the unions had come close to running the Mexican railroads and were a critical factor in the management of PEMEX, the state-owned petroleum company, and other state enterprises. When the government became serious about privatization, it often first had to "break" the union. In many private industries the government also was a party to suppressing labor, since when the government replaced union leadership, it did so in an authoritarian way and did not go the route of free elections.

Other countries also were able to register significant progress in reducing their debt burden in the late 1980s. This was true for Chile, Colombia, Costa Rica, the Philippines, and Uruguay. By 1991 the World Bank was able to list these countries as "moderately indebted," as against "heavily indebted" in the mid-1980s.

Multilateral Action: Structural Adjustment Lending

Among the actions taken by the Bretton Woods institutions, structural adjustment lending is of special interest. It was innovative and represented a departure from previous practice in that it widened the institutions' policy involvement in the affairs of their borrowers, and it enabled the World Bank to be more flexible and make rapidly disbursing loans not attached to specific projects. It was, however, criticized, especially in Africa, by both economic experts and ethicists.

Structural adjustment lending (SAL) emphasized policy reform with the aim of strengthening countries' creditworthiness and ability to resume growth. SAL operations reached more than $10 billion per year in 1989–1993 for the two Bretton Woods institutions. A wide range of policy understandings accompanied these lending operations, directed to lower budget deficits and improve the composition of investment, strengthen balance of payments management, control inflation and Central Bank credit expansion, privatize state enterprises, deregulate the economy, decontrol prices, liberalize trade, and, where necessary, make the exchange rate more flexible. This combination of measures conformed to what later was termed "The Washington Consensus," described in more detail in the 1991 World

Development Report, marking that the set of policies was widely agreed upon among Washington agencies. They were later adopted by an increasing number of countries in East Asia and Latin America, but continued to meet with reservations in some African countries.[21]

The World Bank's evaluation of its own operations suggests that countries that pursued adjustment policies fared better in reestablishing equilibrium and achieving at least moderate growth than those that did not undertake adjustment. But in many countries, especially in Africa, the operations were less successful, mainly because of weak supply response and poor institutional readiness. In some countries, for example Zambia, the World Bank and others made faulty policy prescriptions.[22]

An obvious criticism of SAL was that the World Bank attached too many conditions to its operations. The average number of conditions *per loan* rose from thirty-nine in 1980–1988 to fifty-six in 1989–1991 (Killick, 1994, p. 9). In Uganda alone the World Bank imposed eighty-six specific policy commitments in three years (1991–1994). Follow-up on such a multiplicity of conditions is complex and difficult for both the borrowing country and the lending agency. The IMF's conditionality carried it well beyond its own conventional financial requirements (monetary expansion, exchange rate policy, and balance-of-payments restrictions) into the domestic price structure, management of state enterprises, and the quality of public investment, areas in which the IMF had to work closely with the World Bank.

A further objection to the policy conditionality of SALs was the rigidity and uniformity with which it was applied. For instance, in many situations countries were pressed to liberalize imports too rapidly. In practice, the conditions of SALs were not uniformly implemented by the recipients (Killick, 1994). Essential strengthening of institutions and reform in the financial sector (banking, credit allocation, and interest rate policy) often lagged well behind initial objectives. Some observers and African experts have therefore suggested that homegrown programs would be more successful than those imposed by external agencies and advisors. Increased lending for various types of structural reform might best be confined to countries that are indigenously committed to the necessary reforms. These issues are bound to remain of concern, since policy adaptation is a continuous process.

Critics in the religious and NGO communities pointed out that the strong emphasis on exports can reduce the supply of food for home consumption, to the detriment of the poor. Moreover, young women employed in export industries are often dismissed after a few years and find themselves looking for other jobs with little hope. Export production can also harm the environment by encouraging overcultivation of fragile soils or otherwise call forth undesirable conditions. For example, in Brazil land consolidation associated with expanded production of soya beans for export has pushed small farmers off their land; they subsequently emigrated to the Amazon region, with ill effects for the rain forest. Such developments pose genuine issues in the complex of economic policy formation that could not be found in old textbooks. But they can be dealt with through stronger antipoverty orientation and environmental policies without negating the importance of structural adjustment.

The behavior and policies of lenders and borrowers suggest crucial guidelines for managing capital flows in the interest of strengthening antipoverty efforts, which are consistent with the conditions for avoiding debt crises set forth earlier. Specific investments receiving foreign capital must be economically justified, with benefits that justify the costs, and a sufficiently high return that provides a base for servicing and paying off the loan. Further, when governments or enterprises borrow for general purposes (i.e., not tied to specific investments), the policies of the country must generate sufficient growth in output and exports to cover the cost of servicing the loans. In all situations it is wise to be cautious, because external circumstances can change swiftly to the disadvantage of the borrowers. Debt forgiveness, if it comes at all, will be slow in coming. The borrowers, and especially the people on the spot, pay the price for untoward developments. This will be borne out by a review of the consequences of the debt crisis for the poor.

CONSEQUENCES FOR THE POOR

The 1982 debt crisis caused a sharp break in the growth momentum that had prevailed in the previous two decades. The stagnation of the 1980s weighed most heavily on the poor, since they bear the brunt of lower real wages and higher unemployment. This also raised, of course, serious moral issues, to which we turn at the end of the chapter. Elimination of subsidies, introduced to restore balance to public sector finance, brought higher prices for food and other essential consumption items. Real wages declined by 25 percent or more in Brazil

TABLE 6.4   Growth Momentum of Indebted Countries

	Average % Change per Year	
	1965–1980	*1980–1986*
Production Growth	6.6	0.7
Industry Growth	7.7	-0.2
Gross Domestic Investment	8.4	-6.3
Consumption: Government	7.0	0.6
Private	6.6	0.7
Inflation Rate	26.5	91.6

Source: World Development Report, 1988, Tables 1, 2, and 4.

and Bolivia. Unemployment increased to levels (such as 18–25 percent in Mexico and Bolivia) unknown since the Great Depression. In addition, social expenditures benefiting the poor (education, health, and housing) were severely cut back (see Table 6.4).

The outward transfer of resources associated with the cessation of private bank lending reversed the earlier capital flows, since now the poorest countries had to send their scarce funds to the creditor banks in the rich countries. The change from a positive inward transfer of $18 billion in 1981 to a negative outward transfer of $26 billion in l986 caused a *reversal shock* of $44 billion, equivalent to 5.6 percent of the combined GDP (gross domestic product) of these countries and one-fourth of all investment in these countries. *In the public sector, the shock was of the same magnitude as all expenditures on education and health combined.*

These comparisons barely bring out the extent of the pressures on the social programs of the debtor countries. As these countries were coping with the reversal shock, they also had to reduce their budget deficits, which for the central governments amounted to a total of 7.6 percent of GDP in 1986. Together with the transfer shock, this added up to 13.2 percent of GDP, more than the total outlays on health, education, and housing. This explains how, in the circumstances of the 1980s, strict adherence to the conventional standards of financial stability would have severe consequences for the social programs for improvement of the conditions of the poor.

Reviewing conditions in the Latin American countries, Guy Pfeffermann, chief economist of the International Finance Corporation, concluded that the economic decline and stagnation worsened the precarious livelihood of the poor. Even the distribution of income appears to have deteriorated as a result of the crisis: the rich benefited by being able to send capital abroad, while the poor became poorer because of the rise in unemployment and the sharp decline in real wages. To resume growth, the Latin American countries had to undertake a tremendous effort to boost manufactured exports. The importance of increased diversification and policies to support a more open economy, less dependent on primary exports, is evident from a comparison between Latin America and the East Asia–Pacific countries that managed to avoid the debt crisis. Exports of East Asia and the Pacific showed a steady rise—a total of 159 percent in 1980–1990, as against only 34 percent for Latin America and the Caribbean. Fortunately, Latin American export growth improved after 1987, reaching 36 percent in 1987–1990.

In his analysis of the impact on poverty of the growth slowdown in the 1980s, Pfeffermann (1986) concluded that governments are well advised to take action to make their social agencies more efficient and to direct their social expenditures more effectively toward the poorest groups. His advice preceded the 1987 call by UNICEF to give adjustment a human face. Without special attention to the poor, better focused measures to promote growth and stability will be detrimental to the poor. Adjustment efforts, especially those formulated with the assistance of the IMF under the energetic managing director Jacques de Larosiere, were initially aimed exclusively at restoring balance in the external accounts and government budgets, and were designed to work through a combination of classical measures of stabilization. But in the 1980s the effectiveness of these policies was lessened by sluggish external demand and weak commodity prices, heavy debt burdens, and a shortage of external capital. In the absence of growth, adjustment weighed heavily on the poor through a combination of factors: contraction of aggregate demand, increase in unemployment and lower real wages, and cutbacks in public sector employment and social programs.

Governments in adjusting economies can take various measures to bring the poor into the economic mainstream: undertake productive investment and provide better education and health facilities; increase agricultural prices and enhance the return on land owned by the poor; provide access for the poor to productive assets through irrigation, credit, electricity, fertilizer, and land reform; and improve the functioning of labor markets for the urban poor and help them to get better jobs. Measures of this kind aim at improving the primary income-generating activities of the poor, rather than giving them temporary help that does not change their basic condition. They permit the adjustments so badly needed for financial reasons to become a catalyst for more effective poverty alleviation and more fundamental reform, but often they require a reconsideration of fiscal priorities, which is politically difficult and controversial (Zuckerman, 1989).

By the early 1990s a number of debtor countries had taken major steps to improve economic policies and lay the basis for debt reduction, renewed foreign investment, and growth. Enrique Iglesias, president of the Inter-American Development Bank, pointed out in September 1993 that the Latin American countries had reduced budget deficits to 1 percent of GDP or less, lowered import protection from 40 to 10 percent, and reduced the operating deficits of state enterprises. They were growing by 6 percent per year (except for 4 percent in Brazil). Looking to the future, Latin America will still need to persist in social reform measures, improve the structure and collection of taxes, and pay greater attention to social programs for the poor.[23]

The many dire consequences for the poor make one wonder what are the prospects for further reduction in the debt burden on the poorest population segments. What are the most significant forces that will determine the debt developments in the years ahead?

INTERNATIONAL DEBT MANAGEMENT: PERSPECTIVES AND PROSPECTS

Mitigation of the immediate effects of the debt crisis depended critically on the willingness of the banks to accept some losses and on the financial backing creditor governments were willing to provide for debt-reduction plans. An obvious way would have been for the World Bank to triple or quadruple its loan operations in support of a more adequate debt-reduction scheme. The World Bank can increase its loans without imposing significant new burdens on weary taxpayers in the creditor countries. Failing such an increase, the World Bank itself became a drain on the LDCs and joined the commercial banks in the outward transfer of financial resources from the major debtors, a strange posture for an official lending institution. The Bretton Woods institutions are now finally taking steps to reduce the multilateral debts still owed by some of the poorest countries, but even these steps are highly selective and conditional on good behavior of the debtors.

The creditor countries have also, somewhat reluctantly, taken steps to reduce the official loans outstanding, mostly to the poorer countries. From 1987 on, they rescheduled outstanding loans on increasingly softer terms.[24]

These steps toward substantial debt reduction were deemed necessary to restore the external viability of the poorest debtor countries and place them in a position in which they could meet their remaining obligations without special assistance. Even then, some countries (e.g., Mozambique, Somalia, and Sudan) would still not be able to manage their debt and needed further relief. In a social sense, the cost of debt reduction to the creditors is of course much smaller than the benefits gained by the debtors, which receive relief from an onerous burden.

Most of the poorest countries in the 1980s increased their dependence on concessionary finance. One significant exception was India, which managed to reduce its reliance on soft aid and became an important borrower on private markets as it cut back state intervention in the manufacturing industry and opened its economy to private initiative.[25]

The difficulties of the major debtor countries in the mid-1980s occurred while the industrial economies were no longer depressed, indeed grew moderately, and oil prices declined. The U.S. economy provided important stimulus through a large balance-of-payments deficit. Global growth was, however, less than had been considered necessary for a resolution of debt-servicing difficulties. On the positive side, growth in the developing countries has been substantially higher than in the industrial countries over a period of decades, and continued vigorously after the 1990 downturn in the industrial countries. The developing countries had become a locomotive of global growth.

The aftermath of the debt crisis continues to be harmful to anti-poverty action, even though the crisis has disappeared from the agenda of official discussion in the 1990s, except for renewed consideration of the steps the IMF and the World Bank can take to reduce the debts of the poorest countries. Continuation of a negative resource transfer is a critical issue for the developing countries. Moreover, they face considerable competition from the Eastern European countries, Russia, and the other former Soviet republics, which are in the market for substantial new financing for their reconstruction and transition to a free market. The special demands of Eastern Europe and some Middle Eastern countries could make it difficult for the Latin American debtor countries to raise sufficient capital on reasonable terms. The poorest countries may be left at the short end. International institutions will have to play a key role in assuring that sufficient external help will be available on terms that will not endanger countries' economic strength and ability to fight poverty.

None of these observations suggests that the difficulties confronting the poor in the debtor countries will disappear. The case for continuing action on debt alleviation in the poorest countries is based on both economics and ethics. Continuing difficulties in the economic and financial realm make ethical considerations even more important.

THE ETHICAL DIMENSION

The continuing debt problems of the poorest countries and the often-painful relations between debtors and creditors must be seen in an ethical context. What are the moral obligations to keep the poorest nations out of debtors prison? The religious community was on strong ground when it pointed to the social effects of the debt crisis but, as in other areas of social justice, the story is complex. Before looking at the positions taken by the religious community, it is useful to recapitulate the main economic findings that must now be addressed in an ethical context:

- The debt crisis aggravated the conditions of the poor.
- Strong reliance on the market system contributed to the debt crisis, was not likely to resolve it, and will not prevent similar crises in the future. Official action is needed to supplement or countervail market forces.

Furthermore, none of the parties in the debt crisis emerged with a clean record:

- The banks did not demonstrate a sense of social responsibility, nor did they act in the interest of their clients.
- Creditor governments were slow to realize that they placed excessive reliance on the market system and that special supplementary action was needed.

- The debtor countries overborrowed and needed stricter controls over the use of borrowed funds.

- The international institutions could have set forth and acted on a comprehensive and realistic plan for resolving the debt crisis. The 1980s structural adjustment operations, while innovative, often failed to achieve their objectives, especially in the poorest African countries.

The churches called for a fairer and more equitable way of dealing with international indebtedness and fundamental reform of the international economic system. They continue to have a concern with the external financing of the poorest countries. The position of the religious community is based on what the Bible says about justice among people and institutions, concepts of the common good, and the priorities based on biblical principles.

Biblical Views

There is little doubt that the Bible favors fair treatment of debtors. The essence of the biblical message is that love must be as much in the center of our life as it was in Christ's life. The rule of "Love your neighbor" extends to our attitude toward the countries that surround us. We must deal with them in loving understanding when they face debt repayment difficulties and especially when creditors determine the terms of repayment. But love goes further: it commands debt *forgiveness*, not just fair treatment. The Kingdom of God encourages personal or national growth, conditioned by deep concern for the individual and the environment, and the shackles of indebtedness have no place in God's world.

The Bible gives abundant attention to the poorest among us and speaks of God's forgiveness of debts. Jesus often tells the people who come to him: "Your sins are forgiven, go and sin no more." It may have been wrong to incur too much debt, but Christ wants us to permit the wrongdoers to get on with their lives, not to end them in debtors prison. These points are highlighted by biblical positions on debt and interest payments.

- The Mosaic law recognizes that interest payments are of crucial importance. The faithful are cautioned not to ask interest payments from their poor brothers. No interest is to be charged in the community of faith, and the creditor is urged not to take a pledge from the poor man.

- The Mosaic law also proclaimed the sabbatical year: every seventh year debts must be remitted and slaves set free. It recognizes that severe indebtedness caused poverty, landlessness, and slavery, but in the community of faith people are to be free and not subject to poverty. This freedom culminates in the seventh (sabbatical) year, the year of jubilee, when all slaves are set free and the land is restored to its original owners. The sabbatical year probably was never fully put into practice, but the underlying concept is useful. When indebtedness or landownership becomes oppressive, fundamental corrections must be made.

- The Lord's prayer: "Forgive us our debts as we forgive our debtors" implies that debt forgiveness is basic to the Christian faith. Our life will be burdened with guilt if we are not prepared to forgive the debts others owe us.

- Paul writes: "Be in debt to no one; the only debt you should have is to love one another." Loving a person means getting to know his or her needs. In international relations, this means getting to know the country's needs, what it can bear, and to act accordingly. Such a course may run into conflict with the bottom line of the bankers. There is, in fact, ample space for conflict between the community of faith and the bankers. In one of his early and most public acts, Christ turned over the tables of the money changers in the temple court.[26]

These views are reflected in the position of the churches in the wake of the debt crisis.

The Voice of the Churches

The Catholic Church has given detailed and urgent attention to the various issues raised by the debt crisis. First it focused on critical economic and ethical issues, especially the impoverishment of the debtor countries, the positioning of rich against poor, and the impact of the debt situation on development.

No one has been more outspoken on the questions of poverty and debt than Pope John Paul II: "Christ is speaking of the whole universal dimension of injustice and evil. He is speaking of what today we are accustomed to call the North–South contrast. Yes, the South, becoming always poorer, and the North, becoming always richer. In the light of Christ's words, . . . the poor people and the poor nations . . . will judge those people who take these goods away from them, amassing to themselves the imperialistic monopoly of economic and political supremacy at the expense of others."[27]

The Pope gave his views more completely in the 1987 encyclical letter *Sollicitudo Rei Socialis* (The Social Concerns of the Church), in which he observed that the debt situation acted as a brake on development and in some cases aggravated underdevelopment; it should make us reflect on the ethical implications of economic interdependence (par. 19). Similar observations were made in "At the service of the human community: An ethical approach to the international debt question," which sees the debt problem in the wider context of growth and trade, and of more harmonious relations between rich and poor countries and debtors and creditors.[28] It points out that resolution of the debt crisis depends on growth of the world economy and world trade, as well as on the reduction of protection in the industrialized countries. The message outlined the responsibilities of each of the parties concerned and proposed that the rich countries initiate a new system of aid which, over a period of years, would restore hope to their poor neighbors in the developing world.

Second, in 1989, the U.S. Catholic bishops clarified the relation between economic forces at work in the debt situation and ethical issues, taking note of many injustices in the workings of the international financial system, for example: loans first used to finance capital flight for the rich, subsequently had to be repaid by governments representing the poor; loans were not used for specific projects, but instead for general balance-of-payments purposes, without, however, linking repayment obligations to balance-of-payments conditions; and high interest rates in international markets, beyond the control of the debtor countries, made it impossible for loans to be serviced.[29]

The Catholic bishops urged commercial bankers to place considerations of justice and coresponsibility above short-term financial gain or loss (par. 56 of the 1989 statement). They criticized policies advocating stronger debt repayment capacity through export growth, restraint on real wages and cuts in social services for the poor, and also advocated greater flexibility in a genuine case-by-case approach instead of the uniform conditionality practiced by the IMF and the World Bank (par. 54).

Third, the church explained the consequences of the debt crisis and called for reform of the Bretton Woods institutions so they could deal more effectively with the problems that had arisen. The American Catholic bishops, in their 1986 pastoral letter "Economic Justice for All: Catholic Social Teaching and the U.S. Economy," expressed concern with the inability of the Bretton Woods institutions to cope with the intensification of poverty in the debtor countries (par. 271–77). They were alarmed at the consequences of the programs negotiated by the IMF and called for reform of the Bretton Woods institutions so they may more adequately represent Third World debtors.[30] They felt that the developing countries should have greater weight in policy decisions by the boards of these institutions, in which creditor countries have a dominant position. In actual practice, however, most decisions are taken not by vote but on the basis of consensus, after intense discussion of often highly technical matters. Even so, there may be a new and strong case for reconsidering the operating structure and policies of the institutions in light of their now-universal membership and the continuing integration of the global economy.

The Catholic bishops also called on the U.S. government "to exercise leadership in the World Bank and the IMF to help move those institutions toward lending policies more consistent with equitable development in the Third World" (1989 statement of the U.S. Catholic Conference). They believed that fundamental "changes in the international economic system are needed in order to increase the prospect for social justice and to avoid crises like the debt problem in the future" (par. 47). The bishops' statements are more critical of the international system and call for more thorough reform than those of the Vatican.[31]

The mainline Protestant churches also spoke out against the injustices engendered by the debt crisis, reflecting a priority concern with the poor.[32] They were critical of the conditions the IMF and the World Bank attached to their financial support, in particular the excessive reliance on market forces and the cuts in essential social expenditures under their programs. There are, of course, valid criticisms of the stabilization conditions under the "Washington Consensus," but it should not be forgotten that the policies advocated by the Bretton Woods institutions did place many countries in a stronger position to deal with the problems in their society over the longer term. However, market-oriented policies had to be combined with measures to alleviate poverty and protect the environment. Constructive and valid criticism by the church and NGO community have induced the World Bank to deepen and broaden its programs to improve the human and natural environment.

The Bottom Line

No relationship is more painful, more fraught with errors and false starts, than that between debtor and creditor. It is worse than that between slave and master because it pretends that the contracting parties have independence and honor. It is surrounded with the false aura of "sound finance," but it runs the danger of placing countries in financial servitude. According to the myth of sound finance, a loan for a worthwhile project will pay for itself many times over, and countries will "take off" and produce a surplus with which to pay off their debts and become creditors themselves. But for every country that is successful in this respect, there are others that get mired down in debt and become the beggars of this world. They must present their case over and over again to groups of often-incompetent bureaucrats who represent aid givers and creditors, in negotiations that draw attention away from the real business of development. Economists claim there is a way out and a future for these indebted beggars, and that may be true for some. But a generation later, the poorest are still coming to the debtor table and asking for help, and the debt forgiveness they may receive is highly conditional. No relationship is more degrading than that between a self-righteous donor and the recipients who must make their case over and over again as if they are forever doomed to be in a debtor prison.

No wonder some revolutionaries rejected the externally imposed yoke, stood up with pride and said, "We are free." The Old Testament prophets wiped the slate clean and instituted a year of forgiveness in which all are set free from debt. The religious community of today has joined these prophets in their call for a Jubilee.

After fifty years of pretending that the debtor–creditor system based on "sound" debtor policies and "sound" project finance has worked, is it not time to recognize that many situations did not work out as had originally been envisaged, and that numerous mistakes were made in the original assessment? That there are ill-conceived projects, and that what once were regarded as sound policies made little sense? Out of all the profits made in international finance, a large fund can be set aside to forgive debts and to demonstrate to the world that we tolerate no place for losers, that the country with the poorest "performance" and the poorest prospects has a new chance. For we are all children of God, we all have a chance, and God's blessings are not confined to the creditors of this world or to the successful countries that managed to leap to prosperity.

The often-painful relationship and interchange between debtor and creditor is but one facet of the interaction between rich and poor in human society. The religious community has addressed this relationship in broad ethical terms, discussed in Part Two, "The Ethics of Social Justice."

PART TWO:

The Ethics of Social Justice

The economic diagnosis that emerges from the foregoing text is that poverty is prevalent, has deep causes, and continues manifest throughout modern society:

- In the backwash of the capitalist system;

- In a high proportion of people in the developing countries, even though many now are rapidly integrating with their richer trade partners;

- In the role of women, who are discriminated against in the marketplace and in many respects are the bearers of the poverty burden;

- In the environment, where the poor suffer most from the degradation that occurs in many places;

- In the burden of the military, which weighs most heavily on the poor everywhere; and

- In the often-painful relations between rich creditor and poor debtor countries.

Progress toward eliminating the vestiges of poverty calls for a multipronged attack of general economic policies promoting vigorous growth and job creation, combined with specific measures to promote high-quality education, housing, and health. When these policies fall short of their objectives, welfare measures are needed to provide the poor with an acceptable income and to help them on the road toward a more productive life.

But none of these policies have worked to full satisfaction. The measures taken have often been half-hearted, and simply have not reached the goal of full eradication. Poverty continues on a large scale, even as we seek to reach a steady pace of growth. Moreover, broad new layers of problems have emerged: large segments of the middle class who live in fear of losing their jobs or suffer severe cuts in pay as their jobs are shifted toward occupations with much lower pay. Imaginative and basic solutions to remove these fears are available, but the nation shies away from them because of a prevalent but largely unjustified feeling that government does not work or that our wealthy country cannot afford the extra outlay. Private industry now has become more efficient and profitable, but is loath to take on broader social tasks.

Given the complexities of the issues faced in poverty eradication, all parties need the help of others:

• The poor need the rich;

• The state needs the private sector;

• The city needs the rural economy; and

• Suburbia cannot flourish without vibrant urban centers.

The analysis and prescriptions of economics must somehow be bolstered by recognition of personal responsibility and a lessening of selfishness in our society. The conditions of the poor as analyzed by economists raise major moral questions that society must face: Can we tolerate a vast underclass in the midst of prosperity? Is it right to dismiss the problem by characterizing the poor as undeserving? Can we condone more than 1 billion poor left behind in a rapidly integrating global economy?

To work more satisfactorily, economic policies and communal action must be founded on personal and social conviction of what is right. Hence, we next consider the ethical imperative for action. With this objective, we explore what Judeo–Christian ethicists have to say about poverty, its causes and consequences, and the measures and attitudes we must pursue. In doing so, we also want to probe the economic feasibility of the advice of ethicists, as well as its consistency with the analyses in Part One. As our guide to the views of ethicists, we review the views expressed by the religious community in the United States as well as the Vatican.

The Catholic Church, the mainline Protestant churches, and American Judaism have published statements applying their beliefs to contemporary social and economic issues. Many Evangelicals have also spoken out on these issues, although their churches have mostly refrained from making formal pronouncements. These social justice messages of the religious community provide guidelines to the ethics of poverty issues.

Judaism has addressed a wide range of specific social policy issues, including the cutbacks in social expenditures under the Reagan Administration, hunger, discrimination, housing segregation, and welfare reform.

The Catholic Church speaks in a tradition of over 100 years of social teaching. We take up some of the basic Catholic pronouncements directly concerned with poverty. For understanding antipoverty policies in the United States, the U.S. bishops' pastoral letter "Economic Justice for All: Catholic Teaching and the U.S. Economy" (1986) made a major contribution that is bound to remain as one of the cornerstones of the literature on social justice because of its comprehensiveness, high standards of biblical analysis, and its outright advocacy of constructive support of the poor here and in the developing countries. A number of other Catholic statements, including several by Pope John Paul II, demand attention. The earlier chapters dealing with various economic issues have already drawn on various Catholic and other pronouncements.

Besides important Jewish and Catholic statements, the mainline Protestant churches represented in the National Council of Churches of Christ have expressed their own views on peace and justice. Of these, the United Church of Christ (UCC) and the Presbyterian Church have issued comprehensive statements, while the Lutherans, the Reformed Church in America, the Methodists, and the Episcopalians have issued shorter pronouncements on individual topics which also represent well-defined positions. Of all these, the Lutheran documents and the study paper "Christian Faith and Economic Life" (1987), prepared by the United Church of Christ, along with the United Methodist paper "In Defense of Creation" are particularly forthright and outspoken.

Various Evangelical and Conservative Protestant groups have also put forth their views on a number of social issues. These include the Association for Public Justice, the Evangelicals for Social Action, and the views expressed in the 1990 and 1995 Oxford Declarations on Christian Faith and Economics, as well as the positions taken by some of the Fundamentalist preachers.

The discussion leads off with an overview of economics in the Bible, followed by a review of Jewish statements. Next we will present an economist's look at liberation theology, which profoundly influenced both Catholic and Protestant views and testifies to the work of Christians amongst the poor in Central and South America.

7
Economics in the Bible

The Bible has many different meanings for different people—a book of beauty, comfort, guidance, or history. It is basic to Judeo–Christian ethics. It is a book of faith, recording the history and formation of what Christians and Jews believe. For many it is a source of strength. It speaks in plain language to everyone today, even though its sources are thousands of miles and years removed. The Bible also addresses a broad range of economics topics and uses various economics concepts. This will be clear from our review of Jewish and Christian statements, all of them based on biblical prescriptions. Hence, a reflection on economics in the Bible is a fitting continuation of our economics discussion in Part One.

Written over many ages and in many different circumstances, the Bible was written from the depth of human experience and suffering, but also reflects the height of joy and victory over personal pain and conflict. It is deeply concerned with the human condition and touches on many economic issues that arise in human intercourse. It describes conditions as they are (positive) and as they should be (normative). Its central rule is the prevalence of love in interpersonal relations, including those in the economics sphere. In the Old Testament the rule of love is initially confined to the community of Israel, but later prophets (for example, Isaiah) widened the horizon of love, and in the New Testament Christ made it universal.

Many statements on economics are found in the Bible on such questions as landownership, debt, poverty, and working conditions, all of which concern interpersonal relations. The following are a few examples, none new to the expert in this area or to the regular reader of the Bible. They do not pretend to give a complete picture of the wealth of economic thinking in the Bible.

SOME ECONOMICS CONCEPTS IN THE BIBLE[1]

Wages: You shall not keep back the wages of a man who is poor and needy (Deut 24:14). The worker deserves his wage.

Taxes: Joseph imposed a land tax in Egypt (Gen 41), one of the few biblical events mentioned by Adam Smith in his "Wealth of Nations."

Paying taxes to the emperor: Give Caesar what is Caesar's and God what belongs to God (Mark 12:17). In the books of Kings there are many examples of *paying tribute*.

Property: You shall not steal (8th commandment; Deut 5:19).

Land Transactions: No land shall be sold outright, because the land is mine, and you are coming to it as aliens (Lev 25: 23).

Interest: Israelites can charge interest to a foreigner, but not to a fellow countryman (Deut 23: 19). Don't charge interest to your poor brother, either by capitalizing or by discounting (Lev 25: 35 and 36).

Collateral: Don't enter the borrower's house to take a pledge. Don't keep the pledge given by a poor man (Deut 24:10–12).

Return on Investment: Send your grain across the seas, and in time you will get a return (Eccl 11:1).

Distribution of risk: Divide your merchandise among seven ventures, eight maybe, since you do not know what disasters may occur on earth (Eccl 11: 2).

Weights and Measures: You shall have no unequal weights (Deut 25:13). "A double standard in weights is an abomination to the Lord, and false scales are not good in his sight" (Prov 20:23).

Concentration of Wealth: "Shame on you! you who add house to house and join field to field, until not an acre remains, and you are left alone to dwell in the land. The Lord of Hosts has sworn in my hearing: Many houses shall go to ruin, fine large houses shall be uninhabited. Five acres of vineyard shall yield only one gallon, and ten bushels of seed return only a peck" (Isa 5:8–10).

THE YEAR OF JUBILEE

The sabbatical Year of Jubilee, proclaiming freedom from oppression of various kinds, has a deep meaning for our contemporary society, even though it probably was never put into practice in ancient days. The message is that indebtedness or ownership structures should be changed when they become an obstacle to achieving or maintaining a sane society, which must be made up of free people. Moreover, letting the land lay fallow every seventh year is good for soil conservation. Here are more details from the Old Testament:

Every seventh (sabbatical) year is to be a solemn rest for the land. You shall not sow your field nor prune your vineyard. It shall be a year of sacred rest (Lev 25: 5 and 6).

The seventh sabbatical is the Year of Jubilee. "Proclaim liberty in the land for all its inhabitants" (Lev 25: 10). This liberty includes (a) leaving the land fallow; (b) restoring landed property to its original owner, and (c) setting free all Israelite slaves. The underlying rationale is that the land belongs solely to God and so do the people of Israel; absolute human ownership of either is forbidden (Lev 25: 8–34).

At the end of every seventh year you should make a remission of debts (Deut 15: 1). There will never be a poor among you if only you obey the Lord your God (Deut 15: 4).

When a fellow Hebrew, man or woman, sells himself to you as a slave, he or she shall serve you for six years; in the seventh year, you shall set him free (Deut 15: 13). When you set him free, do not let him go empty-handed, give to him lavishly from your flock, etc. (Deut 15: 14).

Concern for the poor dominates the Bible's view on economics:

It encourages economic behavior that helps the poor—e.g., in taking pledges, not delaying payment of wages, not charging interest, remitting debts after every seventh year. There will never be any poor among you if only you obey the Lord your God by keeping these commandments.

It recognizes the plight of the poor and condemns the rich (Job 24: 1–13):

"The poor rise early like the wild ass
when it scours the wilderness for food.
But though they work till nightfall,
their children go hungry." (Job 24:5).

"They sell the innocent for silver;
they grind the heads of the poor into the earth" (Amos 2: 6–8).

It prefers honest poverty to crooked wealth:

"Better to be poor and above reproach
than rich and crooked" (Prov 28:6).

"A tyrant which oppresses the poor
is like a driving rain which ruins the crop" (Prov 15: 16–17).

Clearly, the Bible is on the side of the poor:

"A man who sneers at the poor
insults his Maker" (Prov 7: 5).

BIBLICAL ECONOMICS IN PERSPECTIVE

The Bible's economic observations are circumscribed by the conditions and attitudes of the times in which they were written. Economic society was simple; there were trade and agriculture, but no manufacturing to speak of. In this simple society lending was an act of charity, and to take interest was to capitalize on another's misfortune (Prov 28: 8). Thus, we find little direct guidance on such contemporary economic issues as concentration of production, employment policies, and the role of market forces, other than that they should be governed by the rule of love. The religious pronouncements on issues of economic justice apply the Bible to more complex contemporary situations. In the final analysis, these carefully prepared statements boil down to some fairly simple and universal rules which can be applied in a wide variety of situations.

Since the Bible reaches out to the souls of people, their deepest emotions, there are of course numerous examples where it goes well beyond economics and deals with the workings of economic forces in a broader perspective. Seeing economic issues in their proper setting is in fact an important task for the religious person. Again, here are a few examples.

Rich and poor are basically in the same condition: "Rich and poor have this in common: The Lord is maker of them all" (Prov 22: 2). The essential human condition extends to all, regardless of their economic status. It will be good to keep this in mind when one listens to what Liberation Theology has to say.

Isaiah uses the terminology of the marketplace in prophesying about a new age. He gives a deeper meaning to life today:

"Come all who are thirsty, come fetch water;
come, you who have no food, buy corn and eat;
come and buy, not for money, not for a price.

Why spend money and get what is not bread,
    why give the price of your labour and go unsatisfied?
Only listen to me and you will have good food to eat,
    and you will enjoy the fat of the land" (Isa 55: 1–2); and
"The Lord shall shine upon you
and over you shall his glory appear"
"Then you shall shine with joy
and you shall possess the wealth of nations" (Isa 60: 2 and 5).

Jesus quotes Isaiah (61: 1) at the very start of his work, announcing the good news to the poor, proclaiming liberty to the captives, to set free the oppressed. Truly, a new Jubilee (Luke 4: 16–19).

Jesus gives the bottom line on economics. Anyone who objects to the messages of present day bishops or synods will have even more trouble with what Jesus has to say. He brings out the conflict between the quest for money and the serving of God:

"No one can be a slave to two masters: he will hate one and love the other; or he will be loyal to one and despise the other. You cannot serve God and money" (Mt 6: 24).

And speaking to the rich man who had obeyed all the commandments from his youth: "You still need to do one thing. Sell all you have and give the money to the poor, and you will have riches in heaven; then come follow me" (Luke 18: 22).

Freedom—freedom from want, from fear, from oppression—is basic to an understanding of how Christian principles are applied in the marketplace. At the very origin of the Judaic religion, the Hebrews are oppressed by the Egyptians and God acts to set them free from political and economic oppression. The Ten Commandments remind us of God's liberating act: "I am the Lord your God who has brought you from the house of bondage."

In the same sense Jesus, in the New Testament, has come to set the people free from fear, from death, from possessions: ". . . Do not be worried about the food and drink you need to stay alive, or about the clothes for your body. After all, isn't life worth more than food? and isn't the body worth more than clothes? . . ." (Mt 6: 25–34). And on property and greed, Jesus warns: "Watch out, and guard yourselves from all kinds of greed; for a man's true life is not made of the things he owns, no matter how rich he may be" (Luke 12: 15).

Paul preaches, in many ways, the freedom we can achieve through faith in Christ. Freedom from the laws that had ruled the life of Jewish society. "Freedom is what we have—Christ has set us free! Stand then as free men, and do not allow yourselves to become slaves again" (Gal 5: 1). He suffered much from oppression, and spent quite some time in jail, but rarely deals explicitly with questions of poverty or property. He does tell us that we should share our burdens and admonishes the richer churches to make contributions to the poorer ones: "Help carry one another's burdens, and in this way you will obey the law of Christ" (Gal 6: 2).

By preaching people's restoration to freedom, becoming a "new being," of which he speaks in Rom 8, Paul lays the foundation for a truly productive life and takes the most important step toward life without want and fear in our contemporary society.

The freedom we find in the Bible is comprehensive. It deals not merely with economic matters, though clearly much of it was written against a background of poverty, and it strongly supports the poor, but at the same time its central message is one of personal salvation for all who accept it. Thus, while it sets a norm of love for the economic system, it also lays the basis for how individuals should deal with that system. A "saved" person, one who has been set free from fear and oppression of all kinds, is better able to deal with the pressures of the job and the marketplace. And in their own particular situation, such persons will be able to make the system work in a more humane way to the benefit of many who work with them or in their sphere of activity.

These verses and views from the Bible are part of a broader vision of economics rooted in the biblical principles of love and justice. We will see how this principle is applied to crucial contemporary issues such as the prevalence of poverty, the emergence of women in the economy, the indebtedness of the developing countries, and the degradation of our environment. We will first review the Jewish roots of social justice, based on the Torah, the Old Testament prophets, and the subsequently evolved Talmud, and next take a brief look at the theology which emerged from the work of Catholic priests among the poorest groups south of our border, a vision of the Bible which is basic to understanding all the churches' contemporary message of social justice.

8

The Jewish Roots of Social Justice

The Jewish community, more than any other in our society, has a long and strong tradition of fighting against all forms of social injustice. Since World War II it has dealt with a broad range of socioeconomic topics—for example, poverty and human dignity, unemployment, teenage pregnancy, the rights of the disadvantaged, provision of basic needs, hunger, the role of charity and welfare, rent controls and affordable housing, civil rights and the impact of discrimination and segregation, business behavior, and international development assistance. The Jews' attitudes and policy views are firmly rooted in the Bible and the later Jewish scriptures.

Most of the texts addressed to economic issues in the Bible are found in the Old Testament. The Mosaic laws and the message of the prophets are basic to the theology of social and economic justice. The scriptural texts have direct applications for the economic realities concerning wages, taxes, landownership, interest charges, and the ethics of business transactions. The sabbatical Year of Jubilee gave new life to the land, the slave, and the debtor. Isaiah gave the basic social–economic rules of the Pentateuch a broader and deeper spiritual meaning.

The Jewish tradition from which these texts stem found its origin in the consequences of oppression by the Pharaos of Egypt and Moses' leadership in overcoming it. The liberation of the Hebrew nation is moving and inspiring history, and presents a true reality of vast contemporary significance. For with Israel's revolt against oppression came the rules for civilized life based on freedom and respect for laws and the individual.

In this brief overview, only some of the highlights of a very rich literature can be noted. It is simply not possible to do justice to the wealth of views expressed over thousands of years. The focus is on the positions taken by the Jewish community on social justice, particularly since World War II, with special attention to Jewish views of poverty and specific actions taken over the past fifty years.

It is one of the great tragedies and lessons of human history that the people who brought us the fundamental concepts of social and economic justice were themselves haunted and persecuted through the ages, from the Babylonian exile to the Holocaust of the twentieth century, itself an aggravation of long dark centuries of pogroms and discrimination that ran through European "civilization." It was often not sufficiently countermanded, and sometimes even encouraged, by the actions and thinking of Christian theologians and churches.[1] It is a strange but wonderful blessing that the pain and distress of these persecutions produced thoughts about a just and better society, not just for Jews but for all people.

In America not so long ago, the Jewish community continued to face discrimination, often subtle, in many walks of life. Only recently have many WASP bastions, like banking, begun to open up to Jews and others. In the immediate post-World War II period, prestigious universities, Harvard not excluded, sought to restrict the number of Jews on their faculty and in their student body. At the same time, the Jews knew well the often-depressing conditions in the urban centers where many of them had lived or continued to live. No wonder the Jewish community was in the forefront of applying basic religious teaching to the social situation of our country. In many ways, they were leaven for our bread.

When Jewish organizations spoke out, they frequently did not give elaborate scriptural interpretation, nor did they make comprehensive pronouncements like some Christian churches. It was as if they were too occupied with the urgency of contemporary social action to have time for more elaborate presentations. Their statements usually made brief references to Jewish social principles and were applied to the specific issues that demanded attention at the time. In addition, the organization of Reform Rabbis presented social justice platforms in 1918 and 1928. Most of the Jewish statements were deeply concerned with poverty.

JUDAISM AND POVERTY[2]

In the Sabbatical Year (Ex 23: 11) the land was to lie fallow so the poor could harvest the marginal crops, and all debts had to be canceled. Land was not the permanent possession of anyone (Lev 25: 23). These rules were based on the realization that unrestricted pursuit of economic interests would result in undue concentration of wealth. The ancient Hebrews sanctioned competition but rejected "rugged individualism." The intent of the Mosaic laws was to restore balance, to give those who had fallen an opportunity to lift themselves up again.

Moreover, Jewish tradition never asserted that property rights have precedence over human rights. Nor did Judaism accept the Puritan emphasis on the acquisition of property and worldly goods as a sign of virtue. The tithe prescribed in biblical law was not a voluntary contribution, but an obligation imposed on all, in order that "the stranger and the fatherless and the widow shall come and shall eat and be satisfied" (Deut 14: 29). No man had absolute control over his property. The man who owned a well in a field had to make the water available to the inhabitants of a nearby community. These requirements evolved out of the fundamental Jewish conviction that material possessions are gifts from God, to be used for the benefit of all.

Jewish sages taught that poverty was the worst catastrophe that could happen to a person. The afflictions of poverty were considered so severe that "the poor man is considered a dead man." Poverty is spiritual death: Judaism has never drawn a dichotomy between body and soul, as other religions and systems have done.

Moreover, there is no word for "charity" in Hebrew. The word used is *tzedakah*, which literally means "righteousness." *Tzedakah* is the fulfillment of an obligation to a fellow being with equal status before God. Injustice to man is desecration of God. "A man who sneers at the poor insults his Maker" (Prov 17: 5). Refusal to give charity is considered by Jewish tradition to be idolatry.[3]

Even greater than *tzedakah* was *gemilut chasadim*, or "acts of loving kindness." The Lord loves a cheerful giver. Moreover, the act of giving must not offend the recipient's dignity. It is sometimes better to lend without the expectation of repayment than to make a grant. Until modern times, every Jewish community had a *Gemilut Chesed* society whose primary purpose was to make loans to the needy without interest or security; some communities still have these societies today.

The great twelfth-century Jewish philosopher (and physician) Maimonides brought order to the many writings of earlier years and wrote a basic commentary on the Mishnah, the codified version of Jewish law. He also gave guidance to the exercise of loving kindness by distinguishing eight degrees of charity, ranging from "He who gives grudgingly, reluctantly, or with regret" at the bottom to "He who gives without knowing to whom he gives, neither does the recipient know from whom he receives" and "He who helps a fellow man to support himself by a gift, or a loan, or by finding employment for him, thus helping him to become self-supporting" at the top of the ladder. [4]

In the Talmudic period, the Jewish community supplemented the obligations of private charity with an elaborate system of public welfare, the first in history. Jewish tradition has always been nurtured in and through the community. So it was only natural for the Jew to look upon poverty as the responsibility of the entire community. The existence of the poor was an indication of social inequity, which had to be rectified by society itself. The system of social welfare became the means of restoring integrity to the community. By the Middle Ages, community responsibility encompassed every aspect of life. The Jewish community regulated market prices so that the poor could purchase food and other basic items at cost. Medieval Jewish practices anticipated "meal tickets" and modern food stamp plans. Jewish communities even instituted rent controls so the poor could get housing at affordable prices.

The concept of President Johnson's "Great Society" was not new to Judaism. Every day Jews pray for a Messianic Era of brotherhood and peace for all people. Judaism does not emphasize individual salvation. Salvation for the individual is inextricably dependent on salvation for the entire people, and salvation of the people is in turn dependent on the salvation of all humankind. [5]

BASIC ATTITUDES

The vision expressed in the Conservative Statement of Principles is that the just society is intended by God as the goal of creation. [6] "Jewish sages ruled that we must give charity to needy non-Jews as well as Jews. The prophetic ideal of social justice found ample expression and concretization in the corpus of the Halakah (Jewish Law) that sought to create a society concerned with the welfare of the homeless, the impoverished, and the alien. Halakah insisted that no human being had the right to ignore the spectacle of injustice in order to engage exclusively in a search of God." The medieval teachers and later movements (e.g., Hasidic), while stressing piety and ritual, never failed to urge us to behave honestly and compassionately toward our fellow creatures.

As mentioned in the *Principles*, the conservative movement has a long history of concern for social justice. It points to the work of Rabbi Sabate Morais and his support of the striking shirtmakers and to Dr.

Abraham Joshua Heschel, who was recognized for his concern for the aged, children, ill, and helpless, and for his espousal of the cause of black Americans.

Jewish policy pronouncements often start with a brief reference to the origins and principles of Jewish social concern. This is reflected in the statements of the Union of American Hebrew Congregations (UAHC or "Union"), the National Federation of Temple Sisterhoods (NFTS or "Sisterhoods"), and the Central Conference of American Rabbis (CCAR or "Rabbis"), all affiliated with Reform Judaism.[7] These general principles reflect the belief of all branches of American Judaism, Reform as well as Conservative and Orthodox. They place policy advocacy in a broad framework of understanding the Torah and other Jewish scriptures.

Since its formation in 1873, the Union has consistently spoken out for civil rights and world peace. From its inception in 1889, the Central Conference of American Rabbis has been in the vanguard of liberal religious thought and action in America. Its social justice platforms of 1918 and 1928 were landmarks of social thought, were widely distributed, and had a powerful impact on opinion in the country. The annual statements of the Commission of Justice and Peace of the Rabbis and their periodic proclamations have set high standards of insight into the processes of democracy. The American rabbis demanded improvements in housing for working people as early as 1918 and again in 1932 and 1935, while the Union called for universal health care as early as 1948.

Reform rabbis have been active in formulating both public statements and direct social action. In the 1920s and 1930s they became involved in labor situations, often in association with representative Catholic and Protestant leaders. The Conservative rabbinate, through the Rabbinical Assembly of America, has also interpreted the teachings of Judaism courageously in every area of contemporary life. The Social Action Commission of Conservative Judaism continues this tradition. Organized in 1954, the commission set itself the objective of organizing local study and action groups, an objective currently pursued by the United Synagogues Social Action (Vorspan and Lipman, 1959, pp. 9 and 14).

Judaism has always demanded that its moral values be applied to the practical problems of society. "The earth and its inhabitants are the Lord's." Jewish prophets viewed the earth, its resources, and the wealth derived therefrom as a sacred trust, to be shared justly by all.

The purpose of society and government is to provide for such sharing, to insure the security and rights of the disadvantaged and the weak. At the same time, Judaism teaches that no economic system is sacred; human beings and human needs are sacred. Any economic system deserves to survive only if it effectively provides for the well-being of the least powerful, least advantaged members of society.[8]

From their own historical experience, the Jews have a particular sensitivity to the horror of the ghetto and to discrimination. In fact, Judaism regards itself as an affirmation of the God-given right of *every person* to equality and justice. The Jewish community confesses a deep commitment to the achievement of a just society in which *all people* can live in dignity and respect. Jewish teaching demands that all people be treated equal; it is directed not just to the Jewish community but to our entire society: "Judaism stands totally opposed to racial segregation and racial discrimination. Judaism believes in the unity of mankind and in the dignity of each personality as a child of God" (Vorspan, 1969, p. 55).

Judaism teaches that poverty constitutes a destruction of human dignity and proclaims that all must endeavor to fulfill the dictate, "There shall be no needy among you." Jewish tradition is distinguished by its sensitive concern for the poor, the weak, the sick, the elderly, the disinherited, and the stranger at the gate, both at home and overseas. It regards as morally indefensible the persistence of poverty in a society possessing abundance to satisfy the material needs of all its citizens. Jewish rabbis consider themselves as the heirs of a prophetic tradition that always sought to repair a damaged world. Jews are called upon to feed the hungry and clothe the naked, an idea that goes back to the Talmud.[9]

The National Federation of Temple Sisterhoods points out that the rule for harvesters to leave enough on the land so gleaners can meet some of their needs is not an appeal to the generosity of the landowners (Lev 19: 9–10). "It confers a right to glean and harvest the uncut edge on those who have no resources of their own. It is perhaps the oldest declaration that the disadvantaged members of society have a right to support from that society and should not be dependent on voluntary benevolence alone—though the latter is stressed as well. Later tradition applies the principle involved to urban conditions."[10]

In facing issues in welfare assistance, the Jewish tradition demonstrates compassion, but also affirms the crucial importance of work as central to the dignity of the human being. Biblical, rabbinic, and

contemporary Jewish tradition are replete with admonitions exalting
the virtues of work as a way to honor God and man.[11]

SPECIFIC ACTION

In their response to particular social issues, the Reform Jewish organizations took positions on a wide range of topics. In 1968, at the time of
President Johnson's war on poverty, the Union of American Hebrew
Congregations set forth a comprehensive set of social justice principles
and policies in its statement "Civil Rights and Social Justice." Based on
the belief that *poverty and discrimination are inextricably related*, the proposals extend well beyond social justice into antipoverty policies.
"What is at stake in the struggle to achieve equality of treatment for
the individual are the spiritual values of our civilization, the economic
well-being of our nation and the moral leadership of America in a
multi-racial world." The statement affirmed that our "national commitment must recognize that the fight against poverty and discrimination requires a truly comprehensive, coordinated approach of all
segments of society, public and private, and the extensive investment
of much more financial resources." The statement calls for programs
that incorporate:

- Provision of basic needs: food, clothing, housing, medical care,
  and education;
- Full employment at adequate wages, and retraining opportunities for the involuntarily unemployed;
- Equitable distribution of public welfare funds, with elimination of procedures which discourage welfare recipients from
  obtaining sufficient employment to leave the welfare rolls;
- Freedom to organize in the pursuit of common economic and
  social objectives; and
- Establishment of indigenous organizations in which the disadvantaged can achieve dignity and self-respect.

The statement also suggests various ways in which the private
sector, including religious institutions, can help achieve greater
equality through local antipoverty programs, financial support for
low-cost housing, equal employment opportunities, urban–suburban
exchange, and service for achieving racial justice and improvement of
community life.

In 1965 a Union (UAHC) statement expressed strong opposition to *discrimination in housing*. In its view, housing segregation tends to produce slum conditions, segregated schools, inequities in employment, and the poverty which haunts millions of African-Americans. It urged congregants to refrain from imposing any qualification about race, religion, or national origin in the sale, leasing, or mortgaging of housing. Later the Union called for greater action toward affordable housing, the creation of a national housing policy envisaging more funding for rehabilitation and new construction, provision of homeless shelters, and the organization of a Federal Office of Affordable Housing (1989). Similar resolutions promoting low-cost housing were passed earlier by the Rabbis in 1946, 1948, 1949, and 1965. Additional resolutions on measures to assist the homeless were passed by the Union (UAHC) in 1983 and the Rabbis (CCAR) in 1984.

In 1965 the Union also declared its wholehearted support for effective programs designed to eradicate poverty. It urged government to implement a policy of "maximum employment, production and purchasing power," such as was first enunciated by the Employment Act of 1946, and to adopt measures to assure everyone willing and able to work a living wage and an adequate income during periods of unemployment.[12] The Union commended local, state, and federal government programs to train unskilled workers and retrain workers displaced by technological changes (1963 and 1977). The United Jewish Appeal, in addition to sponsoring programs abroad, spends a substantial part of its funds for domestic causes in the United States.

The Union urged comprehensive welfare reform combined with income maintenance and incentives for moving recipients into job training and adequate general education, as well as necessary supportive services—day care, family planning, and health and legal services.[13] In 1948 the Union called for medical care to be made available to all at a reasonable price.

In 1993 the Union endorsed a comprehensive overhaul of the American health care system, commending President Clinton's proposed Health Care Security Act, a program which shared many of the Union's objectives. The Union seeks a national health care plan that grants universal access to health care benefits and has adequate provision for education, training, and cost containment. In 1993 the Union also drew attention to neglected issues of women's health and called for more adequate funding for gender-specific health research on conditions such as osteoporosis, breast cancer, and menopause.

The Reform organizations took positions *against* certain government actions that were inconsistent with their principles. For example, in 1951 the rabbis protested against the House Committee on Unamerican Activities and the actions of Senator Joe McCarthy and others. They "affirmed the sacred duty of religious leaders and teachers to act as the conscience of society." The Union opposed the Reagan Administration's cutbacks in funding for public education and the provision of food and Medicaid for the poor, combined with increased military spending and financial burdens on state and local government (1981). The Sisterhoods had called for reductions in military spending even earlier (1969).

In fighting for international solidarity and against poverty, the National Federation of Temple Sisterhoods expressed support for strengthening ties with Latin American nations (1941). It urged the United Nations to speed its expanded program of technical assistance to underdeveloped areas (1950) and strongly supported the United States "Point IV Program" of technical assistance (1953 and 1955).

In 1987 the Union cautioned against cuts in foreign aid associated with the Gramm–Rudman legislation. It urged an increase in overall foreign aid budgets to meet imperative humanitarian requirements, give priority to development assistance over military aid in the allocation of scarce aid resources, and give significant emphasis to the tragic plight of sub-Saharan countries. The Union also urged Congress to continue its commitment to Israel to continue restructuring its economy.

The Sisterhoods also pushed for government programs and private action to cope with the disproportionate number of poor and near-poor who are women and children, eliminate discrimination in pay scales between women and men, and establish pay equity, and they opposed cuts in federal social programs (1985). The Union pointed to the need for action on economic justice for women and removal of discrimination in corporate hiring practices (1983). The Equal Rights Amendment was supported by both the Union (1983) and the Rabbis (1984).

The problem of teenage pregnancy and the importance of breaking the cycle of poverty suffered by teenagers who become pregnant and drop out of school also drew the attention of the Sisterhoods. They encouraged better sex education, health services, family programs, head start, and special tutoring for girls. Local business and religious groups should take part in voluntary programs to provide activities, employment opportunities, and job training for students and dropout teenagers. They supported parental medical leave and wanted employers belonging to Jewish congregations and communities to work toward "eradicating outdated employment practices and implement new policies that meet the needs of today's families" (1987).

Hunger both in the United States and abroad drew wide attention in the 1960s. The Sisterhoods pointed to the government's responsibility to feed the hungry, support private action, and improve the food stamp program (1969). In 1983 the Rabbis noted that hunger conditions had become worse and asked for greater action by local congregations on education of congregants and distribution of food, clothing, and medicines and the provision of shelter, etc. World hunger had to be combated through more effective government policies, as well as moderation in private consumption and action by individual congregations (Union, 1975 and Rabbi, 1985).

These Jewish positions constitute a broad, progressive agenda for action with a strong position against all forms of discrimination. It was developed as specific issues presented themselves, and it demonstrated a willingness to oppose particular government actions inconsistent with the norms of social justice. The pronouncements preceded or ran parallel with those of mainline Protestant denominations like the Episcopalians and Methodists (Chapter 11); Reform Jews expressed appreciation for the social work of Christian churches and have made joint statements with them on specific social concerns.

The Jewish agenda is addressed to government, communities, and congregations. The statements appeal repeatedly to individual congregants to observe principles of social justice in their personal and business lives, including the absence of discrimination in employment practices. They stand for treating people with equality, and hence are in tune with the message of Liberation Theology, to which we turn next.

9
Liberation Theology: Giving the Poor Priority

In the history of salvation that Christians share with Jews, the Bible tells in many ways how God is on the side of the oppressed. He was on Jacob's side when his brother Esau drove him from the land. God prospered Jacob's son Joseph when his brothers sold him into Egyptian slavery. When the people of Israel were oppressed by Pharaoh, the dictator of his time, God sent Moses to guide them toward a new land. Later the people of Israel were exiled, and again God brought a new beginning. The Bible's promise of salvation from oppression is often expressed in the most beautiful phrasing and style, as in the poetry of the second Isaiah (Isa 40 onward).

Again in the New Testament the Jewish nation was oppressed, and Christ brought a new message of hope and salvation, a message most eloquently elaborated by Paul, who himself was put into prison and condemned to death by Roman oppressors.

All this has been articulated in liberation theology, starting in the 1960s, by priests who worked among the poor, men like the Peruvian Gustavo Gutierrez and the Brazilian Leonardo Boff. They saw the results of economic and political oppression in Peru, El Salvador, and other places where thousands of the poor were eliminated by the Pharaohs of our time.

These priests taught us—often against initial objections of some church leaders—that the Christian promise has a special meaning and message for the poor everywhere. Oppression is a universal phenomenon, and the Gospel has a universal message. In our own world we too have to recognize the many forms of oppression—of African-Americans suffering from racial prejudice, of women in the marketplace being underpaid and underpromoted by dual standards, while well-off professional workers may have to put up with often-oppressive forms of regimentation in government and corporate bureaucracies.

Liberation theology demonstrates the richness of the biblical message, once its interpretation is opened up by those whose lives are rooted in the society of the poorest countries and who know first-hand the oppression by the privileged elite. A comparable transformation of understanding and expression can occur when people from the Third World rewrite the textbooks of political science and economics. They identify or highlight new social problems for fresh analysis, phenomena which heretofore were not regarded as worthy of attention.

Liberation theology is fundamental to an understanding of both Catholic and most mainline Protestant messages of the 1980s and later. Robert McAfee Brown, a Protestant who taught at Union Theological Seminary and the Pacific School of Religion, has been an important interpreter of this theology. It explores the Gospel's application to the conditions of the poor. It evolved from the work of Catholic priests among the poorest of the poor. They preached the Gospel of Christ while working with the poor and found in the Bible a rich source of encouragement to strengthen the downtrodden and lift them up to a position of greater dignity and productivity. In contemporary language, God's message empowers the poor. They practiced their views in "base communities" where poor peasants and urban dwellers sought biblical guidance, shared their sorrows, and found a new hope and a new foundation. These communities are the modern equivalent of the Christian church of the first and second centuries.

To understand this particular interpretation of the Bible, one must have seen and felt the depth of poverty in many Latin American countries and the estrangement of the old traditional church from its social surroundings and its poorest members or, even worse, the identification of the church with the elite, the oppressors of their poor neighbors. The "liberation theologians" sought to break this tradition and did so in biblical fashion. They sought to set their parishioners free from oppression and an unproductive tradition by giving them a new insight into the Bible. Few who have seen and felt the pains of oppression in Latin America and have read the Bible in light of the conditions prevailing there can object to this rich interpretation of the Gospel of Jesus Christ.

By reading the Bible with a new understanding, the poor could once again identify themselves with people in the Bible. For example, to them Mary the mother of Jesus had been a gilded queen with a shining crown suspended against the wall of their church, revered but distant. Then they were taught to read Mary's Song of Praise:

God stretched out his mighty arm
And scattered the proud people with all their plans.

He brought down mighty kings from their thrones,
And lifted up the lowly.
He filled the hungry with good things,
And sent the rich away with empty hands. (Luke 1: 51–53)

They understood this language and could identify with a Mary who spoke of conditions close to them and gave them a new promise. Mary had become one of them, and no longer was she an image on a church wall.

Gustavo Gutierrez, the Peruvian theologian and priest and proponent of liberation theology, writes that throughout the entire Bible, God manifests himself as the defender of the weak in the face of the powerful. God upholds the human worth of those scorned by this world, the right of life of the poor who are dominated by the forces of death. God prefers the poor because they are the poor, because they are living in an inhuman situation that is against His will. Gutierrez sees this as the meaning of "Blessed are the Poor." The gospel reveals who God really is: love for all, and especially for the outcast and the oppressed (Brown, 1990, p. 111).

As one would expect, a revolutionary theology of this kind met with wide criticism. It has been criticized on theological grounds, for example, by no one less than Cardinal Ratzinger, the Vatican authority and spokesman on theological interpretation. And it has been condemned on the ground that some authors advocate violent opposition to established power, use Marxist social analysis, and advocate socialist economic policies which are harmful to economic growth and the improvement of the economic conditions facing the poor.

What are the economic consequences of liberation theology? The rich liberation literature was written by priests and theologians who had no systematic training in economics or in the practice of economic and financial policy. These writers draw attention to the unjust effects of certain economic regimes, to the structural deficiencies of industry and agriculture, the economic dependence of Latin American countries on foreign powers, and the belief that raw material producing countries remain poor while the industrialized countries enrich themselves. They seek to empower those who suffer from these economic injustices into a new self-worth and self-respect so essential for a genuinely new economic beginning.

Some critics, like Michael Novak (1993, pp. 92 and 155), have attacked liberation theology on the ground that it was associated with the wrong economic policies. Novak argues that Latin Americans cannot blame poverty in their countries on colonialist exploitation by the United States and other industrialized countries. He maintains that instead they should follow the example of (South) Korea and other Pacific countries and pursue an export-oriented development strategy. He is right that the policy of heavy industrialization and import substitution adopted by some Latin American countries in earlier decades only worked up to a point. It got bogged down in excessive and uneven protection, and it tended to neglect agriculture to the detriment of many of the poor. It missed the challenge of manufactured export expansion that worked so well for Korea, although Brazil did follow it for some years in the late 1960s with remarkable success. But these were faults of economic policy, not theology, and Novak and others were wrong to attack liberation theologians on this ground. One might add that these critics have little explanation for why these countries have such an uneven income distribution, and why the elites of Latin America have had such an adverse impact on social conditions and have so strongly influenced the composition of government expenditures to their own advantage at the expense of the poor.

Liberation theology, or indeed any theology, should not be identified with a particular set of economic measures. A number of Latin American movements that undertook to improve the basic conditions of poverty and social injustice fell into the trap of poor economic policies. They battled the status quo—including the economic powers associated with the United States—and some found solace in the opposing Marxist views. They perceived of Marxism as having concern for the poor laboring classes, but often also pursued policies which in Latin America, and indeed also in Africa, had disastrous effects for overall economic conditions, including those of the poor. This was true in Chile under Salvador Allende, in Cuba under Fidel Castro, and to some extent in Nicaragua under the Sandinistas.

Liberation theology has helped American theologians, both Catholic and Protestant, to focus on the problems of the poor in their own country, even though conditions in the United States are better in several respects than in Latin America. The theology has been given an even broader interpretation by focusing on racial discrimination and the oppression of women and particular social groups. The conditions of the poor in the United States, while distressful by comparison with their better-off fellow Americans, are not as bad as in Latin America. In the United States some 10–15 percent of the population lives in poverty, as against 80 percent in Brazil. In many Latin American countries the ruling elite has shown little sympathy or initiative toward changing society. In the United States there are many more opportunities for everyone, and the upper classes, while often selfish and greedy, do not oppose improvements for the rest of the population and often support these in a constructive way. The spirit in the United States is vastly different from that in Latin America. In considering liberation theology, one has to be mindful of its Latin American roots, something which is easily forgotten.[1]

One should, however, also recognize that the churches have a much broader task than exclusively preaching concern for the poor. True, the Bible is deeply concerned with the poor. But in U.S. society the rich are also in trouble. The Bible brings a message of liberation of the rich from the oppression of wealth and selfishness. Many Americans must work in large business and government organizations or bureaucracies where their own personal freedom, initiative, and innovativeness is severely curtailed in the interest of proper organization, confidentiality, or other constraints. Christ has a message for them, too. Moreover, while to many this may sound ironic, the rich often suffer from their excessive consumption, and the church has the task of inspiring them toward a simpler and more meaningful existence.

In the same vein, some will argue emphatically that liberation theology preaches only part of the many-sided Christian message. The primary news of Christian faith is the salvation brought by Jesus Christ to all people who are willing to accept him. To some, the story of the suffering and crucifixion of Christ has little to say about priority attention to the poor, and neither has the powerful message of the cosmic Christ in John 1. Even so, Karl Barth taught that Christ suffered and died for the oppressed. When seen in the broader context of the world as we experience it, these accounts give even greater force to the Bible's pervasive concern for the poor.

Cardinal Ratzinger has written extensive critiques of liberation theology. He stresses that it places a one-sided emphasis on liberation from servitude of an earthly and temporal kind and that it "seems to put liberation from sin in second place." He accuses liberation theology of reducing sin to social structures, of making the struggle for justice the whole essence of salvation, of reducing the Gospel to a purely earthly gospel. The growth of the Kingdom of God is mistakenly identified with human liberation. Ratzinger says that liberation theology questions whether Christians who belong to different social classes should share the same eucharist. The theology confuses the poor and humble of the scriptures with the proletariat of Marx.[2]

Ratzinger also says that liberation theologians (e.g., Leonardo Boff) hold that church leaders "take their origin from the people, who therefore designate ministers of their own choice in accord with the needs of their historic revolutionary mission." This reality would, of course, appear wrong to a well-established member of the Catholic clergy. However, it also reflects the democratic way in which ministers were selected in Acts, as well as the practice of the churches of the Reformation. The selection of ministers can be democratic and still receive divine guidance.

Latin American theologians will admit that they borrowed some elements from Marxist writings, but claim they did so critically (Berryman, 1987, p. 194). They are not different from many other Latin American intellectuals, who often sought refuge in Marx during the 1950s and 1960s. But the theologians would add that doing so is better than absorbing Western capitalist culture and then claiming that the church is above ideology. In their view, church officials have themselves not risen above economic ideologies. Such an accusation is correct for some officials, as well as for certain Fundamentalist preachers, but in light of the churches' economic pastorals, it is unfair as a general accusation. Gutierrez defended himself vigorously and effectively against often-false accusations; he stressed the Christian basis for his positions on social issues (Brown, 1990, ch. 6).

We can regard Latin American liberation theologians as revolutionaries who sought to be in tune with popular sentiment and experience. Their evangelical work did not fit smoothly into the church establishment. But, argues Hans Kung, such action is in line with the early Christian experience. Jesus did not found a church, as we read in the New Testament, but his life, death, and resurrection set in motion a movement which, over time, took on an institutional form (Kung, 1976, p. 198). If present forms and church organizations do not derive from Jesus himself, then there is room for other varieties. Thus, Hans Kung argues that there is no reason for excluding women from church offices.

Liberation theology set in motion a genuine reformation in the late twentieth century. Much of what is central to this theology can now be found in Catholic social teaching, as well as in contemporary Protestant pronouncements. It was foreshadowed in the documents which came out of Vatican II and reflected in Medellin 1968, the bishops' synods of 1971 and 1974, Puebla 1979, and last but not least in the encyclicals of John Paul II. (Henriot et al., 1988) The underlying theme is that there is a close link between liberation and salvation; the church must make a "preferential option for the poor" and give full respect to basic human rights, including the right to employment and food. As is clear from the 1986 U.S. Catholic bishops' pastoral letter and other teachings, the church calls for an entirely new kind of society.

10
The Role of the Catholic Church

The Catholic Church in the modern world has taught the Christian Gospel by addressing questions of economics as well as faith. It has dealt with a broad range of socioeconomic issues in the late nineteenth and the twentieth centuries, facing up to many critical issues reviewed in Part One: the causes and conditions of poverty and ways of overcoming it, labor–management relations and the role of labor in running enterprises, the social organization of the economy, the weaknesses of capitalism and socialism, and the limits of property rights. Since the 1960s it has directly addressed the problems of poverty in the developing countries, the case for development assistance, the relations between rich and poor countries, and the role of international development institutions. The church's pronouncements in this and other areas have been inspired by the message of liberation theologians, as discussed in Chapter 9.

The Bible has much to say about personal and communal behavior in the realm of economics. The church has clarified and elaborated this biblical message in its papal encyclicals and the pastoral letters of its bishops. It has given substantial testimony of its concern with the many facets of poverty and injustice; many of its institutions are exclusively dedicated to serving the poor. In its social pronouncements the church preaches and practices the Kingdom of God on earth, and expresses a special concern for the poor. A few basic principles can be distilled from the church's pronouncements, but the following list is in no way complete or exclusive:

- Each person, created in God's image, has a right to a full human life and personal dignity.
- All the earth's resources belong to God. All people have a right to share in the endowment and fruits of the earth.
- Private individuals and institutions are the primary agents in bringing about social justice.

- Government has a moral duty to defend and uplift the poor, and to supplement what private individuals and institutions do. Where necessary, the government must step in and help resolve social issues.

After reviewing the history of Catholic social teaching, we discuss some of the major Vatican statements concerning justice for the poor, and conclude by focusing on the major pastoral letter of the American bishops about the application of the church's social teaching to the United States.

A CENTURY OF SOCIAL TEACHING

The Catholic Church has a long history of speaking out for social justice. Since Pope Benedict XIV in the eighteenth century, it has been saying "No" to economic theories that divorce the workings of the economy from moral scrutiny. Church teaching has, of course, evolved over the years, addressing different economic situations and questions, such as the role of private property, labor, and management.

The 1891 encyclical of Pope Leo XIII, *"Rerum Novarum"* ("The Condition of Labor"), has become known as the Magna Carta of Catholic social teaching. Many of its themes are found in greater detail and applied to evolving labor conditions in subsequent social messages of the church (Henriot et al., 1988, p. 7). As the bishop of Perugia, Leo XIII had addressed social issues beyond the then-existing domain of the church. In *Rerum Novarum* he attacked socialism well before it had been radicalized by the Leninist revolution, but was also critical of the beliefs and practices of liberal capitalism (Novak, 1993, p. 41). In the years before this encyclical, a number of discussion groups in Europe, especially Germany, provided an input into the pope's thinking on social issues. Leo XIII spoke out against the inhuman conditions under which industrial workers were employed at the time and urged that just and equitable relationships be maintained between workers, the owners of productive capital, and government. He called for a new reform strategy, including payment of fair wages and the right of workers to join together to protect their interests, and stressed the obligation of the state to intervene where necessary to protect and secure the common good.

Leo XIII attacked socialism on several grounds. In his view, socialism opposed property rights and the freedom of individuals—

for example, the liberty of workers to dispose of their earnings as they saw fit—thus destroying the possibility of increasing their own property and their ability to improve their living conditions. Socialism also opposed marriage and the family, and denied the existence of social differentiation among people. In retrospect, Leo XIII's views on socialism were prescient.

Forty years after *Rerum Novarum,* the world was experiencing the social upheavals of the Great Depression and the Nazi takeover of Germany. In his *Quadragesimo Anno,* the encyclical written to celebrate the fortieth anniversary of *Rerum Novarum,* Pope Pius XI addressed the social justice issues of his time and presented a modern perception of the just wage: If fathers are not receiving wages sufficient to support their families "under existing circumstances, social justice demands that changes be introduced in the system as soon as possible, whereby such a wage will be assured to every adult working man" (Novak, 1993, p. 73). In commenting on the concept of a "just wage," many economists point out that it is an ethical, not an economic, concept and that there is no economic justification for this concept.

The rebirth of the church under John XXIII in the 1960s also gave it new strength to face up to the ever-changing issues of social injustice and poverty. John XXIII internationalized Catholic social teaching and for the first time dealt with the situation in countries that are not fully industrialized, addressing questions of justice between nations in different stages of development and of aid to less developed areas ("*Mater et Magistra*" ["Christianity and Social Progress"], 1961).

In 1965 the Second Vatican Council issued "*Gaudium et Spes*" ("The Church in the Modern World"), seen by many as the most important document in the Catholic social tradition. The people of God must scrutinize the "signs of the times" in the light of the Gospel. Technological and social changes characterize the world and provide both wonderful opportunities and worrisome difficulties for the spread of the Gospel.[1] In the economic sphere, the council stressed that human labor is superior to other elements of economic life; economic activity detrimental to the worker is wrong and inhuman. Workers should participate in running enterprises. God intended the earth for everyone; private property should benefit all. Public authorities must guard against those misuses of private property that hurt the common good. All have a right to goods sufficient for themselves and their families (Henriot et al., 1988, p. 49).

Since the council, the church has addressed major issues in contemporary economic society, including the role of labor and capital, and the special problems confronting the poorest countries.

JOHN PAUL II ON LABOR AND CAPITAL

John Paul II has played a major role on the world scene, especially in the transition from communism to a freer society in Eastern Europe. His contacts with his native Poland were of crucial importance to its liberation from communism. He has developed and deepened the church's views on social issues. He showed his concern with the respective roles of labor and capital in *"Laborem Exercens"* ("On Human Work," 1981) and *"Centesimus Annus"* (1991), written to commemorate, respectively, the 90th and 100th anniversary of *"Rerum Novarum."* On the other hand, John Paul II has not broken new ground on population issues and the role of women in church and society, two areas that are critical in social–economic policy. In his views on the productive process in contemporary society, Pope John Paul II regards labor as cocreator with capital; from a moral vantage point, labor operates on the same level as capital. Two points in *Laborem Exercens* are especially important.

First, he stresses the humanity of labor and objects to the treatment of labor as merchandise or an impersonal agent of production, which clearly conflicts with the biblical concept of human beings created in the image of God (par. 9). Such inferior treatment of labor is also a curse in many American managers' way of looking at their workforce as something to buy at the cheapest price, rather than being treated as part of the total production team to be trained and developed in the interest of the enterprise, as is more common in Germany and Japan (Lester Thurow, 1992, pp. 51–55).

Second, labor policy must aim at full employment, with unemployment benefits provided when the goal of full employment is not reached. Employment is a right of all human beings and should help to reduce the prevailing differences in living standards. In line with the church's earlier position on the just wage, the pope again called for just remuneration of work, wages sufficient to support a family, including social benefits (health care, leisure, pension, accident insurance, and a decent work environment), as well as allowances for mothers who are raising a family (par. 19).

The church is firmly committed to solidarity with workers, "for she considers it to be her mission to be truly the Church of the Poor." In the social conflicts persisting today there is a need for a system that will reconcile labor and capital. Moreover, the right to property is not absolute, should not be a basis for exploitation, and is subordinated to the right of common use.

The church's first major social pronouncement after the breakdown of communism in the former Soviet Union, "*Centesimus Annus*" (1991), discusses the weaknesses of both capitalism and socialism. It directs itself to the social conditions in the developing countries and Eastern Europe, as well as in the industrialized countries of the West. Its theology affirms the "preferential option for the poor." It mentions the issue of widespread poverty in the Third World and discusses the nature of poverty in the industrialized countries, the debt problem, and environmental concerns. It also takes a strong position in favor of human rights and against totalitarianism, especially in its Marxist guise.

Critics from the right such as Michael Novak, a leading ethicist in the American Enterprise Institute, welcomed the recognition in this papal pronouncement of the importance of free markets as "the most efficient instrument for utilizing resources and effectively responding to needs."[2] Right-wing commentators generally endorsed the encyclical, in contrast to their earlier criticism of the Vatican's reservations about the workings of capitalism. However, the encyclical devotes considerable space to outlining ethical and social safeguards on the workings of capitalism. It views the market as a *juridical structure* for accommodating transactions, not an unlimited instrument nor an overarching framework for society. Private property is subject to social limitations and encumbered by a social mortgage.[3]

The letter specifically associates the problems of alienation in our society with excessive emphasis on acquiring goods and treating workers as merely productive agents rather than human beings. The pope has strong misgivings about the emphasis on consumption (consumerism) in Western economies.

Finally, the encyclical elaborates the importance of human freedom in our society. It denounces systematic antichildbearing campaigns which often subject people "to intolerable pressures," based on a distorted view of the demographic problem and presented in a climate of "absolute lack of respect for the freedom of choice of the parties involved." The letter brings out the tension between personal freedom and the social need for constraining population growth. The encyclical views economic freedom as "only one form of human freedom. When it becomes autonomous, when man is seen more as a producer or consumer of goods than as a subject who produces and consumes in order to live, then economic freedom loses its necessary relationship to the human person and ends up by alienating and oppressing him" (par. 39).

The Vatican's view of what determines a just economic system has general applicability in both industrialized and developing countries. The church has, however, also addressed the specific problems of developing countries.

THE CHURCH AND THE POOREST COUNTRIES

In the 1960s the church deepened its social teaching on international development issues. We already saw that John XXIII, as part of the rebirth of the church, addressed development problems in *"Mater et Magistra"* (1961). Later in that decade Paul VI issued *"Populorum Progressio"* ("Development of People," 1967), which focused exclusively on questions of international development and turned the church's full attention to the poorest countries in a comprehensive and understanding manner. Twenty years later, John Paul II updated the church's teaching on development with *"Sollicitudo Rei Socialis"* ("On Social Concerns," 1987). The strong support for the development of poor nations evident in these encyclicals is both significant and encouraging for the cause of international justice.

Populorum Progressio expressed social policy views that were widely accepted at the time, such as the limitations of the market (especially for raw materials and other LDC exports), the need for special measures in support of industrialization, the crucial role of planning in setting development and budget priorities, the case for a more equal income distribution, and the importance of coordination and mobilization of international assistance. The moral ground for development is that God gives the earth's wealth to *all people* and does not want rich countries to monopolize its resources. The church did not support boundless, absolute private property or unchecked "liberalism" leading to the "international imperialism of money," and was deeply concerned with the growing gap between rich and poor countries. Narrowing this gap is urgent and calls for extensive reform. In the development process, the rich countries have an obligation to help the LDCs, and must also welcome and assist immigrants from poor countries.

Both *Populorum Progressio* and *Sollicitudo Rei Socialis* draw attention to the deeper meaning of development and perceive development economics in a wider social and ethical context. The church sees personal conversion, turning a heart of stone into flesh, as critical to overcoming obstacles to development. It observes, with some optimism, an increased awareness of the violations of human rights and a wider recognition of the interdependence of human beings. The 1987 encyclical carries the personal imprint of John Paul II: it explicitly recognizes the right of the poor to oppose an inefficient government, a view that could be based on the pope's earlier experience in Poland. Situations of serious governmental inefficiency have also arisen under some Latin American dictatorships.

The encyclicals establish a strong link between Christian thinking about the individual on one hand and development of people on the other. This link overrides concern of the rich with their own position and wealth, and must open them to the interests of the poor. There is ample moral ground for this view, since in Christ all people are one and recognize their common bond with God. *Sollicitudo* quotes Lk 4: 18–19, where Jesus at the start of his ministry sets out to "preach good news to the poor, proclaim release to the captives and recovery of sight to the blind."

The letter also condemns the arms race (par. 23 and 24). *Populorum Progressio* had called for conversion of military to development expenditures. Many other writers had held that a reduction in military expenditures would free funds for raising the productivity of the poor (e.g., Melman, 1985, ch. 5). Unfortunately, the arms reductions of the early 1990s were not accompanied by larger aid to the developing countries.

Finally, the letter observes that the widening gap between rich and poor poses a moral dilemma. Genuine development, of course, involves more than raising per capita incomes; it entails an improvement in the quality of life, including the environment, health, and education, which may not be fully reflected in conventional national income data. As a matter of mere statistics, an increase in the income gap is almost unavoidable, unless the income level of the rich countries were to come down significantly. A rising gap in the absolute figures for per capita income is almost always going to occur because the rich countries start from a much higher base.

The encyclical identifies several areas where the developing countries had been falling behind—in particular, housing, employment creation, and external indebtedness. The encyclical's assessment of development performance could have been made more realistic by giving explicit recognition to some major economic trends in the past thirty years—for example, the quantum increase in financial integration between the developing and industrialized countries and the much greater emphasis on market-related policies in several countries, notably in China and the middle-income debtor nations. Many countries have been under pressure to reduce their public sector deficits by cutting consumer subsidies and placing state enterprises on an autonomous financial footing. The burden of large external deficits has induced countries to become more efficient through greater attention to competitiveness and bringing their domestic prices in line with those prevailing on international markets.

The Vatican's objection to abortion brings out forcefully the rights of young, even unborn, human life. It took a clear position at the 1994 Cairo Conference on Population and Development. But its strong ethical case does not weaken the need for slowing population growth in the poorest countries, nor is it meant to undermine the case for improving the education of women, who play a key role in bringing down the birthrate. Actual progress in reducing population growth has already been considerable, caused by both economic and social factors, and supported by improved access to contraceptive means. But this progress has bypassed many of the poorest countries, which are actually in greatest need to cut back the birthrate. In these poorest countries, economic development and environmental protection must go hand-in-hand with effective population policy. Wider access to preventive means will also reduce the demand for abortion, which most would like to do without in any case. Greater freedom and better education for women and girls is a basic tenet of population policy and economic development, and should also be supported on ethical grounds.

The church makes a strong appeal on moral grounds in favor of development assistance. Today such appeals are usually greeted with indifference, if not hostility. In fact, aid from the industrialized countries has remained relatively stagnant at a low 0.35 percent of GNP, although a few countries (e.g., the Netherlands and Sweden) are contributing about 1 percent of their GNP, the target level originally set by the OECD (the Organization for Economic Cooperation and

Development, the industrialized countries' club headquartered in Paris) for its members. We may well ask why neither moral nor economic appeals have had much effect. Among the economic reasons, one can point to the realization that development is a slow process, often held back by poor policies and official graft in the LDCs; the view, expressed by P.T. Bauer (1981) among others, that development aid politicizes life in the LDCs by supporting overgrown government bureaucracies at the expense of market forces and the private sector; the intensification of conflicts between industrialized and developing countries, following the 1973 oil shock; and, starting from the 1970s, the increased role of private financial markets.

Both encyclicals express the church's priority concern for the poor. But they run the risk of overemphasizing the role of aid provided by the rich countries, in that aid necessarily plays but a marginal role. Genuine development starts at home and requires deep sacrifice by the developing countries, a view that appears to be missing in the pastorals. The past twenty years have thrown new light on the sources of development, especially the importance of the private sector. The economics embodied in the church pronouncements correctly emphasizes the role of government, but tends to shortchange the critical contribution of private capital, financial integration, and the role of markets in mobilizing and allocating resources.

In these encyclicals the Vatican is doing a genuine service to the international development effort by demonstrating the power and scope of the church's message and the care with which it must be applied in a complex and often technical environment. The American Catholic bishops in turn have made their own unique and powerful case for social justice in the United States.

THE CATHOLIC BISHOPS IN THE UNITED STATES: ECONOMIC JUSTICE FOR ALL

The U.S. bishops' pastoral letter, "Economic Justice for All: Catholic Social Teaching and the U.S. Economy," (EJA) is perhaps the most comprehensive church document dealing with justice in the American economy. It reviews biblical theology and ethics in relation to issues of poverty and injustice in our society, and focuses on selected policy topics. Archbishop Rembert Weakland of Milwaukee chaired the bishops' drafting committee and was the principal author of the pastoral letter.[4]

This basic pastoral letter followed the bishops' work on a peace message ("The Challenge of Peace: God's Promise and Our Response," 1983) that brought a religious perspective to peace issues, dealt with the use and deterrence of nuclear weapons, and recommended specific steps to promote peace. The bishops wanted to write in similar detail on the issues confronting capitalism, and decided that rather than speaking in general terms they would address them in an American context. It took three years of drafting followed by three more years of hearings and redrafting to complete this economic justice pastoral, much longer than the peace pastoral, which was started at the same time but completed in three years. It was drafted in a comprehensive and intense process of consultation and collaboration among many Catholic and other experts, including economists, representatives from other churches, Jewish groups, socially concerned institutions, business, and labor. Earlier drafts or the final version of the letter were welcomed by a number of Protestant churches, as well as the Central Conference of American Rabbis (1985).

Founded on the Christian view that government is good, instituted by God, the letter was discussed in depth at a time when conservatives stood for dismantling many of the arrangements for assisting the poor and for a hands-off government which left society to the free and unregulated play of the market. Everyone interested in social justice issues would benefit from reading this economic pastoral in its entirety.

The pastoral has drawn worldwide interest and inspired bishops in many other countries to address their flock on matters of social policy. A 1993 colloquium in Freiburg, Switzerland, brought together experts from everywhere to consider the unifying theme of some 1,149 bishops' statements issued in various countries on ethics, economics, and development, written since the American 1986 pastoral. It deals directly with the economic consequences and policy implications of the bishops' ethical views, and advocates job opportunities, a key factor in fighting poverty, although the final version of the pastoral did not set specific targets for full employment. Macroeconomic policies must be supplemented by measures in such fields as housing, health, and education (Douglass, 1988; Gannon, 1987). Because of its unique importance, we will comment in some detail on what the pastoral implies for economic policies at home and abroad.

The central theme of the U.S. bishops' pastoral is that the poor should receive priority in the national agenda, in one's view of society, and in shaping economic and international policies. In its theology the letter explains the biblical basis for the priority attention to be given to the poor. In focusing on poverty problems, it analyzes and gives guidelines for appropriate policy action in several areas, such as unemployment, the causes and nature of poverty, the farm economy, and U.S. policies toward the developing countries.

Theological Basis

The biblical theology in the letter stresses that the dignity of the human person, realized in community with others, is the criterion against which all aspects of human life and public policy must be measured. The Bible castigates worship of idols, unrestrained power, and desire for great wealth. From earliest times the church has affirmed that misuse of the world's resources or appropriation of them by a minority of the world's population betrays the gift of creation, since "whatever belongs to God belongs to all." In this view, care for the poor is closely akin to care for the environment.

Every person is created in the image of God. The denial of dignity to a person is a blot on his image. Creation is a gift to all people, not to be appropriated for the benefit of a few. The same God who came to the aid of an oppressed people and formed them into a covenant community continues to hear the cries of the oppressed and creates communities which are to hear his word.

Love is at the center of justice: *there is no justice without love.* As spoken by Jesus, the great commandment is: "You shall love God with your whole heart, mind, and soul," and he adds: "You shall love your neighbour as yourself" (Mk 12: 28–34). In the final judgment (Mt. 25: 31–46), the blessed are those who fed the hungry, gave drink to the thirsty, welcomed the stranger, clothed the naked, and visited the sick and imprisoned. The cursed are those who neglected these works of mercy and love. Neglecting the poor, the outcast, and the oppressed is rejecting Jesus himself.

Jesus warns his followers against greed and reliance on abundant possessions. He underscores this by the parable of the man whose life is snatched away at the very moment he tries to secure his wealth (Lk 12: 13–21). Luke portrays Jesus as living like a poor man; he, like the prophets, takes the side of the poor and warns of the dangers of wealth. This is also confirmed in the Lazarus story (Lk 16: 19–31).

From the earliest stages of Israel's traditions through the later literature and into the New Testament, there is "a constant refrain that the poor must be cared for and protected, and that when they are exploited, God hears their cries." Great wealth is a constant danger. The rich are wise in their own eyes (Prov 28: 11) and are prone to apostasy and idolatry (Am 5: 4–13, Isa 2: 6–8), as well as to violence and oppression. "Since the poor in the biblical sense are not blinded by wealth or tempted to make it into an idol, they are open to God's presence and their human powerlessness makes them a model of those who trust in God alone" (EJA, par 49).

The perspectives expressed by the bishops emphasize the "preferential option for the poor" as put forward by Liberation Theology (see ch. 9). In its attention to the poor, the Bible sets powerful ethical norms for economic life and calls for action to enable the marginalized poor to participate actively in our society. The common good demands justice for all. Moreover, basic human rights extend to the rights of life, food, clothing, shelter, rest, medical care, and basic education. The rights of political freedom must be supplemented by a guarantee of economic rights in an order that assures "minimum conditions of human dignity in the economic sphere for every person" (par. 70–95).

View of the U.S. Economy

The letter's brief and clear description of the U.S. economy applies "economics in which people count." It emphasizes the darker side of the economy, much to the chagrin of the advocates of right-wing policies. The American economy, it points out, has been a marvel of productivity and growth, with the free operation of markets a principal instrument of economic development. However, the market must be supported or constrained and regulated where it does not function properly or has harmful effects. The bishops observe that not all are prosperous and there are many special problems. Many working families are close to the poverty level. Black, hispanic, and other minorities bear a disproportionate share of these burdens of poverty. Poverty problems are reinforced by the effects of *increased global interdependence* of the U.S. economy, including the loss of many manufacturing jobs and the rise in low-wage service jobs. All these problems, however, are merely symptomatic of a deeper need for finding meaning and value in human work and a more equitable form of global interdependence.

Selected Economic Policy Issues

For an economist a crucial question is, of course, how moral teachings can be translated into feasible and achievable policy proposals and actions. The bishops must have realized this for they, like some of their Protestant colleagues, have made a number of proposals in the economic sphere. They recognize that they necessarily speak with less authority on economics than on ethics. But they nevertheless invite discussion of their economic views. They selected four crucial issues for closer consideration: unemployment, poverty, the farm problem, and U.S. relations with the developing countries.

Unemployment, at some 7 percent of the labor force, was of special concern at the time the pastoral was written. The bishops point to the debilitating impact of unemployment, and consider the steps that might be taken to counteract it (par. 136–169). In the mid-1990s the upswing of the U.S. economy, bolstered by judicious monetary and fiscal policies and greater government attention to job creation, brought unemployment down to well below 6 percent. But even at lower rates of unemployment, fundamental issues remain. African-Americans, other minorities, and women suffer most; persistent discrimination makes problems worse. The demand for jobs has been affected by demographic factors such as population increase, immigration and the rise of women in the workforce. The availability of jobs to the poor as well as to broad layers of the middle class and professionals is curtailed by restructuring and technological factors. International competition has caused many plant closings, with adverse effects on the people and communities concerned.

Looking back, in 1970–1985 the economy created some 20 million new jobs, but there continued to be a chronic shortage of work opportunities. Failure to invest sufficiently in certain industries and regions, inadequate training and education for new workers, and insufficient mechanisms to assist workers displaced by new technology have all added to the unemployment problem. It has taken time for the public and private sectors to recognize these issues as major concerns.

The bishops call for macroeconomic and more specific measures, stressing the importance of full employment supplemented by special attention to education, health, and housing along lines set forth in Chapter 1. They highlight the ethical aspects of their policy advocacy, which calls for a consensus that everyone has a right to employment, with the task of securing full employment falling on all: policy makers, business, labor, and the general public. New employment strategies can make further contributions to these objectives. Job sharing, flex time, and a reduced workweek are among the possibilities that should be examined, along with discouragement of excessive use of part-time workers who do not receive fringe benefits. Other possibilities are education and training for those hard to employ, and affirmative action to assist those excluded by racial or gender discrimination.

Guidelines for Antipoverty Action

The bishops make several observations on questions of personal and social behavior that complement the discussion of economic issues in Chapter 1. They emphasize that taking control of one's own life is fundamental to overcoming poverty. Moreover, alleviating poverty "will require fundamental changes in social and economic structures that perpetuate glaring inequalities and cut off millions of citizens from full participation in the economy and social life of our country" (par. 187–215).

Government and private citizens must each play a role, working in tandem. This will work best when private action is fully committed in the fight against poverty. But where the private sector does not make an effective contribution, or where it obstructs the objective of social justice, the government has an obvious need to supplement the involvement of private citizens (Briefs, 1988, p. 70). As also stated by Pope John Paul II in *Centesimus Annus*, the bishops reaffirm that their policy guidelines flow from neither a capitalist nor a Marxist conception, nor do they advocate a third middle way (par. 128–129).

The bishops point to many symptoms of a punitive attitude toward the poor. There is a widespread attitude that stigmatizes the poor, exaggerates the benefits received by them, and inflates the amounts of fraud in welfare. The belief persists that the poor are poor by choice or through laziness, that anyone can escape poverty by hard work, and that welfare programs make it easier for people to avoid work.

The first line of attack against poverty must be to build and sustain a healthy economy that provides job opportunities at just wages for all adults who are able to work. Moreover, vigorous action should be undertaken to remove barriers to full and equal employment opportunities for women and minorities.

Self-help efforts among the poor should be fostered by programs and policies in both the public and private sectors. An effective way to attack poverty is through programs that are small in scale, locally based, and oriented toward empowering the poor to become self-sufficient. "Poor people should be empowered to take charge of their own future and become responsible for their own economic advancement" (EJA, par. 201).

The tax system should be evaluated in terms of its effect on the poor. Does it raise adequate revenues to pay for the public needs of the poor? Is it progressive, do the richer people pay a higher share of their income? The poor themselves should not have to pay any income taxes.

The pastoral also took a close look at *the complex social and economic conditions in American agriculture* (par. 216–50). Led in this area by Bishop George Speltz of St. Cloud, Minn., the bishops expressed concern for the predicament of the family farm and the increased concentration of landownership, the environmental dangers associated with increased production, the decline of farms owned by African-Americans, the low pay of American farm workers, the especially difficult problems faced by migrant workers, and the consequences of urban pressure on American agricultural resources.

The International System: U.S. Policies toward the Developing Countries

Overriding concern for world poverty and the poor must govern U.S. foreign policy and, in particular, U.S. relations with the developing countries. Writing before the massive breakdown of the Soviet system, the bishops called for a drastic shift in U.S. foreign policy, which for years had been dominated by security considerations. But although East–West tensions have now eased, security continues as a major concern, in a general sense or with regard to regions of special interest such as the Persian Gulf. Putting the poor first proves to be difficult in practice.

In the view of the bishops, the United States must give greater priority to international development assistance, and should in this area assume leadership rather than be a laggard. It has for years been in the embarrassing position of being the richest country but making the smallest contribution to international development.

The pastoral stresses that half a billion people suffering from hunger makes it an especially urgent issue. Relief from hunger must be part of a broader strategy to attack poverty. Studies have shown that mass hunger—e.g., in India—has occurred not because of a lack of food but because of an absence of storage and transport facilities needed to bring food to areas stricken by shortages (The World Bank Policy Study, Feb. 1986). In this context, the bishops draw attention to the connection between hunger and rapid population growth and to the need for population planning. They rightly consider that population issues must be dealt with in a broad social setting. One might add that it should be raised not merely in the context of food, but more generally as part of an attack on poverty.[5]

The bishops end their discussion of U.S. relations with the LDCs with some observations of U.S. responsibilities for reform of the international system. But they also point to some of the many things the developing countries can do for themselves: streamline bureaucracies, improve the allocation of public resources, stop capital flight, and modify price discrimination against rural areas. There is a strong case for policies that make the distribution of income and wealth more equal within the developing countries themselves.

Turning to the contributions the United States can make, the pastoral pays special attention to the use the United States can make of its own economic power for the benefit of the eradication of poverty and the curtailment of sales of military weapons to the developing countries. There exists a sharp disparity between expenditures for military and development purposes. The United States alone budgets much (perhaps twenty times) more for defense as for foreign assistance, and two-thirds of the latter includes military assistance. The LDCs themselves waste enormous funds on their military. The bishops call on the United States to take the lead in seeking an international agreement on arms sales.

In conclusion, the bishops realize that the preferential option for the poor requires considerable sacrifice on the part of the richer countries in the restructuring of international relations. For the United States it would mean that the sacrifices it has brought in the past to extend foreign assistance and provide food for the hungry would be matched by a similar effort for establishing a juster world order today. The bishops call for "a U.S. international economic policy designed to empower people everywhere and enable them to continue to develop a sense of their own worth, improve the quality of their lives and ensure that the benefits of economic growth are shared equitably."

The church has clearly defined the moral issues in the allocation of public resources. In all, the U.S. bishops outlined the major issues of poverty in the midst of much prosperity in our wealthy society and called for a range of policy measures that should be given serious consideration in any comprehensive attack on poverty. They substantially complemented the Vatican statements on social justice issues and applied them to the situation in the United States. Many of their views can be found in the statements of Protestant churches, to which we turn next.

11
Views in Mainline Protestantism

Protestants have expressed their concern with a broad range of economic issues. Starting in the early twentieth century, they addressed questions of labor conditions and strife, including the right to strike and the length of the workday. They pointed to the slowness of overall growth and the need for creating job opportunities, the feminization of poverty, the special problems of housing and health, and the consequences of military programs, as well as questions of environmental stewardship and world hunger. They also drew attention to the moral base of our economic organization, the desirability of the American free-enterprise system, and the importance of equal opportunity.

It is a sign of our times that we can classify the several Protestant churches in America by their stand on social policy issues. "Mainline Protestant" churches are those that have applied their theology to the social–economic problems of our society and taken positions on such issues as unemployment, poverty, discrimination by race and gender, the consequences of excessive military expenditure and, more recently, environmental degradation. On the other hand, the so-called Evangelical and Fundamentalist churches are often characterized by a more right-wing orientation that pays less attention to poverty problems and racial or gender discrimination in the United States.

But there are many gradations that blur this simple classification. As is clear from their theological reasoning, the statements by the mainline churches, like those of the Catholic Church, are evangelical in that their position on social issues is rooted in the Bible. And not all "Evangelicals" are silent on social questions. Some Evangelical groups are explicitly concerned with poverty and other social issues. This is true for Jim Wallis' Sojourners, the Evangelicals for Social Action, and the Association for Public Justice, as well as other groups and individuals in the more fundamentalist churches. President Carter, a Southern Baptist, was clearly concerned with human rights. In his "retirement" he has helped to settle critical international disputes and has been active in housing for the poor. Yet the Southern Baptist Convention itself does not appear to have spoken out on poverty and discrimination in our society.

The mainline church statements of the 1980s and 1990s bear the fruits of work in preceding decades. For a historical perspective on these pronouncements, it is useful to look at the churches' earlier views, starting with the Social Creed of 1908.

THE SOCIAL GOSPEL AND SUBSEQUENT ACTIONS

The current positions of the mainline churches were anticipated in the views of the Gospel that emerged around 1900. In 1908 the Federal Council of the Churches of Christ in America (FCC) adopted the "Social Creed of the Church," according to which the churches "must stand for equal rights and complete justice for all men in all stations of life" and "for the most equitable division on the product of industry that can ultimately be devised." The creed reflected the views of various theologians, such as Josiah Strong, Shailer Matthews, Washington Gladden, and particularly Walter Rauschenbusch. From the start the Social Gospel has been unjustly accused of emphasizing the socioeconomic applications of the Gospel at the expense of the message of faith and personal salvation. The leaders of the Social Gospel were well aware of the necessity of individual redemption; they called for an evangelism that would transform society itself (Bennett et al., 1954, p. 8). For example, in his "Christianity and the Social Crisis," Rauschenbusch (1907, pp. 47–48) did not view Jesus as a social reformer, but pointed to the real secret of Jesus' life: that he knew the Father. In turn, all people need to live as children in the presence of their Father. Rauschenbusch dealt with questions of personal orientation and stressed that the life of selfishness and chafing ambition is no life at all—people must enter into a new world of love and solidarity as well as inward contentment.

The Social Gospel also expressed views on labor–management relations in the progressive era. The "Social Creed" was amended in 1912 to recognize the rights of employers and employees to organize and enter into collective bargaining (Bennett, et al., 1954, p. 6). In 1919 the Social Gospel theologians sought to face up to urgent and practical issues. The Commission on Inquiry of the Inter-Church World Movement dealt with the 1919 steel strike and called for an eight-hour shift in continuous processes, a ten-hour day, and a six-day workweek of fifty-four hours. It also recommended the right of steelworkers to join regular craft unions and advised that unions be reorganized to share in the responsibility for production and in the control of production processes.

Shortly after the steel strike, the theologians took on a more general issue: What kind of society would emerge if Christian ideals were in fact realized? The 1920 report of the Committee on the War and Religious Outlook envisaged "a cooperative social order" in which life was regarded as sacred and everyone could find opportunity for the fullest self-expression.

Following up on the work of the Social Gospel theologians, the FCC made a major effort to deepen ethical thinking about economic issues in the early 1950s. A group of ethicists and economists prepared comprehensive studies of "Christian Values and Economic Life" which covered a wide territory: freedom, organization, justice, the high level of consumption, the role of love in society, human dignity, well-being and survival, etc.[1] The ethicists involved, such as John Bennett, Reinhold Niebuhr, and Methodist Bishop Oxnam were well ahead of their economist counterparts. They articulated critical social justice issues, equality of opportunity, and the consequences of the interconnectedness of people everywhere. Strange to a modern reader, the papers by the participating economists did not focus on any particular social issue, with the exception of international policy. Surprisingly, after the economic upheavals of the 1930s, there is only marginal mention of economic security and the key role of full employment in the economic system; there is scant attention to questions of poverty and none to the problems of racial minorities or single mothers. Thus the economic papers do not reflect the views of many prominent economists like Paul A. Samuelson of MIT, James Tobin of Yale, Lawrence Klein of Chicago and Pennsylvania, and Alvin Hansen of Harvard. The effort did, however, benefit from the participation of Kenneth E. Boulding, a well-known economics professor at the University of Michigan, who wrote widely on questions of ethics and economics. As part of the FCC studies of the early 1950s, he contributed "Economic Progress as a Goal of Economic Life" (Ward, 1953, pp. 52–83).

Boulding points to the dynamic role in society of progressive religions stressing "conversion" or "convincement," including the Protestant Reformation, the Catholic Counterreformation, Quakers, and Methodists. On the other hand, when a religion gets "old," when it comes to rely on the coercive power of the family or of the state and loses its "prophetic" quality, it acts as a damper on change of any kind and on economic progress in particular. In Boulding's view, "the greatest enemy of change is the spirit of orthodoxy, the feeling that the fundamental problems of life have been solved and embodied in writing or organization, and that the main task of each generation is to transmit this solution to the next" (op. cit., p. 61).

According to Boulding, the emphasis of Protestant and Evangelical Christianity on conversion, on individual enterprise in religion, and on the virtues of industriousness, punctuality, thrift, honesty, truthfulness, etc. played a key role in the capitalist revolution. The conversion experience, a radical change in the character of the individual, gives a positive value to change which carries over into all spheres of life. In his view, the individual's responsibility to make peace with God in an unmediated religious experience gives a positive value to enterprise, including economic undertakings. And the emphasis on personal integrity made possible a vast extension of interpersonal relationships in the system of finance, which, while it may be deficient in charity, is based firmly on faith and hope. From this affirmation of the advantages and strength of the capitalist system followed Bishop Oxnam's view, probably shared by most of his fellow theologians, that the American free-enterprise system is by far the best we know for productivity, creativity, and freedom (op. cit., p. 23).

The FCC studies appear well ahead of the views on social ethics held by churches' membership (Bennett et al., 1954, p. 238). Nevertheless, with the hindsight of several decades, the churches expressed little awareness of trends emerging in the 1950s, as, for example, the social consequences of the sexual revolution, threats to the family as a pivotal institution, threats to freedom by McCarthyism, and the consequences of black migration to Northern cities. The churches also refrained from addressing the problems of the family. They seemed to accept as truth the picture of the typical family shown on the Ozzie and Harriet TV show at the time, an antiseptic world of idealized homes in an unflawed America (Halberstam, 1993, p. 508). One wonders whether the church leaders realized that many families were rapidly becoming dysfunctional.

The churches demonstrated their naive view of American life in their attitude toward studies of human sexuality. They protested Alfred Kinsey's study, "Sexual Behavior in the Human Male," when it first appeared in 1949. To Kinsey's surprise, he had enraged not only conservative Protestants and Catholics, but also the most powerful persons in the liberal Protestant clergy—for example, Henry Pitney Van Dusen, head of Union Theological Seminary; ethicist Reinhold Niebuhr, also at Union; Harry Emerson Fosdick of New York's Riverside Church; and Harold Dodds, president of Princeton. Because of his study of sexual patterns, Kinsey, himself a sober and dedicated scientist, was accused of trying to lower our moral standards. In 1953 Dean Rusk, head of the Rockefeller Foundation, refused further support for Kinsey's institute (op. cit., pp. 272–81).

The civil rights struggle of the 1960s blew new life into the churches' social action. The National Council of Churches (NCC), successor to the FCC, had substantial involvement in several areas, as is evident from its statements on the status of women (1972), antipoverty programs (1966), world poverty (1968), human hunger and the world food crisis (1975), and special responsibility toward Africa (1956). Additional NCC statements, referred to earlier, concerned the role of women in society and the consequences of American military programs. These statements foreshadowed in many ways the message that the churches brought in the 1980s and 1990s.

THE TESTIMONY OF THE CHURCHES

Each mainline church, while drawing on the same biblical sources, speaks from its own tradition and with its own voice. We highlight the main points made by the individual denominations and give some background on their work. The comments concern statements published since World War II, but mostly in the 1980s and 1990s.

The denominations addressed a wide variety of issues. To meet these issues they consider many different policies, with primary emphasis on job opportunities and bringing the poor into the mainstream.

We will first review the positions taken by the Episcopal and Methodist churches, both of whom addressed their members on several specific issues. This is followed by a discussion of the United Church of Christ and the Presbyterian Church, which prepared comprehensive statements, and of the Reformed Church in America. The review concludes with a look at the message of the Lutherans, who spoke out on several social issues, starting early in the post-World War II period.

The Episcopalians: The Bottom Line Is People

The General Convention of the Episcopal Church passed many resolutions on social policy—for example, concerning AIDS victims, sexual issues, alcoholism, welfare reform, antipoverty action, low-cost housing, and nuclear deterrence.

In 1987 some eighty Episcopal bishops gave a succinct yet complete overview of poverty and other injustice issues ("Economic Justice and the Christian Conscience," October 1987). They were concerned with slow overall growth, unemployment, the extent of urban and rural poverty, hunger, health care, and the feminization of poverty. They urged clergy and laity to reflect on the moral issues that confront them by focusing on God's judgment against oppression wherever it is encountered; rebuilding a sense of community; entering into the pain of those who are poor or afflicted and joining them in the struggle for justice; challenging the systemic causes of poverty; recognizing the value of labor, not as a commodity but as a worthy contributor to production; and advocating anew the responsibility of government as an instrument of the people in the struggle to assure economic justice for all.

The Episcopal bishops closely aligned themselves with the Catholic bishops' pastoral letter "Economic Justice for All," and emphasized the moral base of their appeal for economic justice: "We have suggested throughout this document that we believe our economic problems persist not so much because of fiscal imponderables as because we lack the moral will as a people to reorder our priorities. We could, if we wished, refashion our American life so as to produce a decent life for all. Our inability to do just that derives from a lack of common consensus on those human priorities which ought to undergird economic decision-making. To help create such a consensus, we believe Christians and other people of good-will should rise up and say 'loud and clear that the bottom line is people'" (Episcopal Church, 1987, p. 17).

The Methodists: Putting Grace before Works

The Methodists, with a history of making social declarations going back to 1908, also issued statements on a broad range of topics, including the rights of women, agricultural policy, hunger, housing, and environmental stewardship. The church is strongly interested in giving guidance on social issues to its large membership, 12 million in the United States and 54 million worldwide.[2]

Certain basic themes recur in these Methodist statements, in particular that *"we do not hold poor people morally responsible for their economic status"* (our italics). J. Philip Wogaman, ethicist at Wesley Theological Seminary and now senior minister of Foundry United Methodist Church in Washington D.C., describes how in our social relations we should *"put grace before works."* The way we treat our fellow human beings should reflect how God treats us:

"If justice is patterned in accordance with the priority of grace, then economic goods should be produced and distributed in such a way as to enhance human well-being and self-acceptance and communal fellow feeling without asking first whether people have deserved what they receive."

"We are brothers and sisters in a moral community because we are the family of God. God's love is the 'given' with which we start." "For he makes his sun to shine on bad and good people alike, and gives rain to those who do right and those who do wrong" (Math 5: 45); and each of us "must be able to function as a member of the community." Ultimately we are one family in God (Wogaman, 1986, pp. 34, 35, and 40).

The practical question which all ethical belief must address is what economic policy will make it possible for our principle to be fulfilled. Wogaman believes that social policy is needed to counteract our self-centeredness. A real community is based on mutual love, not on mutual self-interest. As a comment, we may add that these observations are a judgment against the widely prevailing job insecurity of today, as well as the keenly felt competitiveness in our contemporary workplace (op. cit., p. 41). Wogaman's views are echoed in Michael Lerner's "The Politics of Meaning" (1996).

In "The Great Economic Debate Continues," Wogaman comments that "economics should sufficiently ground our physical existence and sufficiently enable all people to participate meaningfully in the life of the community." The basic values in Christian economics hold that our physical existence itself is good; hence we must provide for our basic needs, such as food, clothing, housing, and health, and thus create material prosperity. Moreover, the way we produce and distribute goods and services can have a substantial effect on our relationships with God and other people; the poor have been excluded from our economic community in a number of ways. Our contemporary American culture is at cross purposes with Christian faith, since it is excessively materialistic and overvalues economic accomplishments.[3]

The papers put out by the other mainline churches are written in the same spirit as those issued by the Methodists and Episcopalians. This is clear from the comprehensive papers on social issues published by the United Church of Christ and the Presbyterian church, to which we now turn.

The United Church of Christ: A Just Peace and a Job for Everyone

A relatively small but highly diverse denomination, with about 1.5 million members, the United Church of Christ (UCC) has often taken forthright liberal positions on issues of social justice. Its synod has a record of calling for social action in different areas, including recognition of the People's Republic of China (1959), women's rights (1969 and 1971), and the adoption of a universal health care system in the United States (1991).[4] The UCC was among the first to call for investment of its own funds in line with its social justice principles (UCC, 1981, par. 272). The church takes pride in its multiracial and multicultural character.

In 1985 the synod declared the UCC a "Just Peace Church" and in 1989 it commended a study paper, "Christian Faith and Economic Life," which had been distributed two years earlier. The 1985 resolution called for action against poverty and other symptoms of social injustice in both the national and international arenas. It follows the "basic needs" approach by emphasizing the need for clean water, food, housing, health care, etc. On international matters the resolution embraced the dependency theory of development, which blames much of the poverty of LDCs on exploitation by the existing "international order" and urges what was commonly called at the time the New International Economic Order (NIEO) or what the resolution simply called a "just international order" (par. 129, 130, and 175 of the study paper). The features to which the dependency theory draws attention and which are mentioned in the study paper—poor indigenous institutions, low prices for raw material and agricultural exports, and other adverse trade conditions—make development more difficult, especially in the poorest of the developing countries. But it is good to recognize that by their own policies many LDCs, facing the same adverse external conditions, have managed to attain and maintain sustained growth. In reality, developing countries can do much by their own domestic action to overcome the many obstacles they face, including measures to achieve greater equality in income distribution, lower protection of imports, less emphasis on heavy state-owned industry, and reduced influence of the richer classes in government. Perhaps the most serious flaw in the study paper's reasoning on the dependency theory is the belief that international cooperation is a zero-sum game, a view widely shared among Christian ethicists that policies designed to make poor countries better off must make the rich countries necessarily worse off. But in actual practice, the positive policies that improve overall economic performance and benefit the poor will make all countries better off through increased growth, investment, and trade from which all countries and classes can profit.

The 1985 UCC synod also invited the church to formulate a theology of a just peace. This was attempted in "A Just Peace Church," a book that, however, does not express concrete ideas on economic policy (UCC, 1986). The "new theology" developed in the book is a Protestant reformulation of liberation theology, which it applies to U.S. and international conditions.

The UCC study paper "Christian Faith and Economic Life" (1987) invited the church to reflect on the conditions of poverty and proposed actions which will permit all members of society to enjoy a satisfactory standard of living. The central theological theme of the paper is the idea that God manages the human household to satisfy both the spiritual and material needs of all its members. It calls God "The Economist," based on the original Greek concept of the economist as manager of the household (Meeks, 1989). In this strand of theology, the Kingdom of God is renamed the Economy of God in which our material needs receive full though not exclusive attention. The study paper recognizes that to become reality the Economy of God must be filled by converted Christians who are fully dedicated and committed to the cause of social justice, giving us a new and broader conception of Christian conversion (UCC, 1987, ch. 8).

In the economic sphere, the proposals of the study paper are similar to those of the Catholic bishops' letter, although in some respects the UCC paper goes further (for example, on the international order and the criticisms of the International Monetary Fund). It urges greater *economic democracy*, for example, through participatory community planning, public ownership, workers' ownership and management,

new and revitalized forms of employee participation in corporate decision making, and more careful environmental management (par. 193–
211 and 212–28).

The paper advocates the adoption of an Economic Bill of Rights
as a constitutional amendment: "The right of the people to access to
employment, food, shelter and health care shall not be abridged." This
call for a legal commitment to provide everyone with a job goes to the
heart of the fight against poverty and is in principle shared with other
churches. It is in line with FDR's 1944 State of the Union message
which proposed an Economic Bill of Rights to establish, "regardless of
station, race or creed," the "right to a useful and remunerative job in
the industries or shops or farms or mines of the nation" and "the right
to earn enough to provide adequate food and clothing and recre-
ation."[5]

A further basic proposal of the UCC study paper concerns the
restructuring of the international system so as to provide greater
power to the LDCs in the management of the system and increased
finance for poverty alleviation and debt reduction (par. 128 and 176).
The paper's suggestion that a new international institution be set up
was, however, bound to meet with little enthusiasm in the international community and the major industrial countries. It is more realistic to improve and build upon existing institutions which, with all
their shortcomings, are the best we have and need active public support against attacks from both the left and the right.[6]

The Presbyterian Church: A Dynamic yet Caring Economy

The Presbyterian church, like other mainline churches, points to a long
history of taking stands on social issues. In 1912 it called for an end to
child labor, a minimum wage, and a shorter workday. In the 1930s it
supported the labor unions and the protection of workers against the
deepening recession. After World War II it advocated full employment
and supported free trade, the rebuilding of Europe, and assistance to
underdeveloped areas abroad. It considers itself as an activist church
fighting to improve our economy, in the spirit of John Calvin.

The Presbyterian church has issued two papers: "Christian Faith
and Economic Justice" (1984) and "Toward a Just, Caring and Dynamic Political Economy" (1985). The first provides the theological–
ethical framework for the social and economic discussion in the

second. The two papers, originally prepared in separate church bodies which subsequently were united, can be read as one. The second paper, prepared by the main Presbyterian body, contains a wide range of policy recommendations.[7]

The *theological discussion* in the 1984 paper is similar to that in the Catholic bishops' 1986 pastoral letter. Central to Presbyterian theology is the knowledge that as a community we have a covenant with a sovereign God, the creator of us all. We are to reflect concern of God in all areas of life. He is a God of Justice, and to disregard the doing of justice is to reject God. A critical dimension of divine justice is particular concern for the poor, the old, and dependent children, reflected in both the Old and the New Testament.

Another aspect of the sovereignty of God is *the economics of respect*. Because God alone is creator and sovereign, all persons must be considered of equal value. Loyalty to God is expressed not only in love of God, but in love of neighbor, particularly the neighbor in need.

The justice of God is not opposed to God's love, but is a manifestation of it: "The Lord is just in all his ways and kind in all his doings" (Ps. 145: 17). Indeed, nothing is more central to the Christian faith than the affirmation that "God is love." The divine love for all humankind has profound implications for economics. God's inclusive love for all binds us as one community. God's unconditional love is the measure by which every person is to be valued. God's special concern for the poor and powerless makes our attitude toward them and actions for them a test of our loyalty to God.

The paper makes no explicit reference to the preference for the poor as set forth in liberation theology, but instead refers to the Swiss Reformed theologian Karl Barth (1957) who stressed that the church must concentrate first on the lower and lowest levels of human society.

The 1984 paper also makes a careful comparison of the pros and cons of democratic capitalism and socialism. In the end, the report does not subscribe to either capitalism or socialism. However, it argues that, as John Bennett (1975) put it, "persons concerned about Christian ethics must press the socialist questions even though they do not accept ready-made socialist answers." Similarly, we must press capitalistic questions (for example, concerning efficiency) even though we don't accept simple capitalistic answers (par. 29.294–29.297).

According to the 1985 report, a just political economy seeks fairness and demands the provision of basic needs, but does not imply equality of income. The issue is not so much the existence of a gap between rich and poor, but how wide it is and whether it is widening or narrowing. Are differences working for the benefit of all the people, or to the detriment of some? Justice demands development of minimal participation in community decisions. The test of a policy is whether it will help the poor and minorities to become more active participants in the economic, political, and cultural life of society (p. 10).

The cornerstone of a just political economy is founded on a sound, caring, nurturing experience of life in our "families." *A just political economy needs a strong spiritual component.* It is essential that Christians share their religious or spiritual roots and acknowledge and celebrate them in the economy. We do not live by bread alone, but by the Word of God that includes and transcends the material world. Christians think of possessions differently from those who have only humanistic values. Jesus spoke repeatedly about the perils of affluence and the spiritually corrupt nature of human greed, especially when it is expressed without any sensitivity for its effects on others (Lk 12: 15 and Mk 8: 36).

Significantly, the 1985 Presbyterian statement *also shows concern for the problems of the nonpoor, and it deals with broad issues of macroeconomic policies that affect us all.* The same God who liberates people from their oppression can also liberate the nonpoor from their addiction and fascination with material things. "Economic justice, including racial equality, is at the heart of a just political economy, but our society needs to move beyond economic justice to a society where love, community, and friendship can be freely expressed. This will be possible not only with the public and private sectors working cooperatively together but with voluntary groups of citizens and individuals in their family lives. The cohesiveness of the political–economic fabric is worn and frayed. Formal legal arrangements cannot provide the healing and the hope needed for viable social interaction. Impersonal, rational systems are necessary, but the human race must nurture primary relationships that reweave and humanize the complex systems to ease the terrible strains in the tapestry. The church is well-equipped to provide models and leadership for this human-scale, political economic activity" (p. 12).

As the economy and economic institutions become more complex, decisions are made in a less personal manner and conditions become more competitive, and hence it becomes harder to evaluate the human consequences of our decisions. Economic policies raise many ethical issues; the technical decisions made in the Federal Reserve or the International Monetary Fund all pose moral issues, for example. Higher interest rates and lower taxes on capital gains favor the haves over the have-nots; tax deductions on home ownership (mortgages) help us buy homes, but by subsidizing homeowners and not renters, the government has contributed to the decline of center-city neighborhoods; new highways speed up traffic, but also cut up existing neighborhoods; and subsidizing corn and wheat and selling it at subsidized prices abroad may help the poor in LDCs but may also put farmers in those countries at a disadvantage.

Despite our great wealth, millions have been left out and suffer from lack of basic necessities: children, single women with dependent children, various minorities, older people, people with handicaps, undocumented persons, Native Americans, etc. Many in these groups, each of which has its own special problems, are left out culturally, politically, and socially. They have little impact on business and political decisions and thinking. At the same time many Americans, including Presbyterians, have wrong thoughts about poverty. They blame poverty on the poor. Presbyterians believe that they have the power to improve their own lot, so why should not others? But middle-class people get many advantages—e.g., education, good neighborhoods, democratic institutions, etc. Many others do not have the same advantages. *Ours is a harsh, punitive economy; we must strive to turn it into a caring, sharing economy.*

Many policy recommendations are scattered throughout the paper. It takes a position against the myths that "the market" always corrects itself and will deal with our social problems if only left free. It also opposes the view that the government is our enemy and our biggest problem. In short, the paper advocates affirmative action to keep pressure on employers; quality education for black Americans; honoring the land and mineral claims of Native Americans; pay equity for women, although introduced gradually; increasing social security taxes and making social security payments subject to the same taxation as other income; greater and more effective public assistance for children in poverty; more progressive taxation, including capping the mortgage interest exemption and increasing the inheritance tax; commitment to a full-employment policy through macroeconomic policies and structural measures making the labor market more flexible and upgrading labor skills; slowdown in deregulation, especially of financial markets; advance notification of the closing of large plants; provision of public sector jobs to supplement the private sector; and restrictions on imports from countries which suppress the labor movement.

The paper has a progressive cast and its economics is mostly mainstream. It has a well-thought-through focus on major issues of macroeconomic policy as well as structural measures to improve the efficiency of the labor market and to upgrade jobs and workers' skills. Its advocacy of greater progressivity in the tax system runs contrary to the predominantly upper-middle-class character of most Presbyterian churches.

Church members are urged to assume responsibility to make sure that positive social policies and objectives are being pursued and implemented in their own sphere. Differences on what to do and how to do it should be aired and brought out into the open through frank discussion. *If the Presbyterians actually adopted in their personal and business lives the recommendations of this paper, they could have a considerable positive impact on our country's economic thinking.* Presbyterian views on theology and economic practice are similar to those of the Reformed church.

The Reformed Church in America: Against the Two-Tiered Society

The Reformed Church in America (RCA) has, since 1959, carried out studies and adopted resolutions on a variety of social issues, including poverty and the inequality of income distribution in the United States, nuclear arms production and warfare, international debt, and the environment.[8] Most of the RCA studies were designed to urge members to reflect on the social issues taken up by the church's General Synod. The church also has sought to influence corporate behavior by direct discussion with management of individual companies on various topics of social concern (as, e.g., nuclear arms, pesticides production, race relations, and investment in South Africa). In the course of its study of poverty issues, the 1985 General Synod expressed "the sincere and deep appreciation of the Reformed Church in America" for the Catholic bishops' draft of "Catholic Social Teaching and the U.S. Economy: Economic Justice for All," and urged its congregations to study the bishops' pastoral and communicate their views to local Catholic bishops. The church recognizes that most of its members enjoy family incomes and employment opportunities that are well above the U.S. average.[9]

In "Biblical Faith and Our Economic Life" (1984), the church's Christian Action Committee expressed doubt that the U.S. economy can achieve full employment and a high level of prosperity without effective antipoverty action. The report provides a biblical framework for a Christian response to the conflicting issues of poverty in the midst of a high-income society (Reformed Church, 1984, p. 64). The report also reminds its readers of Calvin's admonishment of the rich.[10]

"The Two-Tiered Society: Inequality Amid the Ascendancy of Capitalism" (1990) addresses the widening gap between rich and poor in our society.[11] On various occasions this church has alerted its members to the obstacles that their possessions and high personal incomes present to Christian life. Even so, the Reformed papers have on the whole a conservative slant, more so than the papers emanating from the Lutheran Church.

The Lutheran Church: A Socially Progressive Commitment

The Lutherans are among the most liberal voices in the mainline churches. This is evident from the documents issued by two of the predecessor bodies of the present Evangelical Lutheran Church of America (ELCA): the American Lutheran Church (ALC), which had its headquarters in Minneapolis (Minn.), and the Lutheran Church in America (LCA), a national body with headquarters in New York City. These churches issued social policy statements well before others had formulated their positions on such issues as women's rights and environmental degradation. Since its formation in 1988 the ELCA itself, with 5.2 million members, has continued in the same liberal tradition; it refused to take a strict pro-life stand in its 1991 general convention.[12]

The Lutheran statements apply theological positions to a wide range of issues of social concern. The churches were keenly aware of social inequities and excessive emphasis on military security as they emerged in the 1960s and 1970s and spoke with a clear voice on policy questions.

The ALC identified its broad social agenda, developed over the years, as "The Unfinished Reformation" (1980), noting in particular the increase in unemployment and threatened cuts in welfare and the inability of government bureaucracies to conduct effective programs and of the private sector to provide social leadership. The statement also says that Lutherans have emphasized a personal relationship to God and a clear understanding of scriptural and confessional teachings. *"Built into the Lutheran confessions, however, is also a recognition that one's relation to God changes one's view of neighbor, of self, and of the institutions and structures of society"* (our ital.).

"The Environmental Crisis" (1970) puts rapid population growth up front in a discussion of the root causes. It raises the question as to *what forms of population control can be effective without destroying basic human and democratic rights and values.* Dramatic growth of technology places additional burdens on the earth's carrying capacity. While opening new horizons, it also places enormous pressure on our resources. A further contribution to the environmental crisis is the *fragmentation of political and economic decision-making processes.* The paper recognizes that difficult choices, often not clear-cut, will have to be faced in paying for the enormous cost of maintaining a cleaner environment. And it calls on Christians to exercise an ethic of stewardship of our resources. The timing of this paper put the ALC well ahead of others in awareness of Christian responsibility to address the scope and costs of environmental pollution.

"Economic Problems of Rural America" (1970) shows how this church addressed rural issues well ahead of the U.S. Catholic bishops (1986). It addressed the severe social–economic problems of the farm communities in Iowa and other Midwestern states, resulting in the impoverishment and even depopulation of entire communities and subregions, problems which are vividly described in "Out West" by Dayton Duncan (1987; ch. 6).

The Lutheran Church in America has likewise made several statements that apply theology to social policy, for example, poverty (1966), ecology (1972), human rights (1972), economic justice (1980), and peace and politics (1984). Throughout these statements and those of its sister church, we find an affirmation of the importance of the human community in our life—in the bringing of God's purposes to reality and realizing the potentiality of individuals. People must live in cohumanity with each other, not in isolation and enmity.[13] This stress on community is in sharp contrast to the role assigned to the individual by capitalist writers, and to some extent also in the Presbyterian papers. But it is echoed in Herman Daly's construction of the "person-in-community," which he prefers over "homo economicus," the maximizer of consumer benefits and profits we find in modern economics (Daly and Cobb, 1989).

"Economic Justice—Stewardship of Creation in Human Community" (1980), one of the more detailed pronouncements, restates and summarizes the earlier statements and gives fresh insights into the Christian view of economics. It discusses the theological foundation of justice and applies it to our values in society and to the role of government. "Formal entitlements to political participation and legal redress and entitlements to basic needs (housing, food, education, minimum income and/or employment) are needed for entrance into the social and economic community." "Property may be held in a variety of ways, but regardless of the way it is held, property is held in trust and its holder is accountable ultimately to God and proximately to the community . . . for the ways the resource or wealth is or is not used."

From the vantage point of the 1990s, the Lutherans' assessment of social issues appears very timely. It reflects a continuous tension and interaction between our understanding of the Word of God and the human economic situation. The human community receives a central place in Lutheran thinking. This implies that much of modern economics must pay more attention to the effects of "orthodox" policies on the community. Such a reorientation requires a major rethinking of economics, much of it already under way. The changes in international markets in the 1980s forced the developing countries to take tough monetary and fiscal measures that had a profound impact on poverty and essential social programs. Global trade policies have the effect of moving hundreds of thousands of workers into the ranks of the unemployed and of virtually destroying whole towns and communities. Is it not time to rethink the social impact of international financial and trade policies? In particular, should governments assume greater responsibility to help communities that are adversely affected by industrial change to take a new course, and to upgrade the skills of our workers?

Economics will have to go some way to adapt its thinking to the changing needs of the human community and in effect "catch up" with ethics in this area. Perhaps economists can be grateful that Christian thinkers set some new objectives that liven up a science which, as practiced by many in the economics profession, has often become unresponsive to the many social issues which received central attention from its earlier writers (Daly and Cobb, 1989, ch. 3).

The social witness of the mainline churches shows considerable variety in emphasis, yet the churches also share a common element that deserves further attention.

DIVERSITY AND UNITY IN MAINLINE TESTIMONY

The mainline churches arrive at similar conclusions in their analysis of social issues. It will, however, be useful to reflect on the differences that arise among the mainline statements and some of the pitfalls in their economic reasoning.

It is worth remembering that the "economic pastorals" of the 1980s were written against the background of recession in the early part of the decade and a subsequent recovery that brought little comfort to the poor in the later 1980s. The Reagan Administration weakened the social safety net and appeared to many indifferent to the plight of the poor. Meanwhile, the developing countries were affected by the aftermath of the debt crisis and structural changes in the international division of labor.

Some observers feel that the pastorals were too bland and reflected their committee-style authorship. The editor of the 1987 UCC paper, Audrey Chapman, wrote later that the pastorals were not sufficiently critical of the capitalist system, but instead sought to educate church members who themselves were entrapped by capitalism. Larry Rasmussen of Union Theological Seminary judged that the pastorals did not address the conflict between the rich and poor classes, which in his view was essential when dealing with the issues of poverty. He expressed an opinion, generally accepted by mainline ethicists, that action in favor of the poor must necessarily penalize the rich.[14] This view contradicts the finding of economists that improvement in policies toward the poor will lift the entire economy, to the benefit of all groups and regions.

The theology in the statements of the U.S. Catholic bishops and the mainline churches is fundamentally the same. Both base themselves on the Bible, assign top priority to protecting the poor, and recognize the essential dignity of the human person created in God's image. God, the Creator, "owns" the earth's resources, and humans are to treat them with love and respect. Love must rule in all our behavior and relationships. The covenant between God and his people has been broadened to a universal community in an interconnected global society. People are called to make a deep personal commitment, with their hearts of stone changed into flesh, and to dedicate themselves to the interests of their neighbor and their community.

At the same time, however, the way individual mainline churches address issues in our society and economy often differs in both tone and substance. The Methodists and the Episcopalians have published resolutions on individual issues which cover the entire range of the churches' social concern. The Methodist and Reformed Church publications are cast as advice to their members. The United Church of Christ has a more negative view of our economy, and its advocacy is broad and sweeping. The economic views of the Presbyterians are more upbeat, come up with specific solutions to the problems they identify, and pay attention to macroeconomic policies which are crucial to overcoming poverty on a broad front. The Lutherans took an early lead in expressing liberal social concerns and balanced economics and theology, without entering into the specifics of economic policy.

Much of the mainline witness is concerned with the disadvantaged position of black America. The many social issue papers make no reference to any consultation by the predominantly white Protestant churches with the black churches, yet these black churches bring an important message to the problems of their members. Many African Methodist Episcopal Church (AME) members have influential positions, as for example former House majority whip William H. Gray III. According to AME Bishop H. Hartford Brookins, "The cradle of black politics in this country was born in the womb of the black church. Without the black church, the black politician would cease to exist."[15] The National Baptist Convention USA, which together with other black Baptist churches has close to 17 million members, in its 1991 meeting in Washington, D.C. called for actions to help solve the social ills plaguing the black community, including teenage pregnancy, black-on-black crime, and drugs.[16] Social issues are the direct concern of the black church, and one hopes that in any interchurch witness it will assume a central place.

The Protestant churches would like to see greater equality in living standards and economic opportunity. Some of the writers want to change the economic system and make it more egalitarian. That may be a good ideal, though some would even doubt that, but in any case it is not so easy to accomplish. In the United States income distribution became less equal in the 1980s and the early 1990s; real incomes of the upper 20 or 10 percent increased significantly, and wages of skilled workers rose relative to those of unskilled workers. Many economists, but not all, would agree that making the fiscal system more progressive and spending more on education would go a long way toward correcting at least some of the inequities in the U.S. economy. Western societies face the challenge of establishing greater equality of opportunity while maintaining economic growth and efficiency.

The authors of the church statements recognize that Christian social objectives cannot be fully satisfied under either the capitalist or the socialist system, a point on which they fully agree with the U.S. Catholic bishops. Nevertheless, the breakdown of Eastern European and Soviet communism had a profound impact on Christian social justice thinking. The collapse of communism, occurring after most of the economic pastorals were written, teaches us how not to do things, even though we may be dissatisfied with some aspects of our own system.

It is no secret that many mainline theologians had prosocialist sympathies. The breakdown of communism after 1989 left something like a vacuum in Protestant ethical thinking. Thus the 1990 convocation of the World Council of Churches held in Seoul, South Korea, focused on environmental issues, but ignored the ethical issues posed by the collapse of communism. Max L. Stackhouse, a well-known Princeton theologian, writes in *The Christian Century* (January 16, 1991) that for mainline ethicists "democracy, human rights and socialism were the marks of the coming kingdom. For all their prophetic witness in many areas, they were wrong about socialism" (Hollenbach, 1992, pp. 78–79).

Full employment is widely advocated as a policy objective in the churches' statements. This is an ideal objective shared by both theologians and economists. Some economists see difficulties in achieving this objective, while others, for example Alan Blinder, give it top priority and believe the inflationary danger of full-employment policy has been exaggerated. It must be an integral part of any comprehensive policy that wants to make full use of our enormous resources in a responsible way. Yet even reasonably full employment is not sufficient to eradicate poverty and fear of being downgraded or laid off in today's economy of rapid structural change.

The churches must strike a balance between speaking out for their Christian principles and applying them to our economic situation. When their economic judgments become too specific or detailed, they can soon find themselves in deep water. Economic policy making is an art; it requires vast amounts of information, and it deals with a steadily changing environment. Church authors can, moreover, have trouble with the intricacies of economic institutions. This is clear from the opinion expressed by some that the International Monetary Fund was conceived in the sin of having excluded the poor at its formation and ignored social justice in its subsequent operations. Nothing would have been farther from the thinking of its founders or the subsequent actions of the people who made the institution work. The World Bank, on its part, has made a deliberate effort to listen to constructive views of church representatives, as is clear from the Bank's vastly increased attention to environmental issues, its dialogue with NGOs, and its new policy of having them participate in its projects.

It remains essential that the churches address the social problems of *both the rich and the poor*. Otherwise both economics and theology become one-sided and divorced from the full biblical message. This is of course especially important in view of the predominantly middle-class character of the church's members. True, they must be educated in the problems of the poor, but higher income families have their own problems in living in a highly competitive corporate environment. The Presbyterian and Reformed churches went farthest in recognizing that they are predominantly middle class, and at least began to address some of the problems of the majority of their own membership. It is good to recognize that the free-market economy has disadvantages for both rich and poor; it works at the cost of keeping down the living standards of the poor, but it may also have a detrimental effect on the psychological well-being of all people, both rich and poor.

One hopes that the churches will gear themselves to address the problems of middle-class professionals. Churches often do not extend the reconciliation of Christian faith and economic reality to the problems of this group. All Christians must and can cope with social and economic pressures. A life of faith and dedication to the principles of Christ can overcome the adverse consequences of life in the modern corporation and of personal and economic competition and uncertainty. The church can do much to strengthen its members' ability to withstand the pressures and selfishness in our society. But to do so it must have a more explicit message of personal Christian commitment in the marketplace.

We may well ask: How are the churches' social pronouncements accepted in the pew? Could it be that the pastorals themselves are now largely forgotten, even by the staff working in denominational offices? This seemed evident from the 1989 conference "God's Justice in a New Century: The Future of Religion and Economic Justice," held to assess the impact of the pastorals and what they hold for the future (Interfaith Action, 1991, pp. 2–3). One hopes that the social views of the churches will continue to influence both the thinking and the personal, professional, and business behavior of their membership and that the churches will continue to develop and apply these views in line with their biblical mandate in a changing world. Their witness is even more important should government policies once again come to endanger the objectives of full employment and the legitimate concerns of the poor.

In their social pronouncements, the mainline churches differ from the Christian Right and the more fundamentalist churches, which lean more toward the capitalist system and have made few if any statements on poverty issues. At the same time, the social views of some Evangelicals are similar to those found in the mainline churches. As related in the next chapter, Evangelicals have addressed many socioeconomic problems since the early decades of the twentieth century.

12
The Evangelicals

Evangelicals express a wide diversity of economic views. Some, as strong advocates of free-market capitalism, pay little attention to its "backwash" effects and the price paid by the poor. Others show concern with the unequal distribution of income in the United States and the gap between rich and poor countries, and even advocate drastic steps to bridge the gap. They are divided on the attention that should be paid to the poor and on the role of the military. What holds these diverse groups together is their unifying faith in the Bible as the Word of God.

With deep roots in our country, the socioeconomic views of Evangelicals go back to the progressive positions taken by William Jennings Bryan, the standard-bearer of the Democratic Party at the turn of the century. In 1896 Bryan gave his "Cross of Gold" oration, a clarion call for social action by a thoroughly Evangelical Christian. Protesting the strangulation of American workers by conservative bankers and calling for vigorous remedial actions, he brought his attentive audience at the Democratic convention to a frenzy:

"Having behind us the producing masses of this nation and the world, supported by the commercial interests, the laboring interests, and the toilers everywhere, we will answer their (the bankers') demand for a gold standard by saying to them: *You shall not press down upon the brow of labor this crown of thorns, and you shall not crucify mankind upon a cross of gold*" (Burns, 1986, p. 231).

Other Christian leaders also spoke out on the social conditions of their times. In 1891 Pope Leo XIII issued his *"Rerum Novarum"* ("The Condition of Labor"), which has rightly become known as the Magna Carta of Catholic social teaching (Henriot et al., 1988, p. 7). In the same year the formidable Dutch theologian-statesman Abraham Kuyper opened a Social Congress with his "The Social Question and the Christian Religion."

For understanding the range of political views among present-day Evangelicals, it is useful to recall the progressive character of Bryan's positions. Bryan was, of course, a Democrat; and like him, until the 1960s, Evangelicals were more likely to be Democrat than Republican. He supported a wide range of progressive causes: monetary expansion and reform, enfranchisement of women, direct election of senators, and a graduated income tax. He collaborated, as a cabinet member, with President Woodrow Wilson, a reformist and progressive president, Calvinist *par excellence*, who introduced among others the Federal Reserve system, the Federal Trade Commission, and the income tax. But in 1915 Bryan broke with Wilson on the issue of peace, acting against Wilson's more internationalist course which led to the 1917 U.S. intervention in World War I, the subsequent allied victory, and the establishment of the League of Nations. Bryan's opposition foreshadowed the isolationism of the 1920s.

Like other outstanding Evangelical leaders, William Jennings Bryan was a great orator and shared in the Evangelical tradition of not acting through a particular church. As we search for Evangelicals' positions on social–economic matters today, we cannot draw on church statements like those of the Catholic and mainline Protestant churches, but must resort instead to the writings and speeches of individual Evangelical leaders or groups. Bryan, and others after him, acted as an individual, even though his advocacy had important consequences in the form of progressive Wilsonian legislation. Neither Bryan nor present-day Evangelical leaders appeal to past theological authority such as Luther, Calvin, or more recent theologians concerned with social issues. In this respect they are very different from Leo XIII, who appealed to Thomas Aquinas, or from Abraham Kuyper, whose writings are spiced with numerous historical and theological references. However, Bryan did refer to Thomas Jefferson and Andrew Jackson's opposition to the influence of the banks (Noll, 1991, p.11).

In the 1920s and 1930s many Evangelicals turned politically inactive, becoming primarily concerned with Christian life at "the end of the age." They were absorbed not by the message of the Bible for our personal and corporate life in the present, but by passive interpretation of current events in the light of a literal reading of the Bible. Of course, many were personally involved with help to the poor and hungry. But the Fundamentalists stood on the sidelines in the 1930s as our country struggled to come out of the depth of economic and social depression, and the New Deal attempted to reinvigorate and reform the economy. And some, like Billy Sunday, openly opposed the New Deal and other forms of social activism (Neuhaus and Cromarty, 1987, p. 42).

This chapter first discusses the Evangelicals' turn to the right after World War II. It then looks in more detail into the thinking of different groups, the "Christian Right" and the more moderate views in the center, as well as Evangelicals' views on education, which are of direct concern to improving the position of the poor. Next, it discusses those Evangelicals who are concerned with excessive emphasis on the military and fighting world poverty. The chapter concludes with a review of the economic thinking in different groups of Evangelicals, and of the Oxford Conference on Christian Faith and Economics, a major effort to reach a more unified position on social issues.

THE POST-WORLD WAR II ERA

After World War II the Evangelicals did an about-face and once again began to engage themselves in politics, some might say even aggressively. They did not act in unison and often took opposing positions on social issues. In a way, they went back to their populist roots, many striving once again to direct their public actions in the light of God's Word. But while they turned back to the populism of Bryan, many also took a sharp turn to the right in their politics.

Many of these newly active Fundamentalists gladly embraced free-market capitalism, believing it to be the economic system preferred by the Bible. But leaders like Billy Graham showed little social awareness of what went on in our economy at the time, were silent on civil rights when it really counted, and supported a strong military posture.[1]

It should be clear from the start that not all Evangelicals subscribe to the same social–economic or even theological views. The main characteristics which bind them together are a belief in the truth of the Bible, personal conversion as the natural outgrowth of the Gospel's meaning, active practice of faith in obedience to divine law, and stress on the suffering of Christ as the key to human well-being (Noll, 1991, p. 3). Neuhaus gives a more "Fundamentalist" and perhaps more rigid lineup of principles, including the "inerrancy" of the Bible on any subject on which it speaks; the virgin birth of Jesus; the atonement of Jesus Christ; his bodily resurrection; authenticity of miracles; and "premillenialism" (Neuhaus and Cromarty, 1987, p. 5). The difference in tone and content of these two characterizations reflects some of the variation in attitude and thought among Evangelicals.

The American political system has not produced a significant political party based on biblical principles like the Christian Democratic parties of Europe. In their search for a political home, the Evangelicals increasingly turned to the Republican Party in the 1980s.

What brought the Evangelicals into the political arena were the 1961 outlawing of prayer in public schools, perceived as secularization of public life, and the 1973 Roe v. Wade decision legalizing abortion on demand. Earlier Southern Evangelicals had established Christian academies to avoid racial integration and to be free to teach creationism and traditional values. Evangelicals felt that the moral foundation of life was crumbling, witness the high divorce rates, the high proportion of unwed mothers heading families, and the increase in the numbers of children born out of wedlock. The New Right was born out of concern with this moral deterioration. Not all New Right leaders are Evangelicals: some like Weyrich and Viguerie are Catholic, and Phillips is Jewish.

At first the Evangelicals supported President Carter, but they turned away when he did not cease federal funding of abortion and did not appoint Evangelicals to high positions. Reagan, however, went out of his way to appeal to Fundamentalist Christians (e.g., in Dallas, 1980). He was richly rewarded with strong Fundamentalist support, and in return he went as far as to remove the ban against racial discrimination in private schools, a ban subsequently upheld by the Supreme Court.[2]

Consistent with Reagan's philosophy, many Evangelicals supported a strong defense. They believed this was called for so that America could play its assigned role in the prophesied final days of history. They also supported a freer rein for the private sector. Jerry Falwell, the Baptist preacher from Lynchburg, Virginia, and founder of the Moral Majority, found that the Book of Proverbs supported the free-enterprise system.

At the start of the 1990s, the political agenda included the adoption of some instrument overthrowing Roe v. Wade; legal restriction of pornography; an end to the "harassment" of Christian schools (or rather, giving Christian schools the same fiscal support as public schools); objection to feminist and pro-gay-rights legislation; termination of social programs that increase the dependency of the poor; and increased defense spending.

The Fundamentalist approach is basically different from those of many other Christian leaders who apply their principles within the framework of existing contemporary society. As Harvey Cox points out, Evangelicals (as distinct from Fundamentalists) and liberal theologians accept a reduced role of religion and theology. Evangelicals differ from liberals on the content of faith, but both accept the world as the arena in which the theological task has to be accomplished; the argument between the two is about the message, not the world. On the other hand, Fundamentalists and liberation theologians both want to work for a *different* world, not to refine doctrine or to translate the message into the world's terms, but to remake the world in the image of the message.[3] At the same time, Fundamentalism impresses outsiders as "authoritarian, intolerant and compulsive about imposing itself upon the rest of society. It is a mindset which sees everything as black and white and for which compromise is alien" (Naisbitt and Aburdene, 1990, p. 279).

In Harvey Cox's view, Fundamentalists are not likely to shape American society in their image. First, the many "rednecks" in their midst cannot be merged easily with the mainstream of American religious and political life. Second, their belief that the end of the age is near produces a cynical sense of powerlessness and makes it difficult for the movement as a whole to push for constructive social or political change.

Last but not least, there may be an inherent tension in the Fundamentalists' use of technology, especially TV. Cox rightly wondered, "What happens when a profoundly anti-modernist attempt to reassert the primacy of traditional values utilizes a cultural form that is itself thoroughly modern and anti-traditional?" There is tension between content and form, message and medium. It could well be that TV technology will strike a mortal blow to the "Old Time Gospel" and traditional religion, exactly what the Fundamentalists are trying to defend (Neuhaus and Cromarty, 1987, p. 109). It is great to see TV technology used for the Kingdom of God, but it is hard to envisage that it can make the true message of Christ be understood in all its depth and simplicity and its compelling urge to sacrifice oneself. In practice, most TV preachers are in constant danger of crowding out the Gospel with their money-raising efforts, as is borne out by the unfortunate, but perhaps unavoidable, experience of right-wing TV preachers like Jim Baker, Jimmy Swaggart, or Oral Roberts. On the other hand, it is critically important that television be used to bring the Christian message to modern society; people are more likely bound to listen to their TVs than to go to church, where the message may or may not be fully relevant to their real-life problems. There is a wide opportunity for the church to enter this field more aggressively and bring its full message of reconciliation and love, and to help both rich and poor find more meaningful lives.

THE CHRISTIAN RIGHT WING

Spearheaded by Jerry Falwell and Pat Robertson, the Christian Right has recruited the shock troops to fight the political battles for a socially active agenda and substantially less government intervention on social–economic issues. Their political objectives are different from the Evangelicals for Social Action and others who emphasize greater attention to the poor and reduced military expenditures.

Jerry Falwell, writing on the political agenda for the 1980s, takes a traditional stand on the family and supports equal rights for women—i.e., a commitment to ensure that in state governments every woman can earn as much as her male counterpart and have the same opportunity for advancement. But he regards the Equal Rights Amendment as the wrong vehicle for achieving equality, since it could put women in combat positions, sanction homosexuality, and financially penalize widows and deserted wives. He supports the return of voluntary prayer to public schools.

Falwell's "Moral Majority" sought to mastermind and activate the Christian right wing in the 1980s until the demise of several TV preachers reduced the flow of contributions. Subsequently, he seems to have disappeared from public attention, but has remained a factor in the Christian Right. However, not all Evangelicals closed ranks with this movement, and some were critical. Jim Skillen of the Association of Public Justice, for example, judged that the "Moral Majority" did not develop the biblical base for the role of a just government in a differentiated society, nor did it offer a convincing rationale for the Christian character of America. Instead, it started out with confidence in the compatibility of America's original moral character with biblical revelation—at best a romantic vision of the past (Skillen, 1990 a, p. 53).

E. Calvin Beisner (1988) maintains that the fight against poverty is not a government task. Caring for the poor is a church function, to be exercised following the criteria set forth in 1 Tim 5: care for those who are left alone without support and those who serve the church.

He tries to demonstrate arithmetically that the churches can actually handle the problem of American poverty. With some arithmetic manipulation, he reduces the number of poor from the official figure of 31–36 million to 3.9 million, a number he claims can easily be managed by the churches.[4]

The enthusiasm for limiting the government's role in poverty alleviation and other social problems is rooted in a belief that private organisms should be given full chance to be effective and to prove that they often can perform better than government. In this view, government should not obstruct what can be done by private institutions, the family, the church, or business and voluntary organizations. Working in the American Enterprise Institute, Michael Novak articulated the importance of these "mediating structures" in the mid-1970s. He wants welfare to focus on empowering families, schools, and neighborhoods as the major agents of social change (Neuhaus and Cromarty, 1987, p. 86). Neuhaus has written in a similar vein.

The same writers strongly advocate a public policy role for the church. In fact, they accuse the "liberals" of having pushed religion into a private corner. Nothing could be worse than to have the church in such a quiet private corner. Indeed, Christ has a message for all parts of our society and claims them as his. But in fact, the mainline Protestant churches and the Catholic Church have spoken loudly and clearly about their and their members' public responsibilities—theirs is not a private affair, nor have they acted like a candle put under a bushel. It is the more Fundamentalist and conservative churches who have officially kept their silence on critical social issues, even though they encourage their members to be active in right-wing politics.

Evangelical authors on the right often appear rigid. Carl F. H. Hendry, founding editor of the journal "*Christianity Today*," shows but meager interest in active poverty alleviation (Neuhaus and Cromarty, 1987, p. 99). He would restrict public action in favor of volunteerism. He points out that American political documents champion the pursuit of happiness but do not guarantee it, an interpretation that seems to oppose social action.

The story of the Christian Right would not be complete without mentioning James Dobson, whose "Focus on the Family" is heard over more than a thousand radio stations, and Pat Robertson, who on his radio and TV network preaches the scriptures with a distinctly political and conservative slant. Like his father, a U.S. senator from Virginia, Robertson is highly conservative on racial and social issues, fiercely anticommunist and promilitary, and critical of deficit spending and welfare programs. His foray into presidential politics did not, however, generate a distinguishable Christian approach to politics and government (Skillen, 1990a, p. 37). Yet Robertson, with Ralph Reed, the executive director of the Christian Coalition until 1997, has shown great acumen in mobilizing a potent force in the political arena.

Robertson founded CBN (Christian Broadcast Network) University, but he and other like-minded leaders have a long way to go in building up institutions of higher learning which can bring forward well-trained professionals versed in our country's economic and social problems. They might learn from the efforts of seventeenth- and eighteenth-century New England Calvinists, as well as from the more recent work of Jesuits in building institutions of higher learning. Or they might look at the work of the Free University of Amsterdam, originally Neo-Calvinist and now more than a century old. Our society can only benefit from responsible and well-prepared leadership from all quarters, and the cause of Christianity would be furthered by well-founded and broadly perceived presentations by people who profess to base their actions on the Bible.

Ralph Reed has shown himself a shrewd and able conservative political activist. But he does not search for a biblical message on which to base his political positions in his "Active Faith" (1996). There is no question that the life of family, prayer, and public witness must be central in our society, and that the Judeo–Christian spirit of charity and care must govern our politics. But Reed preaches moral values as if they are autonomous rather than being a consequence of our faith in Christ. Care for the poor comes as an afterthought in his book, and his attack on welfare spending clearly sidesteps the foundation of our Christian faith as formulated by Jesus at the start of his ministry (Luke 4: 16–22) and in his advice to the rich young ruler: "Give everything you have to the poor, and come follow me" (Luke 18: 22).

MORE MODERATE VIEWS IN THE CENTER

Not all Evangelicals agree with the views of the Christian Right. There is in fact enormous diversity of opinion among Evangelicals. For example, Senator Mark Hatfield, an active Baptist layman and moderate Republican, questioned the choice of issues put forth by the Religious Right: "Many Evangelicals share my concern that the grievous sins of our society are militarism and materialism, rather than the Taiwan treaty, the Equal Rights Amendment, or the Panama Canal." The National Association of Evangelicals, under Robert Dugan, edged toward the political arena in the early 1980s, but avoided identification with what Billy Graham called the "hard right" (Neuhaus and Cromarty, 1987, pp. 86 and 90).

James W. Skillen's Association for Public Justice seeks to apply Christian principles and thinking to the political and social issues of our differentiated society. The monthly report of the association brings to the attention of its readers a wide range of Christian writings on these issues. He repeatedly urges that one should make full allowance for the diversity of social–economic experience in our country and see it in historical context. In 1991, with the collaboration of Emory University, he helped to organize an interdenominational and international "Conference on Christianity and Democracy" in which Jimmy Carter was a lead speaker.

In his "The Scattered Voice: Christians at Odds in the Public Square" (1990a), Skillen describes the wide variety in sociopolitical views among Christians, ranging from conservatives to liberals. In this book he warns against oversimplification of the biblical message and cautions against using the Bible for specific political purposes. In his view, Christians are called back to thankful living in all areas of life. Christian obedience calls for civic responsibility that promotes justice. He believes that the Bible has everything to do with earthly politics, provided that we understand it properly in relation to the world in which we live. But the biblical interpretation is often difficult and does not by itself offer a shortcut to assessing the divergent Christian approaches to contemporary politics. (op. cit., pp. 26–27).

Skillen lays special emphasis on differentiation in our world. He urges that Christians take cognizance of the complexities of our political system and see it in a historical context. He recognizes the prevailing gross economic inequalities and the consequences of racial discrimination. But he would be cautious of direct government action to deal with them. Thus he warns that liberal Christians—the Catholic bishops and the mainline churches—often address public injustice, especially economic injustice, as if society were a simple whole; they do not allow for the differentiation in our society. On the other hand, conservatives like Novak and Neuhaus do emphasize the differentiation in our society and its need for freedom from an overinvolved government. In Skillen's view, a comprehensive political perspective needs to reconcile or synthesize the contrasts and conflicts between these two points of view (op. cit., p. 208).

Against this reasoning one should, however, point out that a careful reading of the church statements shows that their authors were fully aware of the differences in the causes and problems of poverty experienced by various groups in our society. (See, for example, the 1985 Presbyterian statement.) Further, Christians are operating under the biblical perception that the poor must be healed and restored; once poverty is more fully alleviated, there still remains ample room for differentiation in our society. Differentiation in a Christian society need not be based on the level of people's incomes. But above all, a Christian society does not permit the poor to be forced to live outside it as if they were outcasts, a point repeatedly stressed by the Catholic bishops.

If the publications of the Association for Public Justice suffer from a general weakness, it is that they often raise questions to which they do not provide or even seem to seek specific and constructive answers. The papers prepared for the 1994 conference "Public Justice and Welfare," organized by the association, are a good example of this ambiguity. The conference's keynote paper "A New Vision for Welfare Reform" is written with the idea that many elements come into play when society seeks to improve the well-being of the poor, in particular, personal responsibility and the religious community (Carlson-Thies, 1994). However, criticizing the state of welfare (preceding the 1996 legislation) was easy and not new—for example, the main outlines for essential welfare reform were formulated more than thirty years ago by Reform Judaism—but coming up with realistic proposals for job creation and reform in the central cities is something quite different. Carlson-Thies' presentation sounds rather remote from the real situation of life in the ghetto, as depicted for example by Jonathan Kozol (1995). Our society, including the conservative Christians, cannot escape responsibility for coping with the consequences of the sweeping socioeconomic changes that have occurred, the massive move of manufacturing from the Northeast to the South and beyond our borders, and the white flight from the central city. One cannot absolve oneself from one's own coresponsibility of helping to uplift those who are stuck in the inner cities without hope and real prospects, and confine oneself to depicting them as undeserving and preaching that the victims of social upheaval and neglect should assume their responsibility.

Besides welfare reform, many Evangelicals have pushed hard for getting better educational standards in the schools. In this connection they have taken positions on the management and finance of schools in general. This topic is of direct interest in fighting poverty because the poor deserve to get better schools.

POVERTY, PRIVATE EDUCATION, AND RELIGION

The poor are directly concerned with what is done about education. They are easily left out and are put at a severe disadvantage in the struggle for educational excellence, which decides one's place in society or our country's place in the world. Educational reform is a crucial element of antipoverty action. Evangelicals' views about reform deserve careful consideration. They want parents to be free to choose the right education for their children. Their views have implications for the organization and financing of the educational system in general. In our differentiated world, the privileged can usually see to it that their children get the best education available, but the poor are in a weak position to do so.

Skillen has given a good example of the views of Evangelicals. He has written extensively about his preference for free choice in education.[5] In a differentiated society it is important that all parents are free to choose the schools to which their children shall go. He means to extend this freedom to schools that teach religion. He appears to call for public finance of religious education, since in the absence of such government support parents pay a financial or legal penalty for sending children to the private schools of their choice. His position is similar to that of other Evangelicals; many also call for permitting prayer in public schools.

Skillen and other Evangelicals want to strengthen the Christian school in our society. However, public support for private schools could easily endanger the very independence and spirit of these schools.[6]

The issues raised by the interaction of government and religion in our educational system are complex and we cannot do full justice to them here. Much of the debate is about finance and is of broad economic interest. One widely discussed plan would give parents a voucher with which they can pay the "private" school of their choice. The voucher would offset in part the taxes all must pay for public schooling. The voucher plan could bring a welcome element of competition between different schools, and it could be beneficial to both public and private schools. Milton Friedman was an early proponent of the plan, though he holds no brief for Christian education (Friedman and Friedman, 1980, p. 158).

Beyond questions of finance, one would hope the complex issues of state–church relationship will not distract from the importance of having education of the highest quality. Whatever happens to private schools in the United States, all citizens have a stake in strengthening public education available to all, something of clear interest to the poor and marginalized groups which must be made part of the economic mainstream. Quality education is essential in helping the poor to improve their condition.

The Christian concern with the nature of educational improvement is shared by many socially active Evangelicals. The "Evangelicals for Social Action," among others, have a broad social agenda that deserves further comment.

THE EVANGELICAL CONSCIENCE

Some Evangelicals have expressed concern with huge military expenditures and luxurious lifestyles in the face of world hunger and poverty. On moral and ethical grounds, they have argued for cutting back consumption and increasing help to the poorest of the poor. And, unlike the Christian Right, they protested our defense buildup even though it was directed against communism.

The 1973 Chicago Declaration, supported by both Carl Henry on the conservative side of the spectrum and Jim Wallis on the more liberal side, challenged the misplaced trust in economic and military might which promotes a national pathology of war and violence victimizing our neighbors at home and abroad. Domestic and international injustice are the result of an inherent bellicosity in American economic and military structures. In its view, global justice is predicated upon the United States renouncing its use of power. There are no legitimate uses of American power because American institutions are inherently unjust. The Declaration established peace and justice as the central concern of the Evangelical social mission, presupposing that American economic and foreign policy institutions are unjust.[7]

In the Spring of 1978 some 200 Evangelical leaders issued a "Call to Faithfulness," committing themselves to total abolition of nuclear weapons, noncooperation with U.S. preparedness for nuclear war, and "resistance in the name of Jesus Christ." Billy Graham also revised his earlier hands-off position and, in 1979, urged Evangelicals to reconsider their support of U.S. strategic policy. He confessed that previously he had "confused the Kingdom of God with the American Way of Life." This Evangelical conversion experienced another high in May 1983 when the Pasadena Conference on "The Church and Peace Making in the Nuclear Age," with over 1,400 Evangelicals attending, was dominated by Evangelical "peace activists" who had championed the earlier Chicago Declaration.

In practice, however, Evangelicals were quite conformist on the issue of war and peace. According to a 1983 Gallup poll, commissioned by the National Association of Evangelicals, 61 percent of Evangelicals approved Reagan's way of dealing with the nuclear arms situation. The poll also found that 77 percent of Evangelicals favored an immediately verifiable freeze in testing, production, and deployment of nuclear weapons, a percentage only slightly different from that of the general public. And 85 percent found that "a person can be a good Christian and still support possession of nuclear weapons." The just war tradition seeks to be faithful to biblical ethics in the reality of the world in which we live. Some form of peace is possible, but we know, in the words of Cardinal John J. O'Connor, that peace must be "prayed for, worked for, negotiated for, and even as a last resort fought for" (Neuhaus and Cromarty, 1987, pp. 237–42).

Other Evangelical groups, especially those led by Ronald J. Sider of the Evangelicals for Social Action (ESA) and Jim Wallis, editor of the journal "*Sojourners*," have turned their attention to the plight of the poorest in the developing countries.

Ronald Sider emphasizes that the Bible is on the side of the poor. His reasoning is similar to that of the Catholic bishops and many mainline Protestants.[8] In "Rich Christians in an Age of Hunger" (1990), Sider elaborates his theology, analyzes the political economy of international poverty, and sketches a whole range of policy and voluntary actions which he feels are called for by his Christian belief. He states that, "Millions of people die every year *because* rich folk like you and me have ignored the Bible's clear teaching that God measures the integrity of our faith by *how we respond* to the poor." This view, held by many Christian ethicists, may appeal to the guilt feelings of some, but it is faulty economics. (See, for example, the discussion of the UCC paper "Christian Faith and Economic Life" in Chapter 11.) The book seeks to mobilize broad support for all forms of assistance in the fight for poverty eradication.

Sider takes a careful look at the structural and fundamental causes of international poverty, the debt crisis, environmental degradation, exploitation by multinational corporations, etc. He gives top priority to a simpler lifestyle of the rich at home, less conspicuous consumption, and a corresponding release of resources for assistance to the poor. And he calls for a variety of structural changes in our foreign policy, not dissimilar to the recommendations of the Catholic bishops, to do more for the poor and less for the defense of large corporate interests. He also urges that foreign aid give greater attention to the poor, leave ample role for the work of private agencies (including NGOs), extend credit to small business, and operate with a long-range view. He recognizes that effective development is possible only when individuals are determined to help themselves, and believes that Christian conversion gives the right motivation and empowers people to take on the arduous task of development.

The book expresses confidence in what faith can accomplish and gives welcome advice on how to change the focus of external assistance. It does not, however, confront the conservative critics of foreign assistance, and it wants private voluntary agencies to play a larger role. These agencies make, of course, an essential and often highly motivated contribution, but what they do is not enough. There is need, and ample space, for contributions by private banks and corporations, and for assistance from multilateral institutions. Sider's proposal for the government to subsidize these voluntary agencies deserves careful study.[9] The book mentions the problems of global warming, deforestation, and other environmental concerns, but it says little about the adverse effects of rapid population growth and what to do about it. Elsewhere Sider and his associates have, however, pointed out that population issues must be treated in the broader context of health, education, and environmental policies (e.g., *ESA Advocate*, June 1991). At the same time they urge that family programs not be coercive, and that contraceptive techniques be developed so no resort needs to be taken to abortion.

Jim Wallis is, like Sider, concerned about the disparity in income between the rich industrialized nations and the poor in the developing countries, much of which he regards as the responsibility of the United States.[10] In his view, poverty in the developing countries is maintained by the economic and political system of the United States. He chides the Evangelical churches for practicing "compassionless inactivity" and declares that American overconsumption is a theft from the poor. He also believes that people in the developing countries are poor because residents in the United States are rich and pursue destructive policies toward the poor. To improve this imbalance, there must be a *massive redistribution of the world's wealth*. Again, this sounds like good ethics; we can well imagine that Jesus would have said something like this in our day (and Wallis quotes a mass of Bible texts to bolster his argument). It is a task of Christian economic statesmanship to show how international poverty can be eradicated. In the spirit of Wallis' overriding concern, the financial and human resource constraints under which development assistance is now operating must be relaxed so the fight against poverty can be waged on a more comprehensive scale.

But simple redistribution of wealth would not do. No massive improvements can be achieved unless the developing countries themselves are ready to adopt drastic policy reform and development programs. Many countries have done just that, with proven success. Strengthening the human resource base, through education and health measures, and physical infrastructure are both essential elements of domestic policy. These initiatives should be supported by external help. Some redistribution of resources might, of course, be involved— for example, through a tax on luxury consumption and major cutbacks in resource consumption by rich countries in the interest of global environmental policies. But the fiscal sacrifice would be accompanied (and probably be paid for) by a much improved growth environment for the international economy and the poorer countries in particular. At present, world poverty is a drag on the well-being of both the poor and the rich countries, and it is the task of a well-motivated economic policy to remove this obstacle. Jim Wallis is thinking in the right direction, and many of his proposals would be supported by present World Bank operations and a high level of lending on grant-like terms by the International Development Association.

The economic thinking underlying the views of Wallis and other Evangelicals deserves further attention.

ECONOMICS IN THE EVANGELICAL SPECTRUM

There are deep differences in the economic philosophy of the various Evangelical groups. The more Fundamentalist-oriented, typified by Falwell and his Liberty University, revere free-market capitalism. On the other side of the spectrum, the Evangelical conscience is deeply concerned with world poverty and practices economics with a human face, but it plays down what poor countries can do for themselves. Put simply, the first group blames poverty on the poor, the latter blames it on the rich.

Despite Falwell's enthusiasm for the free market, the links between Evangelicals and capitalist philosophy are not firm. As one student of Evangelical economics puts it: "A strong free-market consensus remains at best a prospect for the future. Moreover, rank and file Evangelicals show no signs whatsoever of embracing a distinctive, religiously motivated, economic ethic. They are just as open to income redistribution as other Americans and just as supportive of government programs to promote health, education, and urban renewal, and to alleviate the problems of race, poverty, and the environment. This contrasts sharply with their attitudes toward many moral issues, which are indeed different from and more conservative than those of other Americans. . . . Evangelical leaders with a serious, religiously-oriented commitment to conservative economic principles remain few, their best hopes a distant prospect" (Iannaccone, 1991).

The diversity of economic views among Evangelicals can perhaps be explained in part by the fact that the Bible on which they seek to base themselves does not advocate any particular economic doctrine, except to teach a deep concern for the poor and underprivileged.

Falwell's Contemporary Economics and Business Association (CEBA) underlines the idea that a free-enterprise-based system of political economy can only be successful if it has the underpinning of Judeo–Christian moral values, a value system which has been the basis for most of its great achievements.[11] This point, made earlier by the eminent economist Kenneth Boulding, is indeed very important for life under capitalism. The rules of Christian ethics apply to the capitalist system of economic organization and, with equal strength, to a socialist system such as is still found in China. Other Evangelicals have stressed the importance of personal attitudes and the role of churches in empowering the poor to cope better in an often-hostile world.[12]

In brief, the Christian Right advocates the economic principles of the Chicago school, with its strong reliance on free pricing and disdain for corrective action by government. Perhaps what it does not appreciate is that leading advocates of the Chicago school have shown little use for Christian ethics. In the years immediately following World War

II, Frank Knight, the distinguished philosopher of free-market economics at the University of Chicago, lectured with a distinctly anti-Christian slant. His summer course on the history of economic thought would customarily attract clergy–teachers, whom Knight severely embarrassed with numerous antireligious remarks. Milton Friedman, a leading spokesman for the free market, similarly demonstrated disdain for ethical judgments in his Chicago lectures. Perhaps Fundamentalist economists should look elsewhere for better friends. It is also perplexing that the Christian Right has not faced up to the limitations of the free market. Are they not aware of the adverse effects of unbridled unregulated "free" markets and the many efforts made to mitigate the impact of markets or that, as mentioned in Chapter 1, on many occasions government has had to come to the aid of the free-market system? The market system has inherent instabilities that have damaging effects on poor countries and the poor amongst us. When prices plummet on world markets, it is the poorest economies that suffer most, for they are most dependent on exports of a few commodities. No praise of free markets will help the poor countries when external conditions turn against them. Moreover, the Fundamentalist preachers have not begun to realize that most corporations, the pillars of capitalism, do not operate by Christian principles, but instead are single-mindedly interested in the bottom line at the risk of enhancing selfishness and endangering the rule of love.

The procapitalist bias of the Christian Right is shared by many economists writing in the *Bulletin of the Association of Christian Economists*. They are generally emphatic in their support of free markets and their fear of government intervention. Many are also opposed to giving preferential attention to the poor.

Against the background of praise of capitalism from Fundamentalist quarters, it is useful to listen again to what J. Philip Wogaman, the Methodist ethicist and clergyman, taught in "The Great Economic Debate, an Ethical Analysis" (1977). In his view, "*laissez-faire* capitalism" tends to encourage and institutionalize the expression of human greed. Self-centeredness becomes a culturally approved attitude toward life. (Wogaman, 1977, p. 121; and Michael Lerner, 1996). Wogaman also believed that the market may not deal adequately with the expression of public needs, such as education and transportation; nor does it deal with the dumping of toxic waste by private industry, or the use of public facilities (harbors, roads) by the private sector. The free-market economy must therefore be complemented by government

action in selected areas, as it is in the mixed economy (or what Wogaman called social–market capitalism). In retrospect, the case for the
mixed economy has been reinforced by the experience of stronger free-
market policies since the 1980s. Many countries have found that the
private sector can play a vital role in designing and financing infrastructure projects which earlier had been the exclusive domain of the
public sector. This has been amply demonstrated by the work of the
International Finance Corporation and the restructuring of the public
sector and industry in Latin America.

Our discussion of the divergence in economic thinking among
Evangelicals concludes with a review of the Oxford Conference on
Christian Faith and Economics, a serious attempt to reach a more uni-
fied Christian position on social issues.

THE OXFORD CONFERENCE ON
CHRISTIAN FAITH AND ECONOMICS

Against the contrasting economic philosophies of the different Evangelical groups, the Oxford Conference on Christian Faith and Economics, organized by Ron Sider, the head of Evangelicals for Social Action,
has sought to unite the various strands of Evangelical economic thinking. In 1990 the conference produced a Declaration which "represents
a significant consensus on the importance of both democracy and the
market economy but also on the centrality of God's demand for justice
and the need to correct the injustices of present-day capitalism" (Sider,
1990, p. 213). Like the earlier statements of the Catholic bishops and
the mainline Protestant churches, the declaration sees shortcomings in
both capitalism and socialism. In the words of the declaration, humanity is confronted by the two challenges of "selfish individualism,"
which neglects the human community, and "rigid collectivism," which
stifles human freedom. Christians and others have often pointed out
both dangers. "But only recently have we (the signatories) realized
that both ideologies have a view of the world with humanity at the
center which reduces material creation to a mere instrument" (par. 4).
The declaration reflects many of the positions Sider takes in his book
"Rich Christians in an Age of Hunger" (1990).[13]

The declaration reaffirms Christian views on the environment
and discrimination. Its views on full employment are, however, rather
garbled and reflect a good deal of give-and-take among the authors. It
sees the right to work as part of the freedom of the individual to

contribute to the satisfaction of the needs of the community. The right to earn a living imposes an obligation on the community to provide employment opportunities. Employment cannot be guaranteed where rights conflict and resources may be inadequate. However, the fact that such a right cannot be enforced does not detract in any way from the obligation to seek the highest level of employment which is consistent with justice and the availability of resources (par. 25 and 26).

On poverty and justice, the statement considers the fact that one in five human beings lives today in extreme poverty that is offensive to God. While God extends his love to all, he is the "defender of the poor." In every part of scripture, the Bible expresses God's concern for justice for the poor. Furthermore, the obsessive or careless pursuit of material goods is one of the most destructive idolatries in human history. The declaration recognizes the many complex causes of poverty operating at the global, national, local, and personal level. Poverty results from and is sustained by both constraints on the production of wealth and the inequitable distribution of wealth and income. Every society must provide people with the means to live at a level consistent with their standing as persons created in the image of God.

In brief, the declaration summarizes well how Christians must think of the roles of individuals and governments in the attack on poverty and prevailing injustice. It also has a grasp of both domestic and international economic issues (par. 42–45). And it draws attention to the importance of the informal sector in poverty eradication in developing countries and of credit to small enterprises (par. 64).

The declaration confines itself to general statements and (with the exception of a proposal for making credit available to small business) does not enter into specific measures. Some feel this is a distinct shortcoming—as, for example, Jim Skillen in his critique of the declaration (Skillen, 1990). It is, of course, above all a consensus document, and Sider himself would have preferred to have gone further on full employment and other issues (par. 26). Government is seen as a source of evil as well as of good, but the declaration adds, "It is the responsibility of Christians to work for governmental structures that serve justice" (par. 60).

The declaration of the 1990 conference was the basic reference for the further deliberations held five years later at Agra, India, where the participants held wide-ranging discussions and spent much effort on the formulation of positions that necessarily reflected different theoretical and cultural perceptions. The resulting Affirmation (1995) is a basic statement on the ethical norms for economic behavior and underlying economic systems. It envisions the church's calling of helping to bring about a just society, reflecting the fact that the poor were a priority in Jesus' ministry. This includes exploring the possibility of debt forgiveness when appropriate (affirmation 27). The Report on the Conference's Findings deals with the functioning of a market economy, including the preconditions for a "responsible economy" that fights poverty. It stresses that "eradicating absolute poverty and alleviating socioeconomic inequity require immediate, focused and convergent action from all sectors of society." A transformation of the poor must make them *active participants* in their own and the overall development effort. This will involve developing the human capital of the poor, organizing and empowering them, encouraging self-employment, and sustaining economic growth without leaving the poor to the blind operations of market forces. The report cautions against excessive government intervention and advises that policies "set a balance between environmental care and human needs." The background paper by Linwood T. Geiger, "Market Activity and Poverty," gives a careful overview of development economics with emphasis on the role of the market, especially in export development, but also discusses the consequences of more liberal trade and pricing policies for the poor.[14]

One can only hope that the growing and highly diverse Evangelical movement will continue to make progress on the path taken by the Oxford Conference. More agreement must be worked out on action in critical social areas, such as health, population policy, education, and environmental protection. A truly concerted national effort in these fields would benefit from fuller cooperation of the Christian Right, for which common faith in the Bible should give ample ground.

The ethical base for cooperation is the foundation on which all the different elements in society must work together toward the eradication of poverty. The essence of collaboration is the main theme of the next and final chapter.

13
Working Together to Eradicate Poverty

The causes of poverty are complex and can only be addressed through close collaboration among many different elements in our society. Such comprehensive action must be based on moral conviction and be justified as well by economic considerations. Integration of the poor into the mainstream will contribute to higher output and income in the entire nation and will reduce welfare and other social assistance.

To give sharper focus to what can be done, it is useful to take perspective on the many causes of poverty and what all, in both the private and the public domain, can do to fight poverty.

MANY DIFFERENT CAUSES

The discussion in Part One focused on the economic causes of poverty and the policies necessary to address them. The pastorals of the churches pointed to the moral case for action, but also dealt with economic problems. When we look at the forces that bring individuals into poverty, we realize that there are both economic and noneconomic causes (Freedman, 1993). Moreover, our systems of economics, politics, and morals all suffer from failure, with often painful consequences for people in poverty.

Even with a positive outlook on life, we cannot ignore the failures in the social systems that affect our well-being, failures that are felt most acutely by the poor among us. Our society suffers from a prevailing sense of selfishness which suppresses genuine care for neighbor and the community at large (Lerner, 1996).

- The *Economic System* has often failed for various reasons. The free market does not always function smoothly and leaves deep pockets of poverty. Industrial and agricultural change have depressed incomes in some regions, often below poverty levels—e.g., in the Monongahela Valley, the hollows of Appalachia, and the parts of Iowa that have been depopulated. The low economic growth of many past years has accentuated the problems of poverty and the inadequacy of health insurance, and has reduced our ability and willingness to take adequate action. Vigorous growth would basically change the prospects of the poor and enhance the feasibility of effective action.

- The *Government* has failed to provide universal health care and has not always given sufficient support to crucial local initiatives and efforts. Both government and the electorate have let poverty and despair fester in our inner cities.

- Our *Welfare System* was not designed to make recipients productive in the marketplace. It failed to encourage recipients to seek work and to bolster the family, the cornerstone of a just society. The real value of welfare payments has been going down drastically, and as a result more welfare recipients have been falling below the poverty line.

- Our *Education System*, both public and private, still does not produce a sufficient number of skilled workers able to make a living wage in a technically advanced society. It has been slow to accommodate itself to the social problems faced by students.

- Our *Transportation System* has failed to provide sufficient mobility and flexibility so poor people can move to where the jobs are.

- Our *Morals and Personal Discipline* have failed; witness the disintegration of family and marriage, irresponsible sexual behavior, the use of drugs and alcohol, and the spread of homelessness.

- Our *Social Mores and Legal System* have often failed to maintain racial and gender equality, with resulting higher poverty rates for women and minorities.

- Our *Society* has failed by becoming more violent, with the poor paying the highest price for the disturbance of peace in their neighborhoods.

- *Genetic Failure* is often the cause of alcoholism, which places individuals at risk, even though they remain responsible for their own behavior.

- Our *Disaster Relief System* fails to prevent many victims from falling prey to poverty for short or even longer periods.

The ethnic and cultural diversity of our society makes it imperative that the different issues be tackled with care and that solutions allow for the special problems faced by different groups. This is especially important for the African-American community. The future of this community is critical to the outlook for poverty eradication. While economic issues are central, spiritual and moral health are of equal importance. The black community is deeply divided on how to grow into an accepted part of society. It is aware of discrimination that has continued despite progress on the legal status of African-Americans. Feeling part of society is not just a matter of physical well-being; it requires a deep change in psychological outlook. The growing African-American middle class, more than half working in government jobs, has now risen beyond poverty. But some resent the affirmative action which helped them to get where they are today (West, 1993).

ALL MUST CONTRIBUTE

The great variety of causes means that effective antipoverty action must be comprehensive and not be fragmented. In the changing conditions of our country, experimentation with new approaches will be needed.

Government economic policy can only be part, however critical, of a comprehensive antipoverty effort. Other components are business action; reform of the social service system; assistance to the family; and actions by the local community and school, the religious community, and individuals. No one party in this effort can do the job without the others doing their share.

Among the main areas for action by both government and business, one must mention:

- Increase savings and productive investment;
- Keep the federal deficit under control, restructure government expenditures, and shrink the size of the bureaucracy;
- Increase and sustain the availability of productive jobs;
- Sustain the conversion of the military component of our economy to peacetime civilian production;
- Rebuild our neglected inner cities and bring new hope through housing construction and job creation;

- Modernize manufacturing industries so they can operate without semipermanent special protection from foreign competition (as in steel, autos, and textiles);
- Restore excellence in our schools and provide quality education for all; and
- Reduce the cost of health care and make it available to all.

Government can take a number of direct measures to combat poverty. Cash assistance, food stamps, housing, and other subsidies work to soften the pain of poverty. But public efforts will be most effective when they help people to help themselves. For example, extension of earned income tax credits (e.g., to families below the poverty line) not only provides additional spendable income but also rewards work. More effective education and training of welfare recipients can help them enter the labor market. In addition, the poor can be empowered through home ownership and control of their own neighborhoods, indeed, of city politics. A National Urban Corps, possibly using exsoldiers, can help clean up cities. Programs are needed to create jobs and stimulate conditions for an improved environment for the desperately poor.[1] It may also be possible to start a program, a new Education Corps, that would use unemployed professional and technical workers to educate the marginalized.

These actions would require a concerted effort of the entire community, a new national consensus, so all elements of our society can deal with our social ills. In reality, the measures will have to be pursued in an environment where many forces are undermining our capitalist free-market system, and better financial balance in the public sector requires that the total cost of entitlements be contained. Conservative politicians have been seeking to cut assistance for the poor in the interest of preserving entitlements of richer groups. Moreover, the integration of the United States with the global economy is working against the interests of the poor.

Antipoverty measures work best when the economy is growing vigorously. Maintenance of high levels of employment is a critical ingredient of poverty eradication. Both private and public sectors can contribute to better growth and productivity. Government and business have the tools to create more and better jobs, but action has often been handicapped by assigning too high priority to maintaining price stability. The Federal Reserve has tended to keep the economy on too tight a leash.

The federal budget deficit has worsened the nation's social deficit (Catholic Church, 1993). Restoration of better balance in the budget will strengthen the government's ability to pursue a more positive social policy. However, while most direct assistance to the poor is administered by government—federal, state, and local agencies—many are anxious to limit the role of government and to place greater emphasis on personal freedom and responsibility. Our government agencies are already overextended, although many do a first-rate job in difficult circumstances. Many feel we must find solutions that don't start and end with state intervention.

The view of limited government places enormous responsibilities on the private sector, not the least on the large corporations. When we watch past anemic growth of output, employment, and productivity in the United States, we may well ask what went wrong. What better contribution could big business have made, in innovation, efficiency, productivity, and job creation? In past years, with a few notable exceptions, the large companies were not as dynamic as smaller enterprises. The big companies were not centers of innovation and fell behind in the quest for excellence. Nevertheless, since the 1980s big business has made an important contribution to making our economy more efficient and competitive.

In many cases greater efficiency has come at a high social cost. Corporate management often treats labor like an enemy, an outsider that does not need to be trained and can be dispensed with when times get rough. Corporations put thousands of their best employees out of work to save a few cents per share of profits, by moving abroad and getting the benefit of cheaper labor. What kind of spirit is this? It is bad economics and bad ethics. It does not allow for the cost of plant closings to the community and has been costly in terms of jobs lost and a widespread feeling of insecurity. Continued restructuring of manufacturing is critical, but it should be much more than mere downsizing.

As unproductive jobs are phased out, new ones must be created. Even with the benefits of free trade and international integration, the United States has in many situations the resources at home to make first-rate products at reasonable cost. Many large enterprises have emerged from their harsh restructuring with renewed strength and greater efficiency, and are now able to support a new burst of growth in the U.S. economy. Moreover, our smaller enterprises play a central role in the economy. Government and banks can help smaller businesses with loans and technological assistance. There is a strong case for a new collaboration between labor, government, and business in making the best use of our people and our communities. All will be the beneficiaries, not the least the poorest among us.

Poverty can only be eradicated when individuals take personal responsibility for their lives. But they must be backed up by government assuming its social responsibility. For this our present social service system must be expanded so people will not fail as they proceed through successive stages of life. Our present welfare system, which is only one facet in a comprehensive antipoverty program, is relatively small. It takes up only a small proportion of our GDP and lifts only a fraction of recipients above the poverty line. Our welfare spending is far below that of Western Europe, and it is less effective in bringing people out of poverty. We are good at creating jobs and wealth, but we also suffer more poverty.[2]

Our present social service system remains inadequate, in that people in various phases of life's transitions often look in vain for help. Moreover, funding has been cut for essential institutions like schools and clinics.

It is crucial that *children* get a healthy start in life and receive adequate support as they grow up. We need a child support system so divorce does not hurl children and single parents into poverty. More broadly, a Children's Fund could be set up to complement the Social Security and Health Care Systems for all children. Such a fund could be a logical step in health care reform, quite different from what has been proposed so far. Head Start should be extended to all children at risk. Further, empower the schools, build communities around them, and let them extend essential services.

Families must be bolstered as they face the economic and social storms of our time. Some conservative politicians preach about family values, but propose little help to the hard-working institutions that deserve assistance in this area. Local institutions like schools can share added social responsibilities besides teaching; they can address the physical and emotional needs of children who come to school hungry, neglected, or abused. More broadly, it seems obvious that our welfare practice should not break up poor families while extending necessary financial or medical care. Family Leave has now been enacted into law, but the present child care system is chaotic and full government support for high-quality care is still wanting.

Reform of the health care system continues as a central issue. The failures of the system are all too well-known. U.S. health care is of high quality but continues to suffer from excessive administration and too rapidly rising costs of medicines. Almost 40 million Americans are uninsured, and many more fear their insurance will fail them as they change jobs, a problem now dealt with by new legislation. Sensible ways should be found to simplify the system and make insurance accessible to all, contain rising costs, and give more attention to prevention and to health and sex education.

Social Security, our most successful program, is effective in lifting its beneficiaries out of poverty and has strong political support. In the interest of greater equity, the social security income of the wealthier recipients should be taxed as ordinary income, and scaled down gradually as their incomes rise above a certain level.

The cost of improving the social services system is much less than the cost of the present nonsystem, after allowing for the burden of failure we now bear. This is, for example, clear from the dramatic savings associated with proper prenatal care that many poor women now must forego. The cost of proper child support has been estimated at $15 billion by the National Commission on Children—and this could be financed by cutting part of what Medicare now spends on the care of terminal patients, an obvious area for saving in the present system (Freedman, 1993, pp. 205–35).

In our national reflection on poverty, welfare takes a central place. Many regard it as money ill spent, even a cause of poverty. The welfare debate has brought the shortcomings of the system into sharp focus. But the difficulties of reform must be clear: they are at the heart of the fight against poverty. One conclusion that should emerge is that welfare and growth are closely intertwined.

GROWTH AND WELFARE

There has been a widespread conviction that welfare—formerly the entitlement under Aid to Families with Dependent Children (AFDC)—has needed to be reformed. Unfortunately, the welfare debate has been caught up in the deliberations about balancing the budget, essentially an entirely different objective. The ensuing debate has brought out some of the weaknesses of welfare, but not all negative judgments are correct and the poor have been made the scapegoats of what ails society. For example, there is no evidence that it causes or encourages births out of wedlock, principally by single mothers on welfare.[3] Neither does the system attract a high proportion of recipients to remain on welfare for long periods (Moynihan, 1996, p. 185).

From the 1970s onward, some social analysts have maintained that welfare causes poverty and dependence. The poor are stigmatized as undeserving and belonging to an "underclass," originally an economic term (coined by the Swedish economist and Noble laureate Gunnar Myrdal) which has instead become pejorative.[4]

A main reason for change is to encourage recipients to become productive citizens and get a job. The system, as it was operating until the mid-1990s, suffered from many deficiencies—e.g., it counteracted recipients' efforts at work and asset building. There is also a strong case for simplifying the welfare system. It might best be administered through agencies that are close to the people and communities served. The administrative role of the federal government has been reduced, but federal finance and guidance remain essential. Federal welfare guidelines are important since nationally the system should be fairly uniform, albeit geared to local conditions. We should be able to improve the welfare system without great cost and over the longer term reap important savings. Fortunately, many states have already started to improve the administration of welfare and encourage people to take jobs. As U.S. economic performance improved after 1992, the number of recipients has declined by almost two million and is continuing to go down. Changes in welfare policy are running considerable risks. Some people may turn out to be unemployable, and many may not find jobs in their immediate vicinity. Some mothers will be thrown off welfare rolls without obvious means of support. Some states are bound to botch the administration of programs. Some auxiliary steps must accompany changes in welfare. Thus if they are to move into the labor force, single mothers will need access to child care assistance. Government may have to provide public sector jobs if the private sector does not have sufficient openings (Sawhill, 1995).

The 1996 welfare measures ended the entitlements under AFDC. It makes welfare assistance subject to a five-year lifetime limit and expects recipients to find employment within two years. Working mothers will be helped by an increase of $4 billion in federal aid for child care. The measures cut back food stamps and are particularly harsh on the immigrant population: illegal immigrants and their children are excluded from most federal means-tested benefits; states could deny Medicaid benefits to noncitizens. Under the new law, future legal immigrants are denied most federal benefits during their first five years in the country. The Urban Institute predicted that 1.1 million children will be pushed into poverty by the new policies, and this figure is likely to rise as the full impact of the new law is felt. In all, the reform reflects the spirit of the Republican "Contract with America" which, according to the eminent MIT economist Lester Thurow, targeted the poor, whom it claimed are poor because they are lazy and singled them out as the despised group in our country.[5] The reform as enacted will in any case run up against the scarcity of jobs in the inner cities and certain rural areas. Many welfare mothers were already working at least part-time, but their earnings were insufficient to put them on a self-sustaining basis.

It is well to recall that the welfare debate, along with the reconsideration of Supplemental Security Income (SSI), Medicaid, and Medicare, took place in an environment of relatively slow growth.[6] In the more rapidly growing economy of the 1950s and 1960s, the country was able to start new social insurance schemes without restricting the financing of government services. The possibilities of financing new initiatives are now much less. However, as employment conditions have improved in the 1990s, even the inner city has benefited. Continued favorable performance will help to create jobs, and this in turn will improve the outlook of the inner city and the families living there. It is in the broader national interest for the deliberations about welfare and the budget deficit not to be negative—focusing on cutting back government services—but instead to give more explicit consideration to the possibilities of more vigorous growth. Cutting back government per se does not create prosperity. Instead of emphasizing budget balance, it would be more beneficial to strengthen confidence in government. Controlling expenditures and making the best use of scarce resources are far better objectives than setting targets for budget balance. In some circumstances, a budget deficit is a necessary tool of economic policy. Moreover, anyone who has worked with economic projections over a 7–10-year period knows that they are little more than science fiction; they serve merely as a framework for discussion and decision making. Genuine action takes place in the present or the immediate future.

Growth is, of course, only one policy objective. The poor need more commodities, like housing, appliances, and cars. In addition to growth, we must give priority attention to such issues as assuring jobs for African-Americans and Hispanics, overcoming environmental degradation, keeping our civilian economy efficient and competitive, finding productive employment for those displaced by industrial restructuring and downsizing the military, etc. Child care and job training services are essential in moving people into the workforce. In the past, many public training programs have been costly and ineffective; results-oriented private programs must play a key role.

In the final analysis, welfare makes little sense from an economic viewpoint. The consequences of the absence of welfare, the presence of people in total deprivation and despair, are both morally and economically unacceptable. The essential aim must be that all can live in dignity, even when their living standard is minimal. For these economic and moral reasons, the administration of welfare should recognize the human dignity of the recipient (a point also stressed by early Jewish writers) and in substance it should help to move people into the workforce. Only in a society where work and reward are divorced could one conceive of the greater share of recipients in a permanent welfare status. The overriding motivation and justification remain ethical.

THE MESSAGE OF SOCIAL JUSTICE

Churches, synagogues, and community organs have an obvious role to play in helping and nurturing families, single mothers, and children. Even in a secular society, churches are family for many people, but not all churches provide this kind of support, and less than half of our population regularly attends church. In many situations churches and synagogues extend their influence well beyond their own membership. Other community-based institutions can play a similar role.

In their "economic pastorals" the churches focused their attention not narrowly on moral questions or on their social role in the community, but on economic policies to further social justice. It is worthwhile to listen to what they have to say and explore whether their views make economic sense.

The Christian and Jewish communities have been true *Champions of the Poor* by taking on the issues posed by pervasive poverty. They have spoken out, often against a background of a long history of social witness, in years when the federal administration tended to favor the rich, turned its back on many of the needs of the poor, cut back on job training and other essential programs, and contributed to greater inequality in the distribution of income in our society. The churches expressed themselves in their own theological language. By and large they were united in their social message and recognized the urgency of action required to reduce the suffering of the poor and to build their productivity. They were inspired by a renewed insight into the Bible which, while treating all people alike, recognizes the plight of the poor and calls for priority action against poverty.

In speaking out, the churches play a key role in awakening and keeping alive in their constituency a concern for the prevalence of poverty. They stress that we need to contain our consumption in the interest of our own health and sanity and of our environment. But more important, they explain and proclaim the moral basis for the fight against poverty. To make its message heard, the religious community can go some way in making more use of up-to-date electronic means of communication. It should not leave the use of television and radio to Fundamentalist preachers who express little social concern. Moreover, to be heard they must address the predicament of all in modern society, not just the poor. But while the church must continue to update its message of love in the most effective way, it should have no illusions about its chance of success, because its message is sounded in a hostile world dominated by institutions organized for profit and not for furthering social objectives.

In the United States we have heard much about the importance of "family values." Among the church statements, the Presbyterians stressed that the family must be the cornerstone of a just society. Others will argue that if only we honor the family there would be less trouble in the inner city and there would be less need for welfare. Of course, it is true that if children are cared for by two parents instead of one they are better off. And if men did not leave their wives and children we'd have a better base for fighting poverty. But preaching about family values is much easier than taking practical steps that make sure they are honored. Seeing the moral causes of poverty does not absolve us from looking for solutions beyond condemning the immorality of others. For there is genuine despair among the urban poor in our country, and the situation is much worse because we have neglected the infrastructure of the city, have not created enough urban jobs, and as employers have not treated blacks in the same way as whites. As stressed by Moynihan (1996, p. 226), social decay has continued despite a long streak of noninflationary prosperity in the United States, and new approaches must be developed to counteract this paradoxical trend.

Those who point to immorality as a cause of poverty are not excused for not taking action in the economic sphere. The churches are right to point to the moral basis of antipoverty action, but it is to their credit that in addressing poverty problems, they have gone beyond questions of morality and looked at economic facts and policies.

Issues of morality in our society are not confined to the behavior of poor urban blacks. The whites who ran the savings and loan associations into the ground during the 1980s were clearly in conflict with the law and profited at the expense of the public. And the senior corporate managers who failed to innovate and to raise productivity likewise inflicted damage on our economy and community to the detriment of healthy job creation, and did not live up to their social obligations. Many corporations continue to push consumption of products with doubtful social value, and they continue to greatly contribute to environmental degradation.

Socially concerned religious leaders have an important role in their community. Many church members are relatively well-off, contented people. The message of the churches draws attention to the ethical issues posed by poverty and calls the faithful to arms in an all-out war against poverty. At the same time the churches' message urges the government into action, but while the churches speak with authority, they carry the most weight with their own members. All this applies equally to the community role of synagogues.

The churches seek to reinforce the basic personal attitudes that must underlie effective action. In their view, God changes our inner selves, our motivation, our will, perception, and objectives. So changed, we seek not to engage in acts of injustice, but instead to enter in better relations with our Creator, our fellow beings, and our environment. We want to establish a better order within ourselves and in the world about us. The change that comes when we become new beings in Christ makes us new and different persons. But it does not stop there. We also want to work with God in making the world a better place. We see the hard facts in a new light, and we want to change those aspects of our society that do not conform to God's rule of justice and love. Christ is not a social reformer, but sets people free to start over in their personal lives and to defeat all forms of oppression in the economic system.

The religious community has to work closely with other elements in our society to address poverty issues more forcefully. It must be an essential part of a broad mosaic of many different groups joining in effective action.

WORKING TOGETHER

In the fight against poverty, many players must work together and make their own unique contribution: church, community, business, labor, and government. They cannot succeed on their own. They must attack both economic and noneconomic causes of poverty.

The Christian and Jewish communities need to continue identifying the moral base for antipoverty action and protest the prevailing ethos of selfishness. A new understanding of the Bible focuses on the priority of such action. Many of the churches' and synagogues' members belong to the contented and relatively well-off majority of the electorate. They may be loath to let their tax dollars be spent on the poor. The religious community has a key role in persuading its membership of the urgency of action. It is also well-suited to call attention to the basic importance of noneconomic factors in defeating poverty, such as moral behavior, moderation in consumption, the misuse of drugs and alcohol, and the role of the family. The role of the religious community would become even more important should government once again deemphasize the concerns of the poor and weak in society.

Business, especially the large corporations, has to act with a greater sense of social responsibility. Our American system of limited government cannot work without a dynamic business sector. In this endeavor, labor must work in partnership with business. Productive, well-trained, and well-paid labor is far better for the economy and the fight against poverty than cheap labor operating at low levels of productivity. Our economy is able to maintain wages at remunerative—indeed just—levels that make possible consumption adequate for personal and family lives and also encourage capital investment compatible with the latest technology.

It is in everyone's interest that government and business work closely together to achieve our country's social objectives. Government, including the Federal Reserve, has the main function of setting the right macroeconomic course, taking the lead in a greater savings effort, giving the right signals for a more productive economy, and mobilizing essential assistance for the poor at home and abroad. The government should have the means to take whatever direct supplementary measures are needed to remove poverty from the richest economy on earth. The United States has the means to reduce poverty substantially.

In the global economy, poverty is widespread, and poverty problems in the developing countries are even more intractable than in the United States. The globalization of economic life sharpens the dichotomy between rich and poor. The primary movers in the global economy, large banks and corporations, have demonstrated little social concern. The impact of globalization aggravates poverty and unemployment in many regions and industries in the United States. In the end, each nation must deal with and overcome its own problems, but the rich countries have a moral obligation to assist the developing countries, and it is in their own economic interest to do so. On their part, the international development finance institutions can go further in linking their operations to poverty alleviation and sound environmental policies, and in finding new ways of encouraging the developing countries to save their rain forests (Barend A. de Vries, 1996a and b).

We must expect to make mistakes in this complex endeavor of eliminating poverty. Short-sighted self-interest may prevent some groups from making their full contribution. Many individuals will shy away from assuming personal responsibility and hence will frustrate the best of socioeconomic effort. Others are prejudiced by wrong objectives and wrong information. They believe people are poor because they are undeserving, have not assumed their personal responsibility, and have not made use of what society offers. Or they believe they must save public resources to "balance the budget," a target that cannot be justified by modern economics and could bring us back to the economics of Herbert Hoover and earlier. In other words, these people do not focus on the real issues before us, among them the festering wounds of segregated poor minorities and a stagnating middle class in an economy that has been growing at too slow a pace. Policy must be focused on making everyone better off.

As morally committed people, we know it is not right to let dismay and deprivation fester in our midst. We have the tools and the means to tackle these problems and must go forth and pursue these righteous objectives. We can end the sense of despair that prevails in many quarters. We can pursue policies and solutions that can truly integrate our economy into a whole. Our analysis has identified many measures that will lift the marginalized into a new unity with all. What keeps us from adopting these measures? We can overcome lack of understanding by proper education. Let the word go forth and be illumined by truthful data, as we have sought to put forward. In the end, only comprehensive action will suffice. No one measure, no single actor, can do the job. Both overall economic and social policies and direct assistance are needed. And a moral conviction and motivation must underlie all effort.

Notes

PREFACE

1. See Kenneth Boulding, 1970, and the reference to his writing in Chapter 11, under The Social Gospel.

INTRODUCTION AND OVERVIEW

1. See Danziger et al., 1994.
2. See Chapter 1.

CHAPTER 1

1. The discussion of American poverty is based on the government's official definition. For all their flaws, the "official" measures of poverty in the United States have proved useful to both researchers and policy makers. Since 1965 the government has defined a person or family to be poor when the minimum food package costs more than 35 percent of their cash income. We can define the food package, calculate its cost, and allow for price rises over time. As of 1986, the poverty thresholds were $5,255 for an elderly individual, $11,203 for a four-person family, and $22,497 for a nine-person family (Sawhill, p. 1075). In 1992 the official poverty level for a family of four was $14,335 (*Washington Post*, Oct. 5, 1992); family income rose further to $15,569 in 1995 (*Washington Post*, Sept. 27, 1996).

The official definition raises all sorts of questions, but it is the best we have and does not seriously distort the true picture. Some economists argue that we might better define the poverty level in relation to the median income, say define people as being poor when their income falls below one-half of the median. The official poverty level was at 46 percent of the median level for a family of four in 1965, when the official U.S. poverty line was first introduced; by 1986 it had fallen to 32 percent. In practice, concerns about relative poverty tend to merge with concerns about the distribution of income. In the absence of a marked shift toward greater equality in income distribution, the poor, in a relative sense, will always be with us.

Other problems in the definition are taxation (should the poverty income be defined before or after taxes?), making allowance for the assets of the poor, and the question of the proper accounting period. Depending on the definition used, we find that in 1984 the poverty rate varied from 18.6 percent (the relative poverty rate defined as incomes below 46 percent of the median income), 14.4 percent (the official definition already given), and 5.9 percent (the proportion of people who were poor in every month of 1984). Allowing for the market value of noncash benefits (like food stamps and Medicaid) brings the official poverty rate to 9.7 percent.

Given all the questions about the definition, we should not be surprised at the conclusion of one researcher (Harold Watts): "Our official measures are not grounded in some self-evident principle or expert consensus but are simply a collection of more or less arbitrary and eminently vulnerable rules. Their most remarkable feature is their widespread and persistent acceptance by the public and by those who make and criticize public policies" (Sawhill, p. 1082).

More recently, some economists have argued forcefully that the official definition of poverty, set in the early 1960s, is now out of date. As the nation as a whole has become richer, our concept of what constitutes poverty has also changed. Thus experts constructing a market basket of essential consumer goods in the early 1960s would not have included a telephone, television, or air conditioner, let alone child care for working women, all essential items today in a minimal living standard. When adequate allowance is made for the rise in general standards, Patricia Ruggles of the Urban Institute argues that the poverty line for a family of three should be about $14,000 instead of the official figure of $9,435. But updating the poverty definition in this way would also substantially increase the number of people regarded as poor in the United States. By using the broader definition, some 20 percent of Americans would be classified as poor in 1988 instead of the official 13.1 percent (*Washington Post*, May 4, 1990).

2. Financial wealth, excluding homes and other real estate, is even more concentrated: 54 percent of all financial assets are held by the top 2 percent of families, those whose annual income exceeds $125,000. Of all financial assets, 86 percent is held by the top 10 percent of families (*Washington Post*, May 29, 1995, page A12). In 1995 income distribution became more equal, as the share of the bottom 60 percent rose by 0.5 percent and the share of the upper 40 percent fell; the percentage of incomes between $25,000 and $75,000 rose by 1 percent (*Washington Post*, Sept. 27, 1996). It is not clear whether these changes indicate a new trend.

3. Poverty fell steadily throughout the 1960s, to 12.1 percent in 1969. It remained below the range of 11–13 percent in the decade of the 1970s and increased in the 1980s, reaching 13.6 percent in 1986 and 15 percent in the early 1990s. The U.S. poverty rate in 1995 was 13.8 percent, as against 15.1 percent in 1993 and 14.8 percent in 1992. The poverty rate indicates the percentage of people with incomes below the poverty line, officially estimated at $14,763 per family of four in 1993. Official data indicate that the number of poor was 39.3 million in 1993. These data are based on cash income and exclude noncash benefits like food stamps, free school lunches, Medicaid, and Medicare. If these were included, the poverty rate would be 12.1 percent.

The median wage for full-time male workers dropped from $31,101 (1992) to $30,407 (1993) after adjusting for inflation. Some 39.7 million people were without health care insurance in 1993, or 15.3 percent of the population (1.1 million more than in 1992); this figure rose further to 40.6 million in 1995, or 15.4 percent of the population.

4. The statistics are: African-Americans (14.1 percent) and Hispanics (11.4 percent), compared with whites (6.5 percent). Unemployment on the ten largest Indian reservations was 40–60 percent according to the Bureau of Indian Affairs.

5. The Federal Reserve pursued at first the highly simplistic monetarist theory that to reach stable growth all that was necessary was to permit steady growth of the money supply. The economy would then take care of itself, a truly simplified image of our complex reality. The theory assumed a stable relationship between the growth of money and the real economy. But in the wake of the oil supply shocks of the 1970s, this relationship no longer proved to be stable.

6. In recent econometric work, Harvey Brenner (1993) has shown that high unemployment is positively correlated with insane asylum entries, life expectancy, and infant mortality. More generally, these health indicators are correlated with per capita income, income distribution, and unemployment ("Health and the National Economy" in Human Capital and Development; P.C. Huang, Ed. Greenwich, CT: JAI Press, 1993).

7. Philip Harvey, 1989, p. 50. See also Sumner Rosen, 1996, "Jobs: New Challenges, New Responses"; Annals of the American Academy of Political and Social Science.

8. Krugman, op. cit., Chapter 1. James K. Galbraith points out that improvement in output and productivity may have been underestimated because no allowance is made of the shift toward goods and services of higher quality goods for which issues of price and quality are of greater importance than for the standardized products that are replaced (See Challenge, May-June, 1995, p. 70).

9. After the events of 1989, one hardly needs to point out that Marxism, with its strong reliance on rigid central planning and allocation, obstructs free markets. Yet it also remains useful to recognize that the communist systems, apart from their dictatorial coercion, did allege to pay attention to the material well-being of the average citizen. This is an important characteristic that somehow must be preserved.

10. Kenneth Boulding: "Economic Progress as a Goal of Economic Life," in A. Dudley Ward, Ed., 1953, pp. 52–83.

11. Forty years later Michael Novak (1993) repeated most of Boulding's arguments on capitalism and progress, though perhaps not as succinctly and clearly. (Novak makes no reference to Boulding.)

12. U.S. Senator Albert Gore, Jr., pointed to the Minnesota Emergency Employment Development (MEED) program, which created 25,000 new jobs in two years for workers who had exhausted their unemployment benefits. MEED paid employers $5 per hour for six months for each new job; the cost to the state was offset by $37 million in added state income taxes and lower welfare costs. Gore also raised the possibility of minimum-wage summer jobs for some 700,000 disadvantaged teenagers who meet high academic standards

(Gore, "The Shape of our Destiny: America's Economic Choices," in Gannon, 1987).

Al Gore also pointed to the high demand in the United States for special skills. He observed that the U.S. government trains only 5 percent of the workers who need it, and compared this with the situation in Sweden. Sweden devotes 90 percent of its unemployment assistance to job creation, as against less than 20 percent in the United States. In view of the problems with state-sponsored programs, perhaps the private sector should be encouraged to play a larger role. It is a challenging field with ample scope for improvement and expansion.

13. J. Philip Wogaman, the *Washington Post*, June 15, 1991.

14. In his "Asian Drama" (1968), Gunnar Myrdal describes this phenomenon as the "backwash effect."

CHAPTER 2

1. The economic analysis in this chapter is presented, in greater detail, in the World Bank's World Development Reports (WDR, 1980 and 1990) and in Gillis et al., 1987, especially ch. 4: Development and Human Welfare. The consequences of the cleavage between rich and poor countries was tackled by the French clergyman Joseph Wresinski. Struck by the moral consequences of the separation of the poor from their richer fellows, he started the Fourth World Movement in 1957. From France the movement spread to several countries, including the United States, the United Kingdom, West Africa, Haiti, and Thailand. It has been officially recognized by the French government; the government stated at a meeting of the European Parliament that poverty has no place in a 20th-century industrialized country. Partly at the urging of the movement, the United Nations declared October 17 as the "UN Day against Poverty." (Information supplied by John Kay and "Fighting Poverty: A New Approach," The Fourth World Movement, 1990).

2. In 1980 the World Bank estimated the total of absolute poor at around 800 million, based on data assembled during the 1970s. (See Robert S. McNamara, Address to the Board of Governors of the World Bank, Sept. 30, 1980). Allowing for poverty in China and growth of world population brings the estimate to at least 1 billion in 1990. See Hollis B. Chenery et al., 1974, a study organized at the suggestion of then World Bank President McNamara, which advocated a more gradual approach to economic development.

3. More recent calculations conclude that the world's poor continue to exceed 1 billion (not counting poverty in the Western industrialized countries), but the statistical definition has been changed somewhat. The World Development Report (WDR), 1990 (page 82) draws the poverty line at $370 per capita (in 1985 dollars) and applies this poverty definition to all LDCs, including China, as well as to Eastern Europe. Thus defined, the poor numbered 1,116 million in 1985, of which 180 million are in sub-Saharan Africa and 800 million are in Asia (with 210 million in China and 420 million in India). The estimate for the number of poor in China is highly sensitive to the calculation of the minimal standard of living threshold; by Chinese standards, the threshold is

60 cents per day and the corresponding number of poor is 90 million; on the other hand, by international standards the threshold is one dollar per day, and the corresponding number of poor is 300 million (World Bank News, October 24, 1996).

4. The poverty rate for India was 55 percent, sub-Saharan Africa 47 percent, and China a much lower 20 percent. Some 57 percent of these poor are "extremely poor" (i.e., have a per capita income below $275). Squire (1993) shows slightly different figures. The poverty rate (or head-count index) for all LDCs taken together decreased somewhat during 1985–1990, but it increased in Latin America and the Middle East–North Africa. The poverty gap index reflects the depth of poverty by taking into account how far the average poor person's income is from the poverty line. The index suggests that the poor in Latin America and the Middle East have become relatively worse off during 1985–1990.

5. "Many of the poor are located in regions where arable land is scarce, agricultural productivity is low and drought, floods and environmental degradation are common. This is particularly marked in Bangladesh. In Latin America the worst poverty occurs in arid zones or on steep hill slope areas, economically vulnerable and isolated in every sense" (WDR, 1990, p. 30).

6. "Poverty and hunger among children is of special concern. The very young are highly susceptible to disease, and malnutrition and poverty-related diseases can cause permanent harm. Child poverty is strongly selfperpetuating" (WDR, 1990, p. 31).

7. "Under-five mortality"—the number of deaths per thousand children below five—is 121 for all developing countries, with above-average death rates in sub-Saharan Africa (196), South Asia (172), and the Middle East–North Africa (148). Below-average deaths are recorded in China (58), Latin America and the Caribbean (75), and Eastern Europe (8).

8. It was not until the mid-1980s that Ghana began to enjoy a greater degree of political stability and was able to place greater reliance on the price mechanism and to turn more initiative over to the private sector. It has now become a model of growth with better utilization of natural resources.

9. There are no precise methods for determining priorities in education. One method relies on estimates of "personnel" requirements. Aimed at avoiding shortages of particular skills, this method can easily produce fallacious results because of shifts in industrial staffing requirements and changes in the supply of different skills. Another method is based on the calculation of return to education. The calculations, similar to those made for physical investment, were inspired by Noble Laureate and University of Chicago Professor Theodore Schultz's approach to the role of education in development. They define as the benefits of education the increase in earnings made possible by a certain level of schooling and express these benefits as a percentage of costs. The costs include the direct ("private") costs to the students, for say tuition and books, as well as the indirect costs borne by the families (who have to forego the fruits of the labor of the students) and the education expenditures of the government. Returns to education vary considerably, depending on the country and the level of education. More recent findings confirm that the

return on primary education are in excess of 25 percent, on secondary education between 15 and 18 percent, and on tertiary education between 13 and 16
percent (Fishlow, 1995, page 7).

10. WDR, 1980, p. 61. The publications by the World Bank since 1980
have added detail and more specific observations on particular policies and
measures, but have not changed the basic reasoning presented here. See, for
example, "Poverty and Hunger," a World Bank Policy Study, 1986, of which
Shlomo Reutlinger was the principal author.

11. See also World Development Report, 1984, prepared by a team of
experts headed by Nancy Birdsall. Academic economic literature on population is summarized in Deepak Dasgupta (1995): "The Population Problem:
Theory and Evidence," *Journal of Economic Literature*, Volume XXXIII, No. 4,
December 1995.

12. The World Bank's 1990 World Development Report was entirely
dedicated to a new poverty-reduction effort that became the focus of the
Bank's operations. In the new poverty-reduction effort, bank staff started to
undertake country-by-country poverty assessments that ascertain the who,
where, and why of poverty; identify the need for strengthening the database;
and lay the groundwork for policy discussions with governments. An increasing proportion of lending was dedicated to fighting poverty directly. At the
same time, structural adjustment loans were redesigned to make sure they
would not affect the poor adversely; some loans were made to improve the
delivery of social services to the poorest population groups (e.g., a 1994 loan to
Zambia). In the two years ending June 1993, half of the adjustment operations
paid explicit attention to poverty issues in one way or another (World Bank,
1994, p. 8).

Poverty assessments assemble data that are essential to a dialogue
on poverty issues confronting the countries concerned. They identify, from the
vantage point of the impact on the poor, shortcomings in policy, planning, sector priorities and investments, and the delivery of social services. They consider the impact of long-term economic management on the ability of the poor
to build up assets, as well as the effects which short-term economic measures,
inflation, and cuts in public expenditures have on the poor (see e.g., World
Bank 1993 Annual Report, page 44).

The Bank's lending operations were guided in part by a program of
targeted interventions, loans with the primary objective of poverty reduction
through basic education; productivity of small farmers; basic health conditions; sanitation and water supply, especially for women and children; and
basic infrastructure in regions of concentrated poverty; loans in this category
amounted to one-fourth of investment lending in 1992 and 1993. Moreover, the
Bank's lending for human resource development—education, health, family
planning, and nutrition—has tripled since the early 1980s.

13. A number of religious groups and environmental nongovernmental
organizations (NGOs) lent support to the "Fifty Years is Enough" campaign in
its attack on the World Bank and the International Monetary Fund (IMF). At
the time, these institutions were celebrating the 50th anniversary of their
establishment at the 1944 Bretton Woods Conference. The campaign criticized

the World Bank for ignoring the adverse environmental impact of its projects and programs; for advocating harmful economic policies; and for lack of participation by local, often indigenous, nationals in the formation and execution of loan projects. The campaign also pointed to many difficulties in African development and the continued debt-servicing problems of the poorest countries, and blamed these on the World Bank. The NGOs associated with the campaign have pressured the U.S. Treasury and sought to limit or eliminate new funding for the World Bank, especially its soft lending arm, the International Development Association (IDA).

As an integral part of its own evolution as a development institution, and partly in response to these and other criticisms, the World Bank has in recent years made a large number of institutional and operational policy changes. It has been conducting regular meetings with NGOs to listen to their complaints and to explain new policy initiatives. It has organized an Environment Department under the supervision a new vice president for sustainable development to guide new environmental lending and to assure that its operations have no harmful impact on the environment. It has made local participation a required and essential objective of lending operations. The Bank has also instituted an outside inspection panel which will evaluate complaints about its operations and bring them to the attention of the World Bank's board of directors. And it has made arrangements for greater access to information about various phases of its operations. The Bank also pursued a broad effort to improve the effectiveness of its lending.

14. See esp. ch. 9 of WDR, 1990.

15. Catholic bishops pastoral letter "Economic Justice for All," 1986, par. 287; and *ESA Advocate*, June 1991. The position of the Catholic Church became once again clear at the 1994 Cairo Conference on Population and Development. At this conference the United Nations presented a paper which reaffirmed reasoning on population issues similar to that followed in this chapter. It called for a comprehensive population policy in the interest of the world's social and economic development. The paper gave special emphasis to the importance of strengthening the position of women and girls in the school, the family, and society in general. However, the Vatican representatives at the Cairo conference attacked the paper on the ground that it advocated abortion "on demand," as well as extramarital sex and "innovative" sexual practices (which probably have been around since ancient times). The United States was generally supportive of the UN paper, but like many others did not regard abortion as a tool of birth control. The Vatican was joined in its opposition by certain Muslim countries, probably in part because of their objection to giving women a more equal position.

CHAPTER 3

1. Participation of women in the workforce was highest in the formerly communist countries of Eastern Europe (where the number of women in the 1980 labor force was 90 percent that of men) and lowest in the Middle East, South Asia, and Latin America (30 percent). The other regions are in between, with percentages ranging from 48 percent for Africa to 62 percent for North America. The market economies of the Far East come in with a relatively high 59 percent. For developments in 1970–1992 see World Bank World Development Report, 1994, Table 29.

2. For example, in 1970–1991 the percentage of females enrolled in primary education rose from 63 to 94 percent in low-and middle-income countries, and in secondary education from 17 to 19 percent. For sub-Saharan Africa these figures were 41 to 58 percent (primary) and 5 percent to 16 percent (secondary) (see World Development Report 1994, p. 217).

3. Bergmann, 1996, p. 36. Women over fifty earn only 64 percent of what men earn, as against 72 percent for women of all ages (Washington, DC, American Association for Retired People [AARP] Bulletin, Vol. 32, No. 10, Nov. 1991). The legal rulings underlying affirmative action are reviewed in McWirther, 1996.

4. Judy Mann, The *Washington Post*, December 14, 1990.

5. Such arrangements have been made in Sweden. When a baby is born, there health insurance provides for paid leave which mother and father may share.

6. MIT awarded the first degrees in 1868. In 1873 Ellen Swallows Richards was the first female graduate of MIT. She went on to found the American Association of University Women and to teach at MIT for thirty-eight years. Another example is Sophia G. Hayden, the first graduate of MIT's four-year architecture program who designed the Women's Building for the 1892 Chicago World Fair.

7. In June 1963 the NCCC called for appropriate action on full participation of women in economic life, with equal job opportunities and compensation and equitable conditions of work, and full participation of women also in the life and work of the church. It took a position in favor of laws that will recognize the equality of men and women in family and society. The NCCC gave support to family planning and responsible parenthood "in the best interest of mothers, fathers, children, and society." The NCCC first supported the Equal Rights Amendment (ERA) in March 1975. In November 1983 the NCCC again supported the ERA (reintroduced to congress in January 1983), "because Christian faith and heritage at its best in history had led to elevating the role and status of women." In November 1983 the NCCC welcomed the UN General Assembly action approving the Convention on the Elimination of All Forms of Discrimination against Women. And finally in January 1987 the NCCC acted to sponsor the Ecumenical Decade 1988–1998: Churches in Solidarity with Women. The NCCC committed itself to "a community of communions in which women and men share equally in God's promises to humanity." In its statement it considers the women's movement a sign of hope for the world.

8. Recognition of the wider role of women was recognized in a 1972 statement of the American Lutheran Church, one of the predecessors of the present Evangelical Lutheran Church in America. The statement reviewed the significant changes in the position of women in all walks of life, the family, business and finance, the church, etc. The church confessed its "failure to teach

the whole of God's counsel concerning relationships between men and women. It has tended to accept the ways of society as the way of God. Under the pressure of the times, however, it has reexamined, in the light of the scriptures, its teaching concerning men and women." The church's general president put two questions to its seminaries: (a) "Do you find that the scriptures forbid the ordination of women or service of women in the ministry of Word and Sacraments?" and (b) "Do you find in the Scriptures orders of creation which enunciate a principle of women being subordinate to men which then pertains directly to the role women should serve in the ministry?" The faculties of each of the church's three seminaries, meeting independently, concluded unanimously that the scriptural answer to each question is NO. The Lutheran statement also called for active steps to bring women into leadership roles in the church and welcomed women in the professional ministry of the church.

Action toward greater equality for women was repeatedly addressed by the United Methodist Church. In 1984 it confirmed that Methodists should work to reverse past mistakes and discrimination, support the Equal Rights Amendment, monitor public policies that affect economic conditions of women, strengthen affirmative action, and develop new approaches toward a better life for women and children (United Methodist Church, 1984 General Conference, The Rights of Women).

Protest against discrimination against women was expressed by the United Church of Christ (UCC), which has taken positions similar to those of the NCCC. This was clear from its 1987 statement "Christian Faith and Economic Life," which focuses on the ethics of domestic and international poverty and on measures which might be taken to alleviate or eradicate poverty. It refers to several economic phenomena associated with what it calls "sexism" (i.e., discrimination against women). It mentions UNICEF's recommendation that African women be recognized as having a key role as producers and providers of food for the family. In the U.S. economy it notes the large increase in women's participation in the workforce and the fact that women earn only 60 percent of what men earn and black women only 90 percent of what white women earn. Like the Catholic bishops, the UCC observes that female-headed families bear a disproportionate share of poverty.

CHAPTER 4

1. Cf. John Paul II: "Peace with God the Creator, Peace with All of Creation," Message for the Celebration of the World Day of Peace, Jan. 1990.

2. Where the policies of poor countries are primarily justified by phenomena beyond their control, they may have to be compensated by special external help. This is envisaged under the Global Environment Facility (GEF), set up under the auspices of the World Bank, the UNDP, and the United Nations Environmental Programme (UNEP). The GEF started operations in 1992 for a three-year trial period, with contributions from many donor countries. The facility started out as the interim funding mechanism for the Convention on Climate Change and Biological Diversity signed at the Rio Earth

Summit in June 1992. It helps to finance innovative projects and programs affecting the global environment, such as climate change and the loss of biodiversity. Responsibility for implementing the GEF is shared by the UNDP (technical assistance and project preparation), UNEP, and the World Bank (administration, one of the implementing agencies and repository of the GEF trust fund). In March 1994 more than eighty industrialized and developing countries pledged more than $2 billion for the GEF Trust Fund for the next three years. The participating countries also agreed to manage the facility with a 60 percent majority rule applied to all members, as well as approval by donors representing at least 60 percent of contributions (World Bank, 1994 Annual Report, p. 48).

3. See Sandra Postel: "Halting Land Degradation," ch. 2 in Lester R. Brown, 1989.

4. See Sandra Postel and Lori Heise: "Reforesting the Earth" in Lester R. Brown, 1988.

5. When trees are cleared or harvested, the carbon they contain, as well as some of the carbon of the underlying soil, is oxidized and released to the air, adding to the atmospheric store of carbon dioxide. This release occurs rapidly if trees are burned, but slowly if they decay naturally. In this way deforestation adds greatly to the amounts of carbon in the atmosphere, most of it from tropical forests.

6. See Cynthia Pollock Shea: "Protecting the Ozone Layer" in Lester R. Brown, 1989.

7. The best forecasts currently available from general circulation models predict temperature increases of three to nine degrees Fahrenheit if greenhouse gases in the atmosphere double. A 1991 report of a panel of the National Academy of Sciences, "The Policy Implications of Global Warming," comments: "The mid-point of this range corresponds to an average global climate warmer than any in the last one million years. The consequences of this amount of warming are unknown and may produce extremely disagreeable surprises."

8. The prospect of decelerating grain output is documented in Lester R. Brown, 1989, and Brown and Kane, 1994, Chapter 14.

9. In the United States it is clear that pollution caused by the automobile is directly affected by American transport policy. This is elaborated by Jessica Mathews, writing in the *Washington Post*: "Policies that are both environmentally and economically counterproductive litter the landscape. Nowhere is this more evident than in how we invest in transportation. We pour money into the most energy-consumptive ways of moving people and freight and then deplore our oil import dependence. We build highways and starve transit systems for decades, ignoring irrefutable evidence that this produces more, not less, traffic congestion. We spend more and more to control the pollution caused by cars locked in stop-and-go traffic without assigning the costs to the cause. Then we look at this tangled knot of consequences—pollution, congestion, neighborhood destroying sprawl and a society at risk economically and politically from excessive oil imports—and sigh that regrettably we Americans will never, after all, leave our automobiles" (Mathews, 1991).

10. For example, the cost of soil erosion on Java in one year alone has been calculated at $350–425 million, or almost 0.5 percent of the gross domestic product. The favorable growth figures—the growth of exports and production—in Indonesia and other countries with highly praised macroeconomic policies may often overstate what could be achieved on a sustainable basis—i.e., when full allowance is made for the cost of erosion and degradation. See El Serafy and Ernst Lutz: "Environmental and National Resource Accounting," in Chapter 2 of Gunter Schramm and Jeremy Warford, 1989.

11. The World Bank, Development Committee, 1987, pp. 10–12 and 22–24.

12. The World Bank, Development Committee, 1987, pp. 5–9.

13. Preparation of the 1992 World Development Report was part of the World Bank's growing environmental activities, in rapidly increasing lending as well as technical assistance. These activities involve a rethinking of the economics used in all of the Bank's work which requires new talent and new attitudes. New "environmental assessment" reports on individual countries pinpoint desirable environmental protection policies and lay the basis for future activities. Environmental management and protection programs are under way for the Mediterranean (with the Organization for Economic Cooperation and Development [OECD] and UNDP), the Black Sea, the Baltic, and the Danube River Basin.

14. See, e.g., the 'United Methodists' "Environmental Stewardship," 1984 and "The Church Speaks: RCA Papers of the Commission on Theology 1959–84," pp. 145–48. The 1987 UCC paper "Christian Faith and Economic Life" also had a chapter on the environment.

15. U.S. Catholic Bishops: "Renewing the Earth," 1991, p. 11.

CHAPTER 5

1. This section owes much to the analysis in Ullmann, 1991, and Melman, 1985.

2. At this point the discussion focuses on the impact of defense expenditures on the U.S. economy, not on the broader geopolitical consequences which, while considerable, had only an indirect impact on the U.S. economy. Later in the chapter, the discussion contrasts the decline in U.S. industrial efficiency with the rising competitiveness of Germany and Japan.

3. Renovation of ground transportation and large energy conservation and conversion require major new investments in new equipment—e.g., more efficient home appliances and automobiles, new sources of electricity, and electrification of rail transport. The U.S. rail industry alone could spend over $100 billion on the electrification of some 60,000 miles, closing the gap with the high-speed rail connections in Europe and Japan. U.S. local transit systems need similar attention (Melman, ch. 9).

4. See, e.g., David Gold, ch. 13 in Gordon and McFadden, 1984, p. 195; Ullmann, 1991; and Melman, 1985.

5. Possibilities are office automation, electronic controls for railroads and road traffic, communications equipment, prefabricated houses, railroad cars, electric road vehicles, merchant vessels, and water purification (cf. Melman, 1985, ch. 9).

6. A minority of economists believe that more rapid growth is compatible with reasonable price stability, but their analysis does not address the question of whether the extra jobs created are low-skilled jobs with low pay or better paying, more productive jobs. See, for example, Robert Eisner, "Opening up the Growth Debate," *The Wall Street Journal*, Sept. 25, 1995. Eisner is a Northwestern University professor and a former president of the American Economic Association.

7. High military spenders among the developing countries not shown in Table 5.3 include Angola (29.1 percent of GDP in 1980–1988), Ethiopia (17.7 percent), Libya (15.9 percent), Oman (21.5 percent), Pakistan (7.2 percent), Syria (21.2 percent), United Arab Emirates (12 percent), and the two Yemens (17 and 42 percent).

8. The World Bank, World Development Report, 1988, pp. 106 and 107.

9. Foreword by Kermit D. Johnson, former chief of Army chaplains, in Geyer and Greene, 1992, pp. 9–11.

10. The 1979 General Synod called for a halt to nuclear arms testing. The 1982 General Synod endorsed an immediate nuclear weapons freeze. The 1984 Report of the Christian Action Committee underlined the church's pastoral responsibility toward people who wanted to relocate themselves from military jobs into civilian industry. The 1985 General Synod considered the case against investment in companies engaged in nuclear weapons production and research.

CHAPTER 6

1. The seventeen highly indebted countries suffered a 15 percent decline in per capita incomes in 1980–1987. The fall in output during the five years after 1982 was so painful that the actual 1987 total of $836 billion fell short by some $468 billion below the level these countries would have enjoyed had growth continued in the 1980s at the 6.6 percent pace of 1965–1980. Likewise, the investment opportunities forgone in the 1980s add up to a staggering $210 billion below the level of investment that would have been achieved had it continued to rise at the 8.4 percent rate of 1965–1980, as against the actual decline of 1.5 percent per annum in 1982–1988. (The seventeen highly indebted countries are Argentina, Bolivia, Brazil, Chile, Colombia, Costa Rica, Cote d'Ivoire, Ecuador, Jamaica, Mexico, Morocco, Nigeria, Peru, Philippines, Uruguay, Venezuela, and Yugoslavia [see World Debt Tables, 1988–1989 edition, p. 50]).

2. It is useful to compare the economic performance of EAP with that of the highly indebted countries. Contrast the 1980–1986 growth rate of Korea (8.2 percent) and China (10.2 percent) with that for seventeen highly indebted countries (only 0.8 percent). The Asian Development Bank reported that its developing country membership achieved a GDP growth rate of 8.8 percent in

1988, as against a 1 percent growth rate for the Latin American economies reported by the Inter-American Development Bank. India, a more self-sufficient country than most highly indebted countries, was also able to accelerate its growth from 3.7 percent in 1965–1980 to 4.9 percent in 1980–1986 and a high 9 percent in 1988.

3. In this context, the debt burden may best be measured by the ratio of total debt to exports (D/X) or the debt service ratio (DSR)—i.e., the ratio of debt service (interest plus amortization payments) to export earnings. In simple mathematics, if the interest rate exceeds the growth of exports, the D/X ratio will rise and eventually reach unsupportable levels.

4. Well before the debt crisis of the 1980s, the industrialized countries experienced severe imbalances in their external accounts. Among the major economies, the United States had a persistent balance of payments deficit ($30 billion in 1971), while Japan, the United Kingdom, Germany, and France were in surplus (a combined $21 billion in 1971). Governments had a hard time formulating and adopting the policies necessary to correct these imbalances. The measures eventually taken would lead to the breakdown of the Bretton Woods system of fixed exchange rate parities that had been established after World War II, the cessation by the United States of conversion of official gold holdings, and the devaluation of the key global currency, the U.S. dollar. (Margaret Garritsen de Vries, 1987, p. 94).

5. The oil price increase did not stand by itself, but came about in response to global economic events. The oil producers pointed to several considerations underlying the price hike, such as the U.S. dollar devaluation, the rise in the prices of primary commodities, and the deterioration in the terms of trade of the oil producers while the industrialized countries enjoyed an improvement in theirs. (Margaret Garritsen de Vries, 1985, vol. I, p. 307).

6. The data in Table 6.3 are for long-term public and publicly guaranteed debt; the last three columns are for the Highly Indebted Countries (HICs). The data in this section are from the World Bank's World Debt Tables 1988/89, vol. 1; December 1988). The final column in Table 6.3 shows the percentage of the total long-term public debt contracted on variable interest rates, which fluctuate with the so-called LIBOR rate in the London market. The LIBOR rate is the basis for the interest charged on most private bank loans, in contrast with the usually fixed rates applied by official lending agencies. The sharp run-up in this percentage highlights the increased borrowing by the HICs from the private banks.

7. The private banks' share of total long-term lending to the major borrowers increased from 28 percent in 1971 to 72 percent in 1981. At the same time, the terms on which countries were able to borrow hardened. The maturity of loans shortened from seventeen years in 1972 to thirteen years in 1981 (and eight years for Mexico) (see Barend A. de Vries, 1987, p. 94).

8. Net flows (i.e., loan disbursements minus amortization payments) rose during the 1970s from $2 billion in 1970 to a peak of $30 billion in 1982. Thereafter they fell back sharply to $6 billion in 1986 and $8 billion in 1987. Net flows from official lenders stayed steady at $5–6 billion per year.

Net lending by commercial banks was $9.5 billion in 1980, but was a negative $25 billion in 1984–90:

($billion)

1980	9.5
1984	-20.4
1985	-29.5
1986	-28.6
1987	-30.3
1988	-31.3
1989	-22.3
1990	-16.0

9. Transfers are net capital flows minus interest payments—i.e., the total net payments made by a debtor country to the banks. Net transfers turned around quickly from a positive inward transfer of $18 billion in 1981 to an outward transfer of $9 billion in 1984. The outward transfers stayed above $20 billion after 1985 and, with a renewed increase in interest rates, rose above $30 billion in 1988. In 1990 the developing countries suffered outward transfers of $21.6 billion, of which $10.4 billion came from Latin America alone (World Debt Tables, 1991–1992).

10. By 1987 it became clear to the banks that they were not going to be repaid in full. Faced with a deteriorating situation, the banks decided to set aside substantial loan-loss reserves. Citibank led initially with $3 billion, or 25 percent of its LDC exposure. Other money center banks followed suit, setting aside a total of over $9 billion. Most U.S. regional banks and non-U.S. banks set aside reserves that were even higher in relation to their LDC exposure. As a result, the banks' position to deal with the crisis had been strengthened considerably; their capital and reserves had increased and their loans outstanding to the LDCs had come down. Meanwhile, however, the economic position and the debt burden of the debtor countries had become worse.

11. See The World Bank, World Debt Tables, 1982–1983, p. *vii*.

12. New external debt can be expected to finance the balance of payments deficit and help a country build its official reserves. But in several countries the increase in debt over a period of years was bigger than these two factors alone. The difference can be explained by capital flight. In some countries capital flight exceeded or was a significant proportion of the increase in debt (e.g., Venezuela, 137 percent of the increase in external debt; Argentina, 65 percent; and Mexico, 48 percent). (See World Development Report, 1985, p. 64; and Cuddington, 1989, Table III-1).

13. The importance of sound incentive policies is supported by the empirical work of Balassa and Sachs (See Bela Balassa, 1984a, pp. 955–72 and 1984b; Jeffrey D. Sachs, 1985, pp. 523–64). The efficiency of new investment is a crucial element to be considered. Diaz Alejandro points to the decline in investment efficiency after 1973 in many Latin American countries. His calculations are based on the capital-output ratio. This ratio indicates the amount of investment associated with the increase in output over time—the lower the ratio, the more efficient is the use of capital. The ratio was low in Colombia,

Brazil, and Mexico in 1961–1971 and stayed low in these countries in 1973–1981. But in Venezuela, Argentina, and Chile it was high in the early period and increased after 1973; this suggests that these countries made less efficient use of borrowed funds. (Carlos Diaz Alejandro, 1984).

14. Berg and Sachs have gone beyond simple financial debt ratios and explored the importance of income inequality for debt-servicing difficulties. As explanatory variables, they used the fraction of total income in an economy derived from agriculture and the degree of income inequality (measured by the ratio of the percentages of total household income received by the richest and the poorest 20 percent). They conjecture that "a high degree of income inequality should be associated with a high probability of debt rescheduling, since the income inequality undermines the political stability and political effectiveness needed for successful macroeconomic management." Further, "the share of agriculture in production is included to offer a rough indication of the extent to which governments can derive political backing from rural power interests rather than urban interests." The theory is that a rural power base tends to be more stable and more supportive of export-promoting policies (Andrew Berg and Jeffrey Sachs, 1988). Both a bias against agriculture and high income inequality can be symptomatic of pervasive poverty in an economy.

15. A detailed account of the establishment and operation of the IMF oil facilities is given in Margaret Garritsen de Vries, 1985, ch. 17 and 18.

16. One cannot help but be struck by the parallels between the debt crisis and Germany's default in the 1930s (see Stephen A. Schuker, 1988).

17. These transactions took place at often-significant discounts quoted in secondary markets. Transactions in these markets, operated by the large commercial banks, played an increased role in debt management, especially for Argentina, Brazil, Mexico, and Venezuela, and to a lesser extent Chile, the Philippines, Poland, and Yugoslavia. According to the World Bank, total transactions increased rapidly from some $10 billion in 1987 to $60 billion in 1990 and $100 billion in 1991. Prices quoted in these markets came to reflect countries' creditworthiness. Much of the secondary market business was linked to debt-equity swaps often associated with the wave of privatization in Latin America.

In the "menu" of market options, an interesting role was played by "debt-for-nature" swaps. They are a novel way of linking debt conversion to the promotion of environmental conservation projects. Typically an organization, usually private, purchases debt in the secondary market at a deep discount (around 70 percent) and exchanges it for local currency with the debtor country (at a prearranged price, sometimes at par, but also lower). Thus the exchange is funded by the environmental organization, the debtor country (which exchanges a foreign currency debt for a debt in local currency), and sometimes an additional donor. The environmental organization uses the funds to purchase a rain forest or other lands to be set aside for conservation. Debt-for-nature swaps in 1987–1991 amounted in total to $98 million (mostly owed to commercial banks), of which $68 million represented Costa Rican debts. Other countries included Bolivia, Ecuador, Madagascar, and Zambia (World Debt Tables, 1991–1992, vol. 1, pp. 51–52).

18. Former IMF managing director H. Johannes Witteveen called for a speedy buyback of $125 billion of the $250 billion in nonguaranteed commercial bank loans to major debtors at 40 cents on the dollar. That would cost $50 billion in new debt-reduction resources, or at least double what was contemplated under the Brady initiative. But this proposal was not accepted (The *Washington Post,* June 15, 1989).

19. Direct foreign investment reached $5.3 billion in 1991, double the 1989 level. Mexican corporations were able to raise abroad $2.3 billion in equity in 1991 alone.

20. In June 1989 Mexico received an IMF standby of SDR 3.25 billion, available over three years, in support of a program predicated on a significant reduction in the outward transfer of resources. In parallel, the World Bank made $1.5 billion in quick disbursing sector loans of which $375 million could be used for debt reduction; the individual loans were tied to policy action in the financial, industrial, and public enterprise sectors. By 1990 Mexico was receiving $11.5 billion in capital inflows from all sources and capital repatriation brought in an additional $12.5 billion in 1988–1990. Net transfers moved from a negative (outflow) of $5.7 billion in 1989 (including net direct foreign investment) to a positive (inward) flow of $2 billion in 1990. This enabled Mexico to increase imports substantially and increase its growth rate to 4 percent in 1989–1991.

21. World Bank structural adjustment lending started before the 1982 debt crisis. The first SAL was made in 1980 to the Philippines. The conditions for this loan had been worked out in agreement with the government by an industrial sector mission (see Philippines: Industrial Development Strategy and Policies, a World Bank Country Study, 1980). The conditionality described in the "Washington Consensus," originally formulated by John Williamson, was amended and refined in 1996 to allow for social and institutional factors.

22. Experts on the Africa region were particularly critical of the World Bank report "Adjustment in Africa: Reforms, Results and the Road Ahead" (New York, Oxford University Press, 1994) (see e.g., Sayre P. Schatz: "Structural Adjustment in Africa: A Failing Grade so Far," *Journal of Modern Africa Studies,* 32:4 [1994], pp. 679–92).

23. Enrique Iglesias made these observations in a lecture to the Per Jacobson Foundation, in Washington, DC.

24. This took the form of rescheduling, starting with the 1987 Venice meeting of the G-7 Group of industrialized countries. The terms of these rescheduling operations became more and more liberal as the creditors gained a better understanding of the seriousness of the debtors' problems. Following the 1990 Houston meeting, concessionary debt was to be stretched out to up to twenty years, with a ten-year grace on amortization. By the 1991 Trinidad meeting of the G-7, John Major, then UK chancellor of the exchequer, proposed enhanced relief by a once-for-all debt reduction, with a benchmark of two-thirds of debt to be canceled. The Dutch proposed outright cancellation of all official debts of the poorest countries. In 1991 Poland and Egypt received 50 percent debt forgiveness in their official debt, a cumulative debt reduction over three years, conditional on IMF standby agreements. This reduction had to be matched by parallel action on the part of the commercial banks. Some observers have urged even more liberal terms for reducing debt (see, e.g., the 1990 Craxi Report commissioned by the UN and described in F. Forte, 1991). The World Credit Tables (Eurodad, Brussels, 1996) publishes credits outstanding to developing countries, as distinct from the World Bank's Debt Tables, which are based on information submitted by debtor countries; the 1996 Credit Tables also discuss the costs and benefits of debt reduction.

25. In five years private creditors' exposure quadrupled, from $6.3 billion in 1985 to $25 billion in 1991. The share of private creditors in India's long-term debt rose from 9.8 percent in 1981 to 41 percent in 1991, while the concessionary component fell from 79 to 38.5 percent.

26. Reference texts: Deut 23:19 on interest, Deut 24:10–12 on pledges; Deut 15: 1 and 13, Lev 25: 5 and 6 on the sabbatical year; Lev 25:10 on the year of Jubilee; Rom 13:8, Paul on debt; and John 2:15, Jesus and the money changers.

27. *New York Times*, Sept. 18, 1984; quoted in Schuker, 1988, p. 138.

28. Pontifical Commission *Iustitia et Pax*, December 1986.

29. U.S. Catholic Conference: "Relieving Third World Debt. A Call for Co-responsibility, Justice and Solidarity," 1989.

30. E.g., Potter,1988, ch. 7. Like some other religious statements, the letter erroneously states that the Third World countries were not present at the 1944 Bretton Woods conference which set up the IMF and the World Bank. In reality, distinguished and influential representatives of both China and India participated in the deliberations, as did a galaxy of economists, bankers, and officials from Latin America; many of these were influential in formulating the charter of the World Bank and were to play important roles in the work of the Bretton Woods institutions later.

31. The Vatican statements *"Populorum Progressio"* (1967), *"Sollicitudo Rei Socialis"* (1987), and *"Centesimus Annus"* (1991) are discussed in "The Church and the Poorest Countries" (ch. 10).

32. For example, in a United Methodist Church journal, a lead article "Latin America Pleading for its Jubilee" states, "The debt burden is unsustainable. The banks have more than received a healthy return on their investment. It is time we as a nation examined a larger vision of forgiveness. It would provide a real cleansing and redemption for the national soul" (United Methodist Church, 1988).

The United Church of Christ's "Christian Faith and Economic Life" (1987) calls for alleviation of the debt burden; it mentions the various options for debt reduction without singling out anyone in particular. It joined the Catholic bishops in calling for a restructuring of the IMF and the World Bank. The Evangelicals for Social Action have also expressed concern with the social implications of the debt crisis (*ESA Advocate*, December 1990).

The 1990 General Synod of the Reformed Church in America considered a church study paper, "Third World Debt: The Churches' Response." The paper considered the impact of the debt burden on the poor and emphasized that a resolution of the international debt problem had to come from both creditor and debtor countries. The Synod also endorsed the U.S. Catholic bishops' 1989 paper, "A Call for Co-Responsibility, Justice and Solidarity," and outlined criteria for dealing with debt issues in a way compatible with justice and the revitalization and sustainable development of debt-burdened econo-mies.

CHAPTER 7

1. Unless specified otherwise, Old Testament quotes are from the New English Bible (Oxford University Press, 1970); New Testament verses are from the Good News for Modern Man Bible (American Bible Society, 1976).

CHAPTER 8

1. For example, Martin Luther conformed himself to medieval anti-semitism. In "Von den Juden und ihren Luegen" (1543), he laid down seven Nazi-like conditions for Jews continuing to live in the electorate of Saxony, where Luther himself resided. These included the destruction of synagogues and of all sacred scriptures, as well as the concentration of Jews in work camps (Balke, 1992, ch. 3). Balke makes a distinction between Luther's views and those of Hitler, in that Luther's objections to the Jews were based on his theol-ogy, not on racial hatred. Jewish history is presented in Chaim Potok (1978) and Paul Johnson (1987). Johnson points out that, after becoming the official church of the Roman Empire, the Eastern church took what can only be regarded as a discriminatory stance against the Jews. Potok relates numerous cases of anti-Jewish violence by European Christians. Episcopal Bishop Spong (1996) has laid the basis for removing the anti-Semitism of the Christian church with his systematic exploration of the Jewish origins and rationale of the Gospels.

2. Vorspan (1969, pp. 99–107), which in turn was based on "There Shall Be No Poor" by Richard G. Hirsch, director of the Religious Action Center, Union of American Hebrew Congregations.

3. Danny Siegel (1986 and 1987) gives many examples of the spirit of *tzedakah* in everyday life.

4. Maimonides' Eight Degrees of Charity are given on p. 335 of the Conservative prayerbook (United Synagogue of America, 1946 and 1984). For further information on Maimonides, see Birnbaum, 1974.

5. Jewish ethics does, of course, recognize personal sin—e.g., in the Yom Kippur liturgy.

6. See Conservative Judaism, Statement of Principles, 1988, pp. 44–46.

7. The Union of American Hebrew Congregations is composed of about 1.5 million Jews, the Central Conference of American Rabbis has 1,500 members, and the National Federation of Temple Sisterhoods represents 800,000 women of the Reform movement.

8. Union, 1981; and Rabbis, 1982.

9. Union, 1965, 1973, and 1976; and Rabbis, 1975 and 1983.

10. Sisterhood: "Poverty: United States and Abroad," 1981.

11. President of UAHC, 1977.

12. Union, 1971; and Sisterhoods, 1965.
13. Union, 1971; and Sisterhoods, 1965.

CHAPTER 9

1. E.g., Robert McAfee Brown, 1978. Brown's 1978 and 1990 books differ in tone; the latter, on Gustavo Gutierrez, was written after Brown had received more exposure to Latin American conditions.
2. See, for example, Phillip Berryman, 1987, p. 185ff. and 191; and Brown, 1990, pp. 137–39 and 146–48.

CHAPTER 10

1. The document was the product of a commission and, at the urging of Cardinal Joseph Suenens of Belgium, was revised by a 2,300-member deliberative assembly. In its final form it represents, according to Peter Henriot, then with the Center of Concern, a significant break from the rigid traditionalism of the council's preparatory commission (Henriot et al., 1988, pp. 45–46).
2. See *Washington Post*, May 3, 1991; and Novak, 1993, pp. 137–38.
3. In the words of one close to the drafting of the encyclical (Archbishop Jorge Maria Mejia), private property must be broadly conceived to include know-how, technology, and skill, all part of "goods" destined for all, but that do not reach everyone and are not enjoyed by all (Hollenbach, 1992, p. 85; see also U.S. Bishops 1986 pastoral, par. 113).
4. Archbishop Weakland has a strong international background as former head of the Benedictines, and had personally known poverty in the depressed coal territory from which he came. The other members of the drafting committee also had a strong personal interest in questions of social justice: De Nellon from Atlanta was the son of a bricklayer and union member from New York City; George Speltz from St. Cloud, Minn., brought a strong interest in agriculture; William Wiggin from Salt Lake City had been a pastor in Colombia for ten years, and Peter Rosazza of the Hartford Archdiocese had worked for ten years in the streets of Hartford ministering to Hispanics.
5. Quoting from par. 285–87 of the 1986 pastoral: "We must recognize that the earth's resources are finite and that population grows rapidly. Whether the world can provide a truly human life for twice as many people or more as now live in it (many of whose lives are sadly deficient today) is a matter of urgent concern that cannot be ignored." "The church fully supports the need for all to exercise responsible parenthood. Family size is heavily dependent on levels of economic development, education, respect for women, availability of health care and the cultural traditions of communities. Therefore, in dealing with population growth, we strongly favor efforts to address these social and economic concerns."

"Population policies must be designed as part of an overall strategy of integral human development." Quoting Pope Paul VI: "The size of population increases more rapidly than available resources, and things are found to have reached an impasse. From that moment the temptation is great to check the demographic increase by means of radical measures. It is certain that public authorities can intervene, within the limit of their competence, by favoring the availability of appropriate information and by adopting suitable measures, provided that these be in conformity with moral law and that they respect the rightful freedom of married couples. Where the inalienable right to marriage and procreation is lacking, human dignity has ceased to exist."

CHAPTER 11

1. John C. Bennett et al., 1954, p. 20; and A. Dudley Ward, Ed., 1953.

2. United Methodist Church, Social Principles, 1988.

3. Wogaman appears to favor a mixed economic system, similar to the conclusion reached in the Presbyterian statements discussed later in this chapter (Wogaman, 1987, pp. 412–19).

4. UCC, 1981. The United Church of Christ (UCC) is a fusion of churches originally rooted in Calvinism, of which the Congregational and the Evangelical Reformed churches are the most important. With the Presbyterian Church and the Reformed Church in America, the UCC is a member of the World Alliance of Reformed Churches.

5. FDR's call was followed by the "Employment Act of 1946" and the "Full Employment and Balanced Growth Act of 1978" (the Humphrey-Hawkins Act). In response to conservative opposition, both of these acts were significantly watered down from their originally proposed versions to make them almost toothless in the eyes of some students (Harvey, 1989, p. 4 and pp. 106–12).

6. The church objects especially to the conditions attached by the IMF to its financial operations. The nature and conditions of these operations are discussed in detail in Margaret Garritsen de Vries, 1976, especially vol. 1, part 5, ch. 25 and 26, and vol. 2, part 12; and 1987.

7. The Southern Presbyterian Church in the U.S. split off the main Presbyterian body in 1860; its 1978 general assembly directed the preparation of "Christian Faith and Economic Justice." Upon completion of the paper, the church was reunited with the main body of the Presbyterian Church. The latter's general assembly approved the paper and had earlier (in 1981) ordered the writing of the second paper.

8. The Reformed Church in America is the oldest continuous Protestant denomination in the United States. It was established by seventeenth- and eighteenth-century Dutch Calvinist settlers in New York and New Jersey. They were joined in the mid-nineteenth century by like-minded immigrants, mostly in the Middle West, who had fled religious persecution and economic distress in the Netherlands and, under the leadership of Dr. van Raalte and others, were anxious to start a new life in the United States. (See, e.g., Bruins, 1970). Present-day descendants and their cobelievers in the related Christian Reformed Church have some 700,000 members in the United States and Canada.

9. Cf. a study by Donald A. Luidens and Roger Nemeth in "The Church Herald," 1987, quoted in "The Two-Tiered Society," 1990 General Synod, Acts and Proceedings, page 66.

10. Calvin wrote: "Let those, then, who have riches, whether left by inheritance or acquired by industry and labors, consider that their opulence is not intended as a means to intemperance and luxury, but for the relief of the needs of their brethren. For what we possess is manna, from whatever quarter it comes. And as in the case of any who, through greed or through distrust, hoarded the manna, what was laid up immediately putrefied, so we may not doubt that the riches which are heaped up to the disadvantage of our brethren are accursed and will soon perish." See 1984 Synod Acts, pp. 65–67.

11. Report of the Commission on Christian Action, 1990 General Synod Acts, pp. 65–72.

12. In arriving at common guidelines to limit abortion, the church shunned dogmatism and showed sensitivity to varied situations and views (*Washington Post*, September 21, 1991). The Lutheran guidelines were similar to those issued earlier by the United Methodist Church. The LCA and the ALC, together with the Association of Evangelical Lutheran Churches, were united into the ELCA in 1988. The more conservative Lutheran Church (Missouri Synod) has not joined with the ELCA; its 1968 report gives scriptural views on the role of government and the military, as well as issues of order in society; this church has not written papers on poverty, the environment, and the role of women.

13. See e.g., "Peace and Politics," 1984, p. 2 and "Human Rights," 1972, p. 3.

14. Interfaith Action, 1991, pp. 1–3 and 71.

15. *Washington Post*, Sep. 2, 1991.

16. *Washington Post*, Sep. 7, 1991.

CHAPTER 12

1. See, for example, William G. McLoughlin, "The Essence of Billy Graham," *Washington Post*, Oct. 25, 1991.

2. F. James Reichley, in Neuhaus and Cromarty, 1987, pp. 71 and 79.

3. Harvey Cox, in Neuhaus and Cromarty, 1987, p. 287.

4. Beisner sharply narrows the definition of poverty, and strongly implies that most poverty is caused by "sloth." He simply rejects the official definition of poverty, 13–15 percent of our population, a total of 31–36 million. He appears to be ignorant of the massive professional work done on the definition and measurement of poverty in America (op. cit., p. 200). Instead, he bases his estimate of the number of poor on some fairly simplistic arithmetic: Take a low estimate for the number of homeless, 363,000 in 1985, and increase it to the midpoint between it and the 3 million figure given by advocacy groups. This gives him 1.68 million, which he then arbitrarily doubles to 3.86 million to allow for hungry people who do have housing. This fancy arithmetic gives him a much more manageable figure (3.86 million) than the unwieldy official estimate of around 33 million. He then divides the 3.86 million by the number of churches, to get the number of poor each church should care for on average. This turns out to be a manageable figure. Even so, one cannot help but feel that his procedure constitutes a rather superficial way of dealing with poverty issues, shallow both conceptually and factually.

5. A summary of his views is in Public Justice Report, vol. 15, no. 2, Nov. 1991.

6. In this context, the experience of Christian education in the Netherlands may be relevant. Like many American Christians, the Dutch Catholics and Calvinists paid a high personal price for their schools and made considerable sacrifices. Once these schools were "emancipated" and started to receive state finance (in 1919), they and their teachers became unavoidably subject to government standards and inspection. Fortunately, the Dutch inspectors were not hostile to the Christian schools and were in fact appointed by a government with a strong and independent civil service tradition and in which Christian political parties had a strong influence. But one may well ask how far this situation can be replicated in America. Would Evangelicals accept inspection by government officials?

7. Cf. Dean Currie: "Confusing Justice and Peace" in Neuhaus and Cromarty, 1987, p. 237.

8. "An Evangelical Theology of Liberation," in Neuhaus and Cromarty, p. 143.

9. *"Prism,"* vol. 2, no. 3; p. 38; Lancaster, PA, Feb. 1995. In a similar vein, Senator Dan Coats (R.-Ind.) has proposed that a tax credit be given for donations to charitable organizations devoted primarily to helping the poor (*Washington Post*, Feb. 25, 1996, page A4).

10. "The Powerful and the Powerless" in Neuhaus and Cromarty, 1987, p. 187.

11. *Christian Perspectives* (Lexington, VA), vol. 4, no. 2, Summer/Fall 1991, pp. 7–9.

12. See e.g., Stanley W. Carlson-Thies, 1996. This is a review of Wayne Gordon: "Real Hope in Chicago, The Incredible Story of How the Gospel is Transforming a Chicago Neighborhood," Zondervan, 1995; John Perkins, Ed.: "Restoring at Risk Communities: Doing it Together and Doing it Right," Baker Books, 1995; and John Perkins with Jo Kadlecek: "Resurrecting Hope," Regal Books/Gospel Light, 1995.

13. See Sider's account in *ESA Advocate*, March 1990, p. 2.

14. The 1995 Agra meetings are related in "Transformation, An International Evangelical Dialogue on Mission and Ethics," vol. 12, no. 3, July-September 1995 (6 E. Lancaster Ave, Wynnewood, PA 19096).

CHAPTER 13

1. Cf. review of Danziger et al., 1994, in the *Washington Post* of Jan. 1, 1995.

2. Freedman, 1993, estimates that 17 percent of AFDC recipients are lifted above the poverty line. On p. 208 he refers to Aid to Families with Dependent Children (AFDC) when he estimates that welfare amounts to a fraction of 1 percent of our GDP. Total federal appropriations for welfare were $125 billion in 1994. See ch. 1, table 1.1.

3. The percentage of births out of wedlock has risen sharply from 5 percent in 1960 (2 percent white, 22 percent black) to 31 percent in 1993 (24 percent white, 69 percent black). There are many causes underlying the increase, like earlier sexual activity, later marriage, and more economic independence of women, as well as welfare. The increase occurred while the real value of AFDC fell by 47 percent. Moreover, the United States has a higher out-of-wedlock birthrate than most other industrialized countries, but lower social welfare benefits; this again suggests that welfare is not a major cause of childbearing outside marriage (Sawhill, 1995).

4. Myrdal originally coined the term "underclass" in "Challenge to Affluency" (New York, Pantheon, 1963). It was composed of the victims of deindustrialization: "an unprivileged class of unemployed, unemployables and underemployed who are more and more hopelessly set apart from the nation at large and do not share in its life, its ambitions and its achievements" (Myrdal, 1963, p. 10) (Quoted in Gans, 1995). In 1973 the term became pejorative. See, e.g., Winston Moore et al. "Woodlawn: The Zone of Destruction" (Public Interest 30, Winter 1973, pp. 41–59); Moore regards the underclass as "the product of urban welfare policies which institutionalize poverty" (cf. Gans, p. 30). "Underclass" is also used as a racial or even ethnic code word. It is a convenient device for hiding antiblack or anti-Latino feelings (Gans, p. 59). This is amply illustrated in Jonathan Kozol's masterful "Amazing Grace: The Lives of Children and the Conscience of a Nation," 1995.

5. "More than half of the $9.4 billion in budget cuts passing the House in 1996, $5.7 billion to be precise, came from low-income housing programs alone." See Lester C. Thurow, 1996, p. 159.

6. The gross domestic product of the United States grew by 4.3 percent in 1960–1970, 3 percent in 1970–1980, and 2.7 percent in 1980–1993 (See World Development Reports, 1980 and 1995). The consequences of slow growth were recently discussed by Madrick. He points out that the average real income of a 25-year-old who went to work in the mid-1970s rose by only 10 percent over the next ten years. In the 1950s or early 1960s, a 25-year-old saw income double in ten years. The disparity was greater for blacks and minorities. The percentage of 25–29-year-olds buying homes was 35 percent in 1993, vs. 44 percent in 1973 (Madrick, 1995, p. 134).

References

Avramovic, D. and Associates: Economic Growth and External Debt. Baltimore, Md., Johns Hopkins University Press, 1965.

Bailey, Anthony: Letter from the Netherlands. *The New Yorker*, August 12, 1991, pp. 52–65.

Balassa, Bela: Policy Responses to External Shocks in Developing Countries. American Economic Review, May, 1984b.

———. Structural Adjustment Policies in Developing Countries: A Reassessment. World Development, 12, Sept. 1984a. (pp. 955–972).

Balke, W.: "Omgang met de Reformatoren," Kampen, the Netherlands, De Groot Goudriaan, 1992.

Barth, Karl: Church Dogmatics, Vol. II, Part I, p. 386. Ed. by G. W. Bromley and T. F. Torrance. Edinburgh, T&T Clark, 1957.

Bauer, P. T.: "Equality, the Third World and Economic Delusion." Cambridge, Mass., Harvard University Press, 1981.

Beisner, E. Calvin: "Prosperity and Poverty, The Compassionate Use of Resources in a World of Scarcity." Westchester, Ill., Crossway Books, 1988.

Bennett, John C.: "The Radical Imperative: From Theology to Social Ethics." Philadelphia, The Westminster Press, 1975.

Bennett, John C., Howard R. Bowen, Wm. Adams Brown and G. Bromley Oxnam: "Christian Values and Economic Life." Federal Council of Churches Study. New York, Harper & Br., 1954.

Benoit, Emile: "Defense and Growth in Developing Countries." Boston, Lexington Books, 1973.

Berg, Andrew and Jeffrey Sachs: The Debt Crisis: Structured Explanation of Country Performance. National Bureau of Economic Research, Working Paper No. 2607, 1988.

Bergmann, Barbara R.: "In Defense of Affirmative Action." New York, Basic Books, 1996.

———. "The Economic Emergence of Women." New York, Basic Books, 1986.

Berkhof, Hendrikus: "Christ and the Powers." Reformed Church in America, 1963, pp. 36–40 and p. 50.

Berryman, Phillip: "Liberation Theology. Essential Facts about the Revolutionary Movement in Latin America and Beyond." New York, Pantheon Books, 1987.

Birnbaum, Philip, Ed.: Mishnah Torah, Maimonides: Code of Law and Ethics, Abridged and Translated from the Hebrew. New York, Hebrew Publishing Co., 1974.

Blinder, Alan S.: "Hard Heads and Soft Hearts—Tough-Minded Economics for a Just Society." Reading, Mass., Addison-Wesley Publishing Co., Inc., 1987.

Bonhoeffer, Dietrich: Creation and Fall; Temptation; Two Biblical Studies. New York, The Macmillan Co, 1959 and 1965.

Boorstein, Daniel J.: "Hidden History." New York, Vintage Books, 1989, p. 220.

Boserup, Ester: Woman's Role in Economic Development. New York, St. Martin's Press, 1970.

Boulding, Kenneth E.: "Beyond Economics. Essays on Society, Religion and Ethics." Ann Arbor, University of Michigan Press, 1970.

Brandt Commission Report (1980): "North-South: A Program for Survival." Report of the Independent Commission on International Development Issues under the Chairmanship of Willy Brandt. (Cambridge, Mass., MIT Press, 1980).

Brenner, Harvey: "Health and the National Economy" in Human Capital and Development, P. C. Huang, Ed. Greenwich CT, JAI Press, 1993.

Briefs, Henry: "The Limits of Scripture: Theological Imperatives and Economic Realities" in R. Bruce Douglass, 1988.

Brown, Lester: "State of the World, 1988" and "State of the World, 1989." Washington, DC, World Watch Institute, 1988, 1989 and 1996.

Brown, Lester, and Hal Kane: "Full House. Reassessing the Earth's Carrying Capacity." New York, W. W. Norton & Co., 1994.

———. "Gustavo Gutierrez: An Introduction to Liberation Theology." Maryknoll, NY, Orbis, 1990. "Theology in a New Key," Philadelphia, The Westminster Press, 1978.

Bruins, Elton J.: "The Americanization of a Congregation." The Hist. Series of the Reformed Church in America, no. 2; Grand Rapids, Eerdmans, 1970.

Brundtland, Gro Harlem: "World Commission on Environment and Development: Our Common Future." Presented to the United Nations General Assembly, October, 1987.

Burns, James MacGregor: "The Workshop of Democracy." Vol. II of "The American Experiment." New York, Vintage Books, 1986.

Carlson-Thies, Stanley W. "Turnabout in the City." Washington, DC, Center for Public Justice, Public Justice Report, vol. 19, no. 3, May-June, 1996, p. 6.

———. "Ending Welfare As We Know It." Lancaster, PA, Prism Magazine, vol. 1, no. 7, June, 1994.

Catholic Church: Bishop John Ricard, Chairman US Catholic Conference Domestic Policy Committee: "How Fiscal and Human Deficits Intertwine," 1993.

———. "Called to be One in Christ." A Pastoral Response to the Concerns of Women for Church and Society. Washington, DC, National Conference of Catholic Bishops (US), Third Draft, 1992.

———. US Catholic Conference. Pastoral Statement: "Renewing the Earth" Nov. 1991.

———. John Paul II, Social Encyclical "Centesimus Annus" May 1991 (Issued for the centenary of Leo XIII's Social Encyclical "Rerum Novarum").

————. John Paul II, Message for the Celebration of the World Day of Peace (Jan. 1, 1990) Peace with God the Creator, Peace with All of Creation.

————. "Relieving Third World Debt: A Call for Co-Responsibility, Justice and Solidarity" US Catholic Conference Administrative Board, September, 1989.

————. John Paul II, On the Dignity and Vocation of Women, *Mulieris Dignitatem*, Apostolic Letter, August 15, 1988; Vatican City. Washington, DC, US Catholic Conference.

————. John Paul II: Encyclical on Social Concerns: *Sollicitudo Rei Socialis* (Dec. 1987; written in commemoration of the 20th anniversary of "*Populorum Progressio*," Pope Paul VI's encyclical). (Washington, DC, Origins, National Catholic Documentary Service, vol. 17, no. 38, March 1988.

————. US Bishops Pastoral Message and Letter: Economic Justice for All: Catholic Social Teaching and the US Economy (Nov. 1986) (Also referred to as "The Bishops' Letter" in the text).

————. US Catholic Conference "The Challenge of Peace," 1983.

————. John Paul II: "*Laborem Exercens*" (On Human Work) Encyclical on the 90th Anniversary of *Rerum Novarum* (May, 1981). Boston, MA, Daughters of St. Paul.

Chenery, Hollis et al.: "Redistribution with Growth." London, Oxford University Press, 1974.

Christian Perspectives, A Journal of Free Enterprise. Lynchburg, Virginia, The Contemporary Economics and Business Association, vol. 4, no. 2, Summer/Fall, 1991.

Church Statements: Directory of Religious Statements on Justice in the Economy. In Centerpiece, Issue 2, March 1988. Berkeley, CA, Graduate Theological Union, Center for Ethics and Social Policy, 1988.

Cleave, John: "Environmental Assessments" Washington, DC, "Finance and Development," March 1988.

Cline, William R.: International Debt: Systemic Risk and Policy Response. Cambridge, Mass., MIT Press for the Institute for International Economics, 1984.

Collier, Paul: "Women in Development, Defining the Issues." Washington, DC, the World Bank, Working Paper WPS 129, 1988.

Conservative Judaism: Statement of Principles of Conservative Judaism, Social Justice: Building a Better World, pp. 44–46, New York, The Jewish Theological Seminary of America, The Rabbinical Assembly and the United Synagogue of America, 1988.

————. United Synagogue of America: Sabbath and Festival Prayerbook. 1946 and 1984, page 335.

Cook, James I.: See Reformed Church in America.

Cropper, Maureen L. and Wallace E. Oates: "Environmental Economics: A Survey." Journal of Economic Literature, vol. XXX (June 1992), pp. 675–740.

Cuddington, John T.: The Extent and Causes of the Debt Crisis of the 1980s in "Dealing with the Debt Crisis." World Bank Symposium Volume, 1989.

Currie, Laughlin: "Accelerating Development, the Necessity and the Means." New York, McGraw-Hill, 1966.

Daly, Herman E. and John B. Cobb Jr.: "For the Common Good." Boston, Beacon Press, 1989.

Daly, Mary: "Beyond God the Father; Toward a Philosophy of Women's Liberation." Boston, Beacon Press, 1973.

Danziger, Sheldon H., Gary D. Sandefur and Daniel H. Weinberg: "Confronting Poverty, Prescriptions for Change." Cambridge, Mass., Harvard University Press, 1994.

Dasgupta, Deepak: "The Population Problem: Theory and Evidence." Journal of Economic Literature, vol. XXXIII, no. 4, December 1995.

DeGrasse Jr., Robert W.: "The Military Economy," Ch. 1 in Gordon and McFadden, 1984.

de Vries, Barend A.: "The World Bank's Focus on Poverty," in Jo Marie Griesgraber and Bernard G. Gunter, Eds.: "The World Bank: Lending on a Global Scale." London, Pluto Press, 1996a. (Vol. III of the report of the June 1994 Conference "Rethinking Bretton Woods" Washington, DC, Center of Concern).

———. "Challenges and Opportunities for The World Bank" in Orin Kirshner: The Bretton Woods-GATT System, Retrospect and Prospect After Fifty Years. New York, M. E. Sharpe, 1996b.

———. "Remaking the World Bank." Washington, DC, The Seven Locks Press, 1987.

———. "The Debt-Bearing Capacity of Developing Countries: A Comparative Analysis." Rome, Banca Nazianale del Lavoro Quarterly Review, March 1971.

de Vries, Christine M.: The Penetration of Women into Male Intensive Occupations. Washington, DC, George Washington University, 1984.

de Vries, Margaret Garritsen: "Balance of Payments Adjustments, 1945 to 1986, The IMF Experience." Washington, DC, IMF, 1987.

———. "The International Monetary Fund, 1972–78, Cooperation on Trial." Vol. I, II, and III. Washington, DC, IMF, 1985.

———. "The International Monetary Fund, 1966–71: The System under Stress" Vol. I and II Washington, DC, IMF, 1976.

Diaz Alejandro, Carlos: "Latin America: I don't think we are in Kansas anymore." Brookings Papers on Economic Activity, Washington, DC, the Brookings Institution, 1984, vol. 2, pp. 335–389.

Douglass, R. Bruce, Ed.: "The Deeper Meaning of Economic Life: Critical Essays on the US Catholic Bishops Pastoral Letter on the US Economy." Washington, DC, Georgetown University Press, 1988.

Duncan, Dayton: "Out West." Viking Press, 1987.

Episcopal Church: Policy for Action (Adopted at General Convention 1982 and 1985; and Executive Council, 1982–85; and Resolutions passed by the 69th General Convention (1988).

———. "Economic Justice and the Christian Conscience." The Urban Bishops Coalition, 1987.

Fei, John C. H. and Gustav Ranis: Development of the Labor Surplus Economy: Theory and Practice. Yale University Economic Growth Center and Richard. D. Irwin Inc., 1964.

Fishlow, Albert: "Inequality, Poverty and Growth: Where Do We Stand?" World Bank Annual Conference on Development Economics, 1995.

Forte, Francesco: "The International Debt Crisis and the Craxi Report." Rome, Banca Nazionale del Lavoro Quarterly Review, no. 179, December 1991.

Fourth World Movement: "Fighting Poverty: A New Approach." New York NY, 1990 (Second Edition).

Freedman, Jonathan: "From the Cradle to the Grave. The Human Face of Poverty in America." New York, Atheneum, 1993.

Friedman, Milton and Rose Friedman: "Free to Choose, A Personal Statement." New York, Avon Books, 1980.

Furnish, Victor Paul: "The Moral Teaching of Paul." Nashville, Tenn., Abbington, 1979.

Galbraith, John Kenneth: "The Culture of Contentment." Boston, Houghton Mifflin Co., 1992.

Gannon S.J., Thomas M., Ed.: "The Catholic Challenge to the US Economy. Reflections on the US Bishops' Pastoral Letter on Catholic Social Teaching and the US Economy." New York, Macmillan, 1987.

Gans, Herbert J.: "The War Against the Poor. The Underclass and Anti-Poverty Policy." New York, Basic Books, 1995.

Garten, Jeffrey E.: "A Cold Peace." New York, A Twentieth Century Fund Book, Times Books, 1992.

Geiger, Linwood T.: "Market Activity and Poverty." Wynnwood, PA, Transformation, an International Evangelical Dialogue on Mission and Ethics, vol. 12, no. 3, July-September, 1996.

Geyer, Alan and Barbara G. Green: "Lines in the Sand. Justice and the Gulf War." Louisville, Kentucky, Westminster/ John Knox Press, 1992.

Gillis, Malcolm; Dwight H. Perkins, Michael Roemer, and Donald R. Snodgrass: Economics of Development, Second Edition. New York, W. W. Norton & Co., 1987.

Gold, David: "Conversion and Industrial Policy," Chapter 13 in Gordon and McFadden, 1984.

Gordon, Suzanne and Dave McFadden: "Economic Conversion: Revitalizing America's Economy." Cambridge, Mass., Ballinger, 1984.

Gore, Al: "Earth in the Balance, Ecology and the Human Spirit." Boston, Houghton Mifflin Co., 1992.

Gottschalk, Peter: "Inequality, Income Growth and Mobility: The Basic Facts." Minneapolis, Minn., Journal of Economic Perspectives, vol. 11, no. 2, Spring 1997.

Hackman, Sandra: "After Rio: Our Forests Ourselves." Cambridge, Mass., MIT Technology Review, vol. 95, no. 7, Oct. 1992.

Halberstam, David: "The Fifties." New York, Willard Books, 1993.

Harrington, Michael: "The New American Poverty." New York, Holt, Rinehart and Winston, 1984.

Harvey, Phillip: "Securing the Right to Employment." Princeton N.J., Princeton University Press, 1989.

Henriot, Peter J., Edward P. DeBerri, and Michael J. Schultheis: "Catholic Social Teaching, Our Best Kept Secret." Maryknoll, New York, Orbis Books, and Washington, DC, Center of Concern, 1988.

Hewitt, Daniel: "Military Expenditures in the Developing World." Washington, DC, IMF, "Finance and Development," vol. 28, no. 3, Sept. 1991.

Hewlett, Sylvia Ann: "Lesser Life: The Myth of Women's Liberation in America" (Warner Books Edition). New York, William Morrow, 1986.

Hollenbach S.J., David: "Christian Social Ethics after the Cold War." In Theological Studies (Boston, MA, March 1992, vol. 53, no. 1).

Iannaccone, Laurence R.: "Fundamentalism and Economics in the US." Association of Christian Economists Working Paper, Grand Rapids, Calvin College Econ. Dept., 1991.

Interfaith Action for Economic Justice: "God's Justice in a New Century: The Future of Religion and Economic Justice." A Conference sponsored by Interfaith Action, Nov. 1989. Summary, Aug. 1991.

International Labour Office: "Toward Full Employment, A Programme for Colombia." Prepared by an interagency team organized by the ILO. Geneva, 1970.

Johnson, Paul: A History of the Jews. New York, Harper and Row, 1987.

Kaldor, Mary: "Problems of Adjustment to Lower Levels of Military Spending in Developed and Developing Countries." Washington, DC, World Bank, Annual Conference on Development Economics, 1991.

Killick, Tony, with Moazzam Malik: "Country Experiences with IMF Programmes in the 1980s." Working Paper 48. London, Overseas Development Institute, 1994.

Knight, Frank H.: "Freedom and Reform: Essays in Economics and Social Philosophy." New York, Harper and Brothers, 1947 (and Liberty Press Reprint, 1982).

Kozol, Jonathan: "Amazing Grace. The Lives of Children and the Conscience of a Nation." New York, Crown Publishers, 1995.

Krauss, Melvyn B.: "Development Without Aid: Growth, Poverty and Government." New York, McGraw Hill for the Manhattan Institute, 1983.

Krugman, Paul: "Peddling Prosperity." New York, W. W. Norton & Co. 1994.

———. "The Age of Diminished Expectations, US Economic Policies in the 1990s." Cambridge, Mass., The MIT Press, 1990.

Kung, Hans: "On Being a Christian." Translated by Edward Quinn. New York, Doubleday & Co, 1976.

Kuyper, Abraham: "Het Sociale Vraagstuk en de Christelijke Religie." Amsterdam, J. A. Wormser, 1891; reissued as "The Problem of Poverty," edited and introduced by James W. Skillen, the Center for Public Justice, Washington, DC, and Baker Book House, Grand Rapids, Mich., 1991.

Land S.J., Philip S.: "Shaping Welfare Consensus. The US Catholic Bishops' Contribution." Washington, DC, Center of Concern, 1988.

Lerner, Michael: "The Politics of Meaning." Reading, Mass., Addison-Wesley, 1996.

Lewis, Oscar: The Children of Sanches, Autobiography of a Mexican Family. New York, Random House, 1961.

Lutheran Churches:
  American Lutheran Church:
    ——. Mandate for Peacemaking (1982).
    ——. The Unfinished Reformation (1980).
    ——. Peace, Justice and Human Rights (1972).
    ——. Women and Men in Church and Society (1972).
    ——. Economic Problems of Rural America (1970).
    ——. The Environmental Crisis (1970).
  Lutheran Church in America:
    ——. Peace and Politics (1984).
    ——. Economic Justice: Stewardship of Creation in Human Community (1980).
    ——. The Human Crisis in Ecology (1972).
    ——. Human Rights (1972).
    ——. Poverty (1966).
  Lutheran Church (Missouri Synod):
    ——. Report of the Commission on Theology and Church Relations: Guidelines for Crucial Issues in Christian Citizenship (1968).
McNamara, Robert S.: Address to the Board of Governors of the World Bank, Sept. 30, 1980.
——. "Reducing Military Expenditures in the Third World, Washington, DC, Finance and Development, vol. 28, no. 3, Sept. 1991.
McWhirter, Darien A.: "The End of Affirmative Action: Where Do We Go From Here?" New York, A Brick Lane Press Book, Carol Publishing Group, 1996.
Madrick, Jeffrey: "The End of Affluence. The Causes and Consequences of America's Economic Dilemma." New York, Random House, 1995.
Matthews, Jessica: "The Myth of the American Car Cult." Washington, DC, *Washington Post*, March 31, 1991.
Meeks, M. Douglas: "God the Economist: The Doctrine of God and Political Economy." Minneapolis, Minn., Fortress Press, 1989.
Melman, Seymour: "The Permanent War Economy, American Capitalism in Decline." New York, Simon and Schuster, 1985.
Methodist Church: See United Methodist Church.
Milne, Pamela: "Genesis from Eve's point of view." *Washington Post*, March 26, 1989.
Moynihan, David Patrick: "Miles to Go. A Personal History of Social Policy." Cambridge, Mass., Harvard University Press, 1996.
Myrdal, Gunnar: "Asian Drama: An Inquiry into the Poverty of Nations." 3 volumes. New York, Pantheon, 1968.
——. "Challenge to Affluence." New York, Pantheon, 1963.
——. "An American Dilemma. The Negro Problem and American Democracy." New York, Harper, 1944.
Naisbitt, John, and Patricia Aburdene: "Megatrends 2000." New York, William Morrow & Co., 1990.
Nash, James A.: "Loving Nature: Ecological Integrity and Christian Responsibility." Nashville, Abingdon Press, 1991.

National Council of Churches of Christ in the U.S.: "Defense and Disarmament: New Requirements for Security." Washington, DC, 1968.

Nelson, Robert H.: "Reaching for Heaven on Earth. The Theological Meaning of Economics." Savage, MD, Rowman and Littlefield Publishers, 1991.

Neuhaus, Richard John, and Michael Cromarty, Eds.: "Piety and Politics: Evangelicals and Fundamentalists Confront the World." Washington, DC, Ethics and Public Policy Center, 1987.

Noll, Mark A.: "The Scandal of Evangelical Political Reflection, 1896–1991." Conference Paper issued by the Ethics and Public Policy Institute Conference "To Be Christian In America To-day," Washington, DC, 1991.

Novak, Michael: "The Catholic Ethic and the Spirit of Capitalism." New York, The Free Press, 1993.

——. "The Spirit of Democratic Capitalism." New York, Simon and Schuster, 1982.

Oxford Declaration on Christian Faith and Economics. (1990) Philadelphia, Evangelicals for Social Action (10E Lancaster Pike, Philadelphia, PA 19151).

Pfeffermann, Guy: Poverty in Latin America, The Impact of Depression. The World Bank, 1986.

Potok, Chaim: Wanderings: History of the Jews. New York, Fawcett Crest Books, 1978.

Potter, George Ann: Dialogue on Debt, Alternative Analyses and Solutions. Washington, DC, The Center of Concern, 1988.

Presbyterian Church (USA): "Restoring Creation for Ecology and Justice" (Adopted by the 202d General Assembly), 1990.

——. "Toward a Just, Caring and Dynamic Political Economy." Committee on a Just Political Economy, 1985.

——. Christian Faith and Economic Justice. 1984 General Assembly.

——. The Church in US Society; Christian Faith and Economic Justice; written in response to a request by the 1978 General Assembly.

Rauschenbusch, Walter: "Christianity and the Social Crisis." New York, Macmillan Co. 1907.

Reed, Ralph: "Active Faith. How Christians are Changing the Soul of American Politics." New York, NY, The Free Press, 1996.

Reform Judaism:
  Central Conference of American Rabbis:
    ——. Environment, 1990.
    ——. Welfare, 1987.
    ——. Economic Justice, 1986.
    ——. Social and Economic Betterment, 1985.
    ——. World Hunger, 1985.
    ——. Homeless, 1984.
    ——. Hunger and Food Banks, 1983.
    ——. Budget and Social Welfare, 1982.
    ——. Hunger, 1975.
    ——. Housing, 1918, 1932, 1935, 1949, 1965.
    ——. Social Betterment, 1928, 1942, 1951, 1954.

————. Public Works, 1938, 1942.

National Federation of Temple Sisterhoods:

————. Social and Economic Justice, 1987.

————. Economic Justice, 1985.

————. Hunger, 1969.

————. Priorities for Peace, 1969.

————. Poverty, United States and Abroad, 1941, 1950, 1953, 1955, 1965.

Union of American Hebrew Congregations:

————. Health Care Reform, 1993.

————. Womens' Health, 1993.

————. Affordable Housing, 1989.

————. Congregational Programs Serving the Hungry and Homeless, 1989.

————. Child Care, 1987.

————. Foreign Aid, 1987.

————. Mazon (Sustenance), 1986.

————. Wage Discrimination, 1985.

————. Economic Justice for Women, 1983.

————. Homeless, The, 1983.

————. Toxic Substances in the Environment, 1983.

————. Legal Services, 1981.

————. Energy, 1978 and 1979.

————. Economic Justice, 1976.

————. Full Employment, 1977.

————. Social Progress, 1973.

————. World Hunger, 1973.

————. Welfare Reform and Income Maintenance, 1971.

————. Environmental Pollution, 1969.

————. Civil Rights and Economic Justice, 1968.

————. Conservation and Development of Natural Resources, 1965.

————. Discrimination in Housing, 1965.

————. Eradication and Amelioration of Poverty, 1965.

————. Unemployment, 1963.

————. Budget, and Social Welfare.

Reformed Church in America: James I. Cook, Ed.: "The Church Speaks." Papers of the Commission on Theology, 1959–1984 (Grand Rapids, Wm. B. Eerdmans Publ. Co. 1984).

————. "The Evangelistic and Social Task of the Church," (pp. 142–44).

————. "A Reformed Theology of Nature in a Crowded World," (pp. 145–48).

————. "Christian Faith and the Nuclear Arms Race: A Reformed Perspective," (pp. 165–181).

————. "Biblical Faith and Our Economic Life" Report of the Christian Action Commission, in Acts and Proceedings, 1984 General Synod, (pp. 51–68).

————. "Christian Peacemaking in a Troubled Economy: The Church's Pastoral Responsibility," (pp. 68–70).

————. "The Church's Peace Witness in the US Corporate Economy," in Acts and Proceedings of the 1985 General Synod, p. 5.

Reformed Church in America (*continued*)

———. "The Two-Tiered Society: Inequality Amid the Ascendancy of Capitalism" in Acts and Proceedings of the 1990 General Synod, (pp. 65–72).

———. "Third World Debt. The Churches' Response," (pp. 72–77).

Reich, Robert B.: "The Work of Nations." New York, Vintage Books & Random House, 1991.

Repetto, Robert: "Economic Policy Reform for Natural Resource Conservation." Washington, DC, World Bank, Environment Department, May 1988.

Riley, Marion and Jo Marie Griesgraber: "Case Study of Women in Poverty in the US." Washington, DC, Center of Concern, 1991.

Rosen, Sumner M.: "Jobs: New Challenges, New Responses." Annals of the American Academy of Political and Social Science, vol. 544, pp. 27–42. New York, Sage Publications, March 1996.

Rosenberg, David and Harold Bloom: "The Book of J." (Translated from the Hebrew by David Rosenberg, interpreted by Harold Bloom) New York, Grove Weidenfield, 1990.

Rosovsky, Henry: "Liberal Arts in the 21st Century." Wooster: 125th Anniversary Issue. Wooster, Ohio, The College of Wooster, 1991.

Rowen, Hobart: "Unemployment Benefits: Out of Sync." *Washington Post*, May 16, 1991.

Sachs, Jeffrey D.: External Debt and Macroeconomic Performance in Latin America and East Asia. Brookings Papers on Economic Activity, 1985, No. 2, pp. 523–564.

Sawhill, Isabell: "The Economist as Madman in Authority." Journal of Economic Perspectives, vol. 9, no. 3, Summer, 1995.

———. "Poverty in the US: Why is it so Persistent?" Nashville, Tn, The Journal of Economic Literature, Sept. 1988, vol. XXVI, no. 3, pp. 1073–1119.

Schatz, Sayre P.: "Structural Adjustment in Africa: A Failing Grade So Far." Journal of Modern African Studies, 32:4 (1994), pp. 679–92.

Schrader, Janet: "Ringside with Welfare." *Washington Post*, p. C1, January 1, 1995.

Schramm, Gunter and Jeremy Warford, Eds.: "Environmental Management and Economic Development." Baltimore, The Johns Hopkins Press, 1989.

Schuker, Stephen A.: American "Reparations" to Germany, 1919–33: Implications for the Third-World Debt Crisis. Princeton, NJ, Princeton University, 1988.

Schultz, T. Paul: Women and Development: Objectives, Frameworks and Policy Interventions. Washington, The World Bank, Working Papers, Population and Human Resources Department, 1989.

Shields, Mark: "Let's Hear it For the Feds!" *Washington Post*, June 1, 1991.

Sider, Ronald J.: "The Oxford Declaration." Wynnwood, PA, The Advocate (July-August 1991).

———. "Rich Christians in an Age of Hunger." Dallas, Word Publishing, 1990.

Siegel, Danny: Gym Shoes and Irises (Personalized Tzedakah). Book One and Book Two. Spring Valley, NY, Town House Press, 1986 and 1987.

Sivard, Ruth Leger: "World Military and Social Expenditures, 1987–88." Washington, DC, World Priorities, 1987.

———. "Women, a World Survey." Washington, DC, World Priorities, 1985.

Skillen, James W.: "The Oxford Declaration on Christian Faith and Economics: Some Comments and Questions." Bulletin of the Association of Christian Economists, Issue No. 16, Fall 1990 (Wenhem, Mass. Gordon College, 1990b).

———. "The Scattered Voice; Christians at Odds in the Public Square." Grand Rapids, Zondervan Books, 1990a.

Spong, John Shelby: "Liberating the Gospels: Reading the Bible with Jewish Eyes." New York, Harper Collins, 1996.

Squire, Lynn: "Fighting Poverty." American Economic Review, vol. 83, no. 2, May 1993, p. 377 (Nashville, TN).

Thurow, Lester: "The Future of Capitalism." New York, Wm. Morrow & Co. Inc., 1996.

———. "Head to Head: The Coming Economic Battle Among Japan, Europe and America." New York, Wm. Morrow and Co. Inc., 1992.

Tolchin, Martin and Susan J.: "Selling Our Security. The Erosion of America's Assets." New York, Alfred A. Knopf, 1992.

Topel, Robert H.: "Factor Proportions and Relative Wages: The Supply Side Determinants of Wage Inequality." Minneapolis, Minn., Journal of Economic Perspectives, vol. 11, no. 2, Spring 1997.

Ullmann, John E.: "Building a Peacetime Economy." Cambridge, MA, Massachusetts Institute of Technology, Technology Review, vol. 94, no. 7, Aug.-Sep., 1991.

United Church of Christ: "Christian Faith and Economic Life." (Edited by Audrey Chapman Schmock); 1987 version prepared by the Board for World Ministries.

———. "A Just Peace Church." (Edited by Susan Thislethwaite) New York, United Church Press, 1986.

———. "Social Policy, The First 25 Years (1957–81)." Edited by Jay Lintner UCC Office of Church in Society, 1981.

United Methodist Church: Agricultural and Rural Life Issues (1988).

———. Economic Justice (1988).

———. Hunger and Poverty (1988).

———. Latin America: Pleading for its Jubilee (Washington, DC, Christian Social Action, vol. 1, no. 6, June 1988).

———. Social Principles (1988).

———. In Defense of Creation (1986) (Foundation Document and Pastoral Letter. Nashville Tenn, Cokesbury, 1986).

———. Domestic Hunger and Malnutrition (1985).

———. Environmental Stewardship (1984).

———. Housing (1984).

———. Hunger (1984).

———. Peace (1984).

———. Rights of Women (1984).

United Nations: Preventing the Tragedy of Maternal Deaths. A Report of the International Safe Motherhood Conference. Nairobi, Kenya, 1987.

United Nations Development Programme: Human Development Report, 1996; New York, 1996.

Volcker, Paul, and Toyoo Gyothen: "Changing Fortunes, The World's Money and the Threat to American Leadership." New York, NY, Times Books, Random House, 1992.

Vorspan, Albert: "Jewish Values and Social Crisis: A Casebook for Social Action." New York, NY, Union of American Hebrew Congregations, Revised Edition, 1969.

Vorspan, Albert and Eugene J. Lipman: "Justice and Judaism." New York, NY, Union of Hebrew Congregations, Revised Fourth Edition, 1959.

Ward, A. Dudley, Ed.: "Goals of Economic Life." Federal Council of Churches Study. New York, Harpers & Br., 1953.

West, Cornel: "Race Matters." Boston, Mass., Beacon Press, 1993.

Will, George F.: "A Moral Environment for the Poor." *Washington Post*, May 30, 1991.

Wirth, Timothy E.: "Easy Being Green." *Washington Post*, Oct. 4, 1992.

Wogaman, J. Philip: "Economics and Ethics. A Christian Inquiry." Philadelphia, Fortress Press, 1986.

———. "The Great Economic Debate: An Ethical Analysis." Philadelphia, Westminster Press, 1977.

———. "The Great Economic Debate Continues." Journal of Economic Studies, vol. 24, no. 3, Summer, 1987, pp. 403–423.

Woodward, Bob: The Agenda: Inside the Clinton White House, New York, Simon and Schuster, 1994, p. 310.

The World Bank: World Development Report, 1980, 1984, 1988, 1990a, 1992, 1993, 1994, 1995.

———. "Adjustment in Africa: Reforms, Results and the Road Ahead." New York, Oxford University Press, 1994.

———. Annual Report, 1993, 1994.

———. "Poverty Reduction and The World Bank, Progress in Fiscal 1993," 1994.

———. "Implementing the Bank's Poverty Reduction Strategy. Progress and Challenges" 1993.

———. "Effective Implementation: Key to Development Impact." Report of the World Bank's Portfolio Management Task Force (headed by Willy Wapenhans), 1992.

———. World Debt Tables, 1988–89 and 1991–92 editions.

———. Women in Development. A Progress Report on the World Bank Initiative, 1990b.

———. Bangladesh: Strategies for Enhancing the Role of Women in Economic Development. A World Bank Country Study, 1990c.

———. "Dealing with the Debt Crisis." A World Bank Symposium, edited by Ishrat Husein and Ishac Diwan, 1989.

———. "Women and Kenya's Economic Prospects." A World Bank Country Study of Women in Development, 1988.

————. Development Committee: "Environment, Growth and Development." 1987.

————. Poverty and Hunger: Issues and Options for Food Security in Developing Countries," Policy Study, Feb. 1986.

————. Philippines: Industrial Development Strategy and Policies: A World Bank Country Report, 1980.

World Credit Tables. Brussels, Eurodad, 1996.

Zuckerman, Elaine: Adjustment Programs and Social Welfare. World Bank Discussion Paper, 1989.

Index